BOKO HARAM:

Pathways to a Solution

Scribble City
PUBLICATIONS

DEDICATION

Dedicated to the memory of my late mother, Lady Jessie A Ezeife;
my late brother, Afam Okechukwu Ezeife;
and my late sister, Nkechi Ifeoma Ezeife.

ACKNOWLEDGEMENT

I wish to acknowledge my learned friends, Charles Spiropolous, Esq. and John Mozie, Esq., for proofing and for offering their critical assessment. All errors, mistakes, and omissions are mine. Much obliged to Barbara Ije Ifezue and Scribblecity Publications; and to my niece Onyinye Nnamdi for helping with the graphic design of the cover page.

To my wife, Nnenna, and my children, Okey, Ifeoma, Tochi and Chioma; thank you for providing a loving and nurturing environment for me to work.

TABLE OF CONTENTS

PREFACE

Nigeria, as a developing nation, is beset by a myriad of growing pains that impedes her ability to grow. Chief among these is terrorism. In the long annals of Nigeria's chequered history, from the colonial through post-independent periods, there have been violent incidents. However, those incidents pale significantly in comparison to the danger that the Boko Haram insurgency poses to Nigeria. One can safely frame the Boko Haram threat in existential terms. What this book seeks to do has become necessary because there is much we still do not know about Boko Haram. The exact details of their operations, size, and structure remain a mystery.

This book begins with the study of terrorism, with emphasis on attempts to define it and other concepts that are linked to its study. The book goes on to attempt an in-depth look at the ignominious history of modern terrorism in Nigeria, with emphasis on the most potent of the terrorists, the Boko Haram insurgency. Along the way, it will also try to understand what drives the Boko Haram insurgency and paint a picture of the impact of this scourge on Nigeria and Nigerians. Then, it will offer an array of ideas and concepts for containing and eventually eliminating Boko Haram in Nigeria. In our concluding chapter, we will try and tie the entire discussion into a neat bundle.

Given the fact that Nigeria's economy is under threat from the insurgency, and is literally in the throes of strangulation by Boko Haram terrorists, this work is timely, if not critical, to assist the authorities and policymakers in their efforts to confront this heinous scourge with the right toolkit.

The sources of the materials for this book are scholarly journal articles, books, conference materials, communiques, legal texts, statutes, newspaper and magazine reports, cases, Charters, Conventions and Protocols.

Chapter 1

Introduction

There is no gainsaying the fact that the world as we know it has been dramatically changed by terrorism since September 11, 2001. **Nsongarua J. Udombana** captures this paradigm shift well when he says that "since the events of 11 September 2001 ('9/11'), the US has redefined the paradigm in the struggle for global order by plodding the international community to launch a global 'war on terrorism,' a 'militaristic jargon' that "views terrorism from a conflict management rather than an exclusively law enforcement perspective." [1]

Terrorism and the fight against it has become the third rail of international geo-politics. It has altered almost all aspects of life, not only for the direct victims of it, but also the general world population at large. It has ushered in unprecedented security measures at airports,

---

[1] **Nsongarua J. Udombana**, *Battling Rights: International Law And Africa's War On Terrorism*, 13 Afr. Y.B. Int'l L. 67 2005, at page 68, available at http://www.ssrn.com/abstract=1806304

seaports, train stations, public buildings and facilities. It has spawned a booming industry in the facilities and personal protection field and has also enriched the military industrial complex of the United States, United Kingdom, China, Russia, Israel, the European Union and elsewhere. Nations have been obliged to augment security budgets in a bid to come to terms with this new phenomenon.

This shift in emphasis on pouring money and efforts into fighting terrorism, even at the risk of neglecting other priorities, has been pointed out by **David Cortright**. Referencing the call by the then United Nations Secretary-General, Kofi Annan, for a balanced approach to the fight against terrorism that will include addressing the environment that cultivates and nurtures terrorism, as well as to strengthen the rule of law and protection of human rights, **Cortright** regrets that:

> Despite these calls for broader counter-terrorism campaign that includes both preventive and protective measures, the global fight against terrorism has focused largely on denial and deterrence strategies. The U.S. concept of a 'global war on terror' has been the dominant political paradigm, and this has diverted international efforts largely towards coercive, law enforcement approaches. The United Nations itself has been influenced by this counter-terrorism fervor and has focused its attention on

protective law enforcement measures, with little to longer range preventive strategies.[2]

Terrorism has created new fronts in national frictions and heightened suspicion amongst nations and peoples. It has increased tension and conflict between religions and cultures. It has ushered in a new "cold war" between "Radical Islam" and the rest of the world and between the West and Middle East. **Sudha Setty** paints a picture of the new post 9/11 world thus:

> Ten years after the attacks of September 11, 2001, it almost goes without saying that the acts of grotesque violence committed on that day have had enormous effects on national security law and policy worldwide. To be labeled a terrorist, or to be accused of involvement in an act of terrorism, carries far more severe repercussions now than it did ten years ago. This is true under international law and under domestic law in nations that have dealt with serious national security concerns for many years.[3]

---

2 **David Cortright**, *A critical Evaluation of the UN Counter-Terrorism Program: Accomplishments and Challenges, A Crime and Global Paper presented at: Global Enforcement Regimes, Transnational Organized Crime, International Terrorism and money Laundering*, held at the Transnational Institute (TNI) in Amsterdam, 28-29 April 2005, available at http://www.tni.org/crime, at page 2

3 **Sudha Setty**, *What's In A Name? How Nations Define Terrorism Ten Years After 9/11*, U. Pa. J. Int'l L, Vol. 33:1 [2011], at page 1, available at http://www.ssrn.com/abstract=1858327,

Terrorism has opened cracks in all the fault lines that had lain dormant for decades, nay centuries, a ticking time bomb poised to explode. One of such fault lines is in the Northern region of Nigeria. The fault line is being exposed by Boko Haram in an orchestrated attempt to embroil the region in a religious, sectarian and ethnic war, quite capable of dragging the rest of Nigeria into a civil war.

The threat and impact of terrorism have also been exacerbated by globalization. It has been suggested that "globalization narrowed significantly the global space – facilitating easy international travel and communication – and the terrorism threat and opportunity and potential for greater damage increased sharply."[4] **Ogbonnaya and Ehigiamusoe** opine that "with the aid of globalization, terrorist groups and organizations have become powerful national security challengers which nation-states in most cases are not adequately prepared to encounter."[5] With globalization, terrorists have a longer reach in terms of who and where they can impact.

They also have ability to source support and logistics farther and faster. **Zumve, Ingyoroko** and **Akuva**

---

4 **United Nations Office of the Special Adviser on Africa,** *"Africa and International Counterterrorism Imperatives" Expert paper prepared by the Office of the Special Adviser on Africa, available at http://www.un.org/africa/.../OSAA-TerrorismPaper-12Nov2010...*

5 **Ogbonnaya, Ufiem Maurice, Ehiagiamusoe, Uyi Kizito,** *Niger Delta Militancy And Boko Haram Insurgency: National Security In Nigeria, Global Security Studies, Summer 2013,* Volume 4, Issue 3, at page 2, available at http://www.academia.edu/.../Niger_Delta_Militancy_Boko_Hara...

capture the trend and say that "the rapid advances in transportation and communication technology associated with globalization have brought about a shift in the nature and scale of the terrorist threat."[6]

There is also the contribution of technology to the spread, impact and efficacy of terrorists. Modern technology has given a boost to terrorism and terrorists. Bomb making technology and other terrorist tactics are easily obtainable online. Terrorists are able to recruit members and sympathizers online. With technology, funds can be accessed and/or moved around clandestinely with ease. Arms, ammunitions and parts for making explosive devices can be sourced online and moved with little or no trace. Crypto currencies and "Go Fund Me" are potential go-to technologies for funding terrorism. Information can also be passed around fast and clandestinely between terrorists and terrorist cells with the use of modern technology. Terrorists have also mastered the act of propaganda with the aid of technology. They now have global reach to disseminate their message and to indoctrinate gullible and susceptible individuals.

Oluwafemi, Adeyinka and Abdulhamid offer the following perspective on the impact of technology on terrorism:

---

6 **Samuel Zumve, Margaret Ingyoroko, Isaac Iorhen Akuva,** *Terrorism In Contemporary Nigeria: A Latent Function Of Official Corruption And State Neglect,* European Scientific Journal March 2013 edition vol.9, No.8, pp 122-140, at page 124, available at http://www.eujournal.org/index.php/esj/article/view/882

The belligerent utilization of modern technology for management of information, communication and intelligence has had a progressive effect on terrorist activities . . . they continue to improve their sophistication and abilities in all aspects of operations and support using these tools ... Today it is common knowledge that terrorists use ICTs and the Internet in recruiting, promoting propaganda, gathering of information, publication of training materials, communications, preparation of real-world attacks, terrorist financing, etc ... Terrorists are now known to plan and communicate with encrypted data even beyond law enforcement's ability to intercept or decode this data. They have utilized other ICT tools, including disposable cellular phones, over the counter long-distance calling cards, internet cafes, to mention but a few. They even employ the use of embedding information in digital pictures and graphics.[7]

Most importantly, modern technology offers terrorists the pedestal to "shock and awe" their victims and target audience, as well as the world in general. With the aid of YouTube, FaceBook, Whatsapp, Twitter, and other technological and online tools, images of terror and recruitment propaganda can potentially reach all nooks

---

7 **Osho Oluwafemi, Falaye Adeyinka Adesuyi, Shafi'I M. Abdulhamid,** *Combating Terrorism with Cybersecurity: The Nigerian Perspective,* World Journal of Computer Application and Technology 1(4): 103-109, at page 104, 2013, available at http://www.hrpub.org

and crannies of the world, hitting computers, cell-phones, handheld pads etc. Quoting **Levitt** and **Jacobson**,[8] the **2013 FATF REPORT**:

> [A]ttribute the evolution in financing sources [for terrorists] to rapid globalization and sustained technological advances, which have enabled terrorist groups to raise, store, transfer, and distribute funds for their operations with ease. In particular, the advent of new technology has spurred changes in how money is transferred, with mobile and online money transfers becoming more commonplace.[9]

The broader threat that terrorism poses to world peace is underscored by the myriad of resolutions and Conventions of the United Nations on the subject, and the extraordinary array of clear guidance the august body has laid for member states, to fight the scourge. Since 2001 there has been a slew of UN Resolutions and Conventions on international terrorism.[10] There was an ushering in of a different regime in the UN attitude

---

8 **Levitt, Mathew, and Jacobson, Michael** (2008), *The Money Trail: Finding, Following, and Freezing Terrorist Finances*, Washington Institute for Near East Policy, Washington DC, United States, available at http://www.washingtoninstitute. org/...

9 **Fatf Report**, *Terrorist Financing In West Africa*, OCTOBER 2013, at paragraph 2.3, available at http://www.fatf-gafi.org,

10 **See Javier Ruperez**, *The United Nations In The Fight Against Terrorism*, sourced from www.un.org/en/sc/ctc/.../2006-01_26_cted-lecture.pdf. [Javier Ruperez was the Executive Director, Counter-Terrorism Committee Executive Directorate, United Nations]; **Sudha Setty**, *What's In A Name? How Nations Define Terrorism Ten Years After 9/11*, U. Pa. J. Int'l L, Vol. 33:1 [2011]

to terrorism, with the enactment of the United Nations Resolution 1373[11] on the heels of the September 11, 2001 attacks on the continental United States. According to **David Cortright**, "these and related efforts placed counter-terrorism at the center of the UN political agenda."[12] A new strategy was invoked wherein all member states were mandated to work collaboratively to fight the scourge of terrorism. Member nations were obligated to pass legislation to punish it; to come up with strategies to fight it; and to collaborate with each other and the international community in a united front against it. Thus:

> By approval of the UN Strategy, UN Member States resolved to prevent and combat terrorism in all its forms and manifestations. To this end the UN Strategy, while endorsing the security-related counter-terrorism measures of the Security Council, also calls on member states to employ a holistic approach in meeting the challenges of international terrorism. The UN Strategy's priorities include measures to address underlying conditions conducive to the emergence and spread of terrorism, highlights the importance of development as an important element of global counter-terrorism efforts, and places equal emphasis on the importance of ensuring that counter-terrorism measures should respect

---

11 *United Nations Security Council, Security Council Resolution 1373* (2001), S/RES/1373, New York, 28 September 2001

12 Corthright, supra note 2, at page 4

human rights and the rule of law."[13]

The effort to fashion a universal definition of terrorism, however, has been hampered by controversy. **Dr. Paul Norman** succinctly captures the problem as follows:

> [T]he development of universal legal norms in this area has been tempered by superpower conflict and competition, national liberation movements struggling for independence from colonialists, and perhaps most prominently today the unresolved 'Palestinian question'. These bases for conflict have hindered the international community's efforts to counter terrorism as a generic phenomena, leading to an imperfect position where particular acts of terrorism and facilitators of terrorism have been legally proscribed via a network of UN conventions but without a universal definition of terrorism being agreed. [14]

Despite the conflict over, and the controversy surrounding, the definition of terrorism, strides have been made by the United Nations to mobilize member states and regional organizations to fight terrorism, its causes, sponsors and those who shelter it. **Professor**

---

13 United Nations Office of the Special Adviser on Africa , "*Africa and International Counterterrorism Imperatives*," Expert paper prepared by the Office of the Special Adviser on Africa, available at http.//www.un.org/Africa/.../OSAA-TerrorismPaper-12Nov2010

14 **Dr. Paul Norman**, *The United Nations and Counter-terrorism After September 11: towards an assessment of the impact and prospects of counter-terror 'spill-over' into international criminal justice cooperation*, Paper to British Society of Criminology Conference 6-9th July 2004, University of Portsmouth, at page 2, available at http://www.britsoccrim.org/new/volume7/004.pdf

Suhda Setty credits the UN for ingeniously getting around the definitional problems around terrorism.[15] The passage of the UN Resolution 1373[16] is seen as a turning point in the universal battle to conquer terrorism. In his assessment of the resolution, **Dr. Paul Norman** says that "overall it can be seen that the passage of SCR 1373 uniquely set an obligatory international legal regime to realize a general UN enforcement strategy against international terrorism encompassing wide range of judicial, criminal, police and immigration cooperation measures." [17]**David Cortright** takes the position that "Resolution 1373 was unparalleled in imposing new legal obligations on states and mobilizing the international community for a campaign of nonmilitary cooperative law enforcement measures to combat global terrorism."[18]

The African Union [AU] and the Economic Community of West African States [ECOWAS] echo the exhortation of the United Nations to Member states to pass legislation against and to put in place strategies to fight terrorism. The grave threat terrorism poses to peace, security and cooperation in Africa and its constituent regions and nations has been identified and recognized

---

15 **Sudha Setty**, supra note 3, at page 15 where he asserts that "without an official definition of terrorism to work with, the United Nations Security Council has established partial measures: either by enacting resolutions that condemn acts of terrorism without defining the parameters of terrorism, or by including general descriptions of acts that fall within the rubric of terrorist activity without purporting to fully define terrorism."

16 UNSCR 1373 of 2001

17 **Dr. Norman**, supra footnote 14, at page 11

18 **Cortright**, supra, footnote 2, at pages 2-3

by the Organization of Africa Unity [OAU] now African Union [AU]. [19]

The Organization of African Union [as it then was called] in 1999 passed a convention on the prevention and combating of terrorism, aptly titled **OAU Convention on the Prevention and Combating of Terrorism 1999.**[20] It was adopted by the 35th Ordinary Session of the OAU Summit, held at Algiers, Algeria, in July 1999.[21] The Convention expressed deep concerns over terrorism and stressed cooperation amongst member nations in a concerted effort to fight terrorism. It recognized that terrorism constitutes a violation of human rights; that women and children are disproportionately impacted by terrorism; that there is growing link between terrorism and organized crime, trafficking and money laundering; that terrorism can be sponsored by states and that terrorism cannot be justified under any circumstances.

The Convention went into force in December 2002. Forty Member nations have so far ratified the Convention. The Convention was supplemented in 2002 by the AU

---

19 See the Constitutive Act of the African Union, available at http://www.au2002. gov.za/docs/key_oau/au_act.htm

20 OAU Convention on the Prevention and Combating of Terrorism, available at http://www.refworld.org/docid/3f4b14.html

21 See, the African Union Counter Terrorism Frame work, available at http://www.peaceau.org/en/page/64-counter-terrorism-ct [last accessed 10/9/2014.]

Plan of Action on the Prevention and Combating of Terrorism.[22] The plan of action was produced at the AU High-Level Inter-Governmental Meeting on the Prevention and Combating of Terrorism in Africa, held in Algiers, Algeria in September 2002. In 2004, a Protocol[23] to the Convention was adopted by the 3rd Ordinary Session of the Assembly of the African Union at Addis Ababa in July 2004. **Kathryn Sturman** opines that the AU "plan of Action is premised on the need to strengthen the capacity of African states through intergovernmental co-operation and co-ordination"[24] to fight terrorism.

The **United Nations Office of the Special Adviser on Africa** summed up the AU efforts in the fight against terrorism in the following passage:

> The AU's adoption of counter-terrorism legal instruments – OAU Convention (1999) and the Protocol (2004) – and the Plan of Action (2002), which establishes a counter-terrorism legal framework, are clear expressions of political will and intent of African States to deal seriously with the issue of terrorism. The Protocol to the OAU Convention, adopted 2004, conferred on the Peace and Security Council of the African Union the responsibility for implementing

---

22 Available at http://www.peaceau.org/en/page/64-counter-terrorism-ct

23 *Protocol To The Oau Convention On The Prevention And Combating Of Terrorism*, Adopted by the Third ordinary Session of the Assembly of the African Union, Addis Ababa, 8 July 2004, available at http://www.au.int/.../protocol-oau-convention-prevention-and-c...

24 **Kathryn Sturman**, *The Au Plan On Terrorism Joining the global war or leading an African battle?*, African Security Review 11(4) 2002, page 103, at page 104, available at http://www.issafrica.org/pubs/ASR/11No4/Sturman.pdf

regional, continental and international counter-terrorism instruments as well as harmonizing and coordination efforts in the prevention and combating of terrorism. The AU Plan of Action provided a framework and a roadmap for African States to implement international counter-terrorism measures as provided in the OAU Convention, as well as the measures mandated by Security Council Resolution 1373 (2001). The Protocol also established and clarified the mission of the African Centre for the Study and Research on Terrorism as a structure of the AU Commission. The ACSRT operates as the operational arm of the AU Commission for counter-terrorism implementation in Africa.[25]

The **UN Adviser** concludes his assessment by positing that "from the African perspective, having established a legal framework and operational framework, Africa's willingness to implement global counter-terrorism standards and practices, and later the UN Global Counter-Terrorism Strategy should not be in doubt."[26] **J. Shola Omotola** offers her assessment of the African Union's counter terrorism measures in not too glowing terms. According to **Omotola**:

> The enthusiasm with which the counter-terrorism call was received in Africa appears to be linked to the possibilities for adapting counter-terrorism instruments for the survival of state power, and for the advancement of the interests of incumbent African leaders. Under

25 The U.N. Adviser, supra, footnote 13, at page 31
26 Ibid

such circumstance, Africans are left with minimal choice between human rights and security in the war against terrorism." [27]

Udombana also, does not share the optimism with which the AU Terrorism Convention is being discussed. He worries that:

The Convention could sweep along its path trade and student union activities as well as purely political demonstrations. It could provide armories in the hands of Africa's dying but desperate despots to pursue repressive policies and clamp down on opposition groups, secure in the belief that their excesses would be ignored. Even the few democratic governments in Africa could take cover under the Convention to adopt measures that run counter to international human rights law. [28]

The Economic Community of West African States [ECOWAS] released a draft ECOWAS Counter-Terrorism Strategy and Implementation Plan[29] on 23 May 2013. The Draft Strategy outlines a historical overview of terrorism in West Africa and assesses the threats, vulnerabilities and causes of terrorism in West Africa. Although it does not define terrorism, it does

---

27 **J. Shola Omotola,** *Assessing Counter-Terrorism Measures In Africa: Implications For Human Rights And National Security, Conflict Trends,* Issue 2 (2008), African Centre for the Constructive Resolution of Disputes (ACCORD), Umhlanga Rocks, South Africa page 41, at page 42, available at http://www.accord.org.za/publications/conflict-trends-20082,

28 **Nsongarua J. Udombana,** *Battling Rights: International Law And Africa's War On Terrorism,* 13 Afr. Y.B. Int'l L. 67 2005, at page 99, available at http://www.ssrn.com/abstract=1806304;

29 Ecowas Counter-Terrorism Strategy And Implementation Plan, available at www.issafrica.org

enumerate what it considers characteristics of terrorism, and they include kidnapping, hijacking, hostage-taking, bombing, suicide attacks and murder.[30] It identifies what it terms "Notorious Terrorist Groups in West Africa"[31] as Boko Haram; Movement for the Emancipation of the Niger Delta; and Al Qaeda in the land of Islamic Maghreb (AQIM). The factors the draft Strategy attribute the rise and spread of terrorism in West Africa to, are as follows: presence of local radical Islamic groups and terrorist cells; conflicts, political instability, collapsed states and the presence of rapacious rebel groups; the porous Sahel region which has become a highway for terrorists and traffickers; poverty and inequality; prevalence of drugs, arms, organized crimes, money laundering and human trafficking which funds terrorism.[32] The object of the Strategy is to accomplish the following:

• Give effect to regional, continental and international counter-terrorism instruments and provide a common operational framework for the prevention and combating of terrorism and related crimes in West Africa;
• Operationalize regional and international counter-terrorism instruments in West Africa;
• Promote and consolidate cooperation, coordination, harmonization, and synergies in national counter-

---

30 Ibid at page 2
31 Ibid at page 8

32 Ibid at pages 9 - 10

terrorism actions;

- Ensure adequate protection of fundamental human rights in states counter-terrorism activities;
- Strengthen ECOWAS[33] role including that of states, civil society organizations and media networks in the prevention and combating of terrorism.

The Draft Strategy identifies its *"Three Pillars" as Prevent, Pursue and Reconstruct.*[34] The Strategy seeks to prevent terrorism in the region by countering radicalization of its people; by improving cooperation between its Member nations and peoples within the nations; by enhancing human support; and by improving intelligence amongst Member states and within states themselves. Terrorists will be pursued with enhanced criminal justice capacity by Member states; with better border controls; and by countering the financing of terrorism. Finally, the Member states will work to protect victim rights and repair the Member states governments' social contracts with its citizen and thus foster peace.

Part of the draft strategy calls for the drawing up of an ECOWAS Counter-Terrorism Training Manual to help develop and strengthen capacity of Member states to effectively implement the Counter-Terrorism Strategy. The Manual will also provide the impacting of specialized skills to aid intelligence gathering, sharing, and education

---

33 Ibid page 15
34 Ibid page 25

and facilitate the effective investigation and prosecution of terrorists.[35] At the 42nd Extraordinary Session of the Heads of States and Governments of Member states held on 27-28 February 2013 at Yamoussoukro, Cote d'Ivoire [Ivory Coast], the ECOWAS Draft Strategy of Combating Terrorism was adopted. 16 Presidents and Prime Ministers of 15 Member states signed for their respective countries.[36]

The **UN Office of the Special Adviser on Africa** gave ECOWAS a big pat on the back for her anti-terrorism capacity building programs. According to its special report:

> The ECOWAS is often seen as being the most effective of the RECs[37] in counter-terrorism programming which falls within its peace and security sector. For example, ECOWAS has established a Warning and Response Network – an information sharing programme addressing security issues. This sub-regional peace and security observation system known as the ECOWAS Warning and Response Network (ECOWARN) is operated by the ECOWAS

---

35 Ibid page 25

36 *Supplentary Act A/Sa.3/02/113 Adopting The Ecowas Strategy For Combating Terrorism, And Its Implementation Plan*; See government of Ghana Official portal, accessed from http://ghana.gov.gh/index.php/2012-02-08-08-32-47/general-news/974-ecowas-adopts-anti...

37 "RECs" is an abbreviation for Regional Economic Communities

Observation and Monitoring Centre (OMC). ECOWARN provides the sub-region with the capacity to evaluate, inform and guide responses to potential threats, including terrorism threats, in the sub-region. ECOWARN is seen as an example to be duplicated in other sub-regions.[38]

On 10 December 1999, ECOWAS established an Inter-governmental Group, Inter-Governmental Action Group against Money Laundering (GIABA) under the auspices of the Financial Action Task Force (FATF)[39] to fight money laundering in the sub-region. Speaking about GIABA, **Ibrahim Abdu Abubakar** takes the view that "the establishment of GIABA as a FATF style regional body (FSRB) is a demonstration of the strong political commitment of member states to combat money laundering and terrorist financing and to cooperate with concerned nations and international organizations to achieve this goal."[40]

---

38 United Nations Office of the Special Adviser on Africa , supra, footnote 13, at page 37

39 FATF is an inter-governmental body established by the G7. It is mandated with setting up standards and to promote effective implementation of legal, regulatory and operational measures for combating money laundering, terrorist financing and other related threats to the integrity of the international financial system: Ibrahim Abdu Abubakar, An Appraisal of Legal and Administrative framework for Combating Terrorist Financing and Money Laundering in Nigeria, Journal of Law, Policy and Globalization, Vol.19, 2013, page 26-37, available at www.iise.org

40 **Ibrahim Abdu Abubakar**, *An Appraisal of Legal and Administrative framework for Combating Terrorist Financing and Money Laundering in Nigeria,* Journal of Law, Policy and Globalization, Vol.19, 2013, page 26-37, at page 34, available at www.iise.org

The Federal Republic of Nigeria is a signatory to the UN Convention on Terrorism, as well as the AU and ECOWAS Conventions, Protocol and Strategy for Combating Terrorism. In adherence to the UN mandate pursuant to Res. 1373, Nigeria has passed key legislation criminalizing terrorism[41] and tackling the financing of terrorists and money laundering.[42] **Abubakar** summarizes the framework of Nigeria's fight against money laundering and terrorist financing as follows:

> The administrative framework in Nigeria is accomplished through the creation and the enactment of EFCC (Establishment) Act 2004 which established the Economic and Financial Crimes Commission; the NDLEA Act Cap No.30 LFN, 2004 which established the National Drug Law Enforcement Agency; the Banking and Other Financial Institutions Act, 1991 which gave the Central Bank of Nigeria (CBN) the power of enforcing the Act. Other institutions responsible for combating money laundering and terrorist financing are the Department of State Security (DSS), the Office of the National Security Adviser (NSA) and the Nigeria Police Force." [43]

---

41 TERRORISM (PREVENTION) ACT, 2011

42 The Money Laundering (Prohibition) Act, 20011; the Economic and Financial Crimes (Establishment) Act, 2004; and The Terrorism (Prevention) (Amendment) Act, 2013

43 Ibrahim Abdu Abubakar, supra, footnote 40, at page 34

In conclusion, we agree with **Udombana**[44] that terrorism is forcing the world to turn this century into the age of security. According to him:

> The twentieth century was justifiably regarded as the age of rights, given the avalanche of instruments that the international community elaborated and the corresponding institutions it established to safeguard and secure human freedoms. The twenty-first century is set to be the age of security, given terrorism's threat to global security.[45]

---

44 **Nsongarua J. Udombana**, *Battling Rights: International Law And Africa's War On Terrorism*, 13 Afr. Y.B. Int'l L. 67 2005, available at http://www.ssrn.com/abstract-1806304

45 Ibid at page 71

Chapter 2

What is Terrorism?

2.1. Definition of Terrorsim

One of the most intractable concepts in modern jurisprudence is a universally accepted definition of the term "terrorism." **Oladimeji** and **Oresanwo** say that "the term terrorism does not have a single definition and thus, become one of the most contested concepts in the world."[1] **David Cortright** aptly captures this conundrum. He says that:

> One of the most long-standing and intractable challenges facing the UN is the lack of an agreed definition of terrorism. The definitional conundrum has entangled the UN for four decades. Some countries condemn as terrorism all acts that endanger or take innocent life, while others seek to differentiate what they consider legitimate acts of resistance against oppression. Others have emphasized the need to include

---

1 **Oladimeji, Moruff Sanjo, Oresanwo, Adeniyi Marcus**, *"Effects of Terrorism on the International Business in Nigeria"* International Journal of Humanities and Social Science, Vol. 4, No. 7(1); May 2014, 247-255, available at http://www.ijhssnet.com/journals/Vol_4_No_7_1_May_2014/30.pdf, at page 248

state-sponsored acts within the definition of terrorism. Middle Eastern states in particular have refused to support counter-terrorism initiatives that might prejudice Palestinian resistance to the Israeli occupation.[2]

Given that being labelled a "terrorist" and an action labelled a "terrorist act" carries far reaching legal consequences, it has become crucial that "terrorism" be defined in precise terms, and that the definition carry universal acceptance. **Ben Saul** stresses the importance of defining terrorism and the risk inherent in failing to put boundaries to the term. He points out that:

> The absence of a definition is not merely of theoretical interest, because the terms 'terrorism' and 'terrorist' have operative legal significance in Res 1373, triggering obligations to criminalize financing of terrorism, suppress terrorist groups, deny refugee status to terrorists, prevent the movement of terrorists, bring terrorists to justice; and, vitally, establish terrorist acts as serious domestic crimes. Resolutions have also implicitly referred to self-defense against terrorism, so lack of definition allows States to unilaterally target 'terrorists' in military operations.[3]

---

2 **Cortright** supra, footnote 2, at page 19

3. **Ben Sal**, *Definition of "terrorism"* in the UN Security Council: 1985 – 2004, Chinese Journal of International Law (2005), Vol. 4, No. 1, 141 – 166 doi:10.1093/chinesejil/jmi005 downloaded from http://chinesejil.oxfordjournals.org/ on 10/9/2014, at pages 159 – 160; See Multilateral Responses to terrorism; The united ed Nations, posted October 2004 by the Anti-Defamation league in its terrorism update, accessed on 10/9/2014 from http://archive.adl.org/terror/tu/tu_38_04-09.html, where it was argued that "One of the main obstacles in forging a united front against terrorism is that there is no internationally accepted definition of terrorism. The decades old refrain 'one man's terrorist is another man's freedom fighter' still reverberates throughout the institution. As a result, there is also no internationally recognized screening mechanism for identifying terrorist groups."

The reality is that the term is difficult to define, and consensus is hard to reach on what the term actually means.[4] According to **Dr Adigbuo**, "Terrorism is a value laden word that defies precise definition. It is a concept that is charged with political motives."[5] The reason for this is that nations and groups, in the interest of self-preservation, are wary of agreeing to terms and phrases that may rope them, or parties they support, in future, as state sponsors of terrorism for actions that might seem proper at the time they were undertaken. Many of the states, especially those in the Middle East and many in other third world countries, that wish to protect the rights of oppressed or colonized peoples to struggle for their freedom and independence, are unwilling to accept any definition that may derogate from the right to self-determination. **Eugenia Dumitriu** aptly captures this divergence of opinions in the following words:

> Terrorist acts have, for a long time, constituted a major concern for the international community. Yet the definition of terrorism has represented an area of international law where the divergence of views between States was significant. For some, the protection of the State and of the democratic values of the society laid at the heart of the debate, whereas others were more concerned with the

---

4 See **Karolyi, George Andrew**, *The Consequences of Terrorism for Financial Markets: What Do We Know?* (May 7, 2006. Available at SSRN: http;//ssrn.com/abstract=904398 or http://dx.doi.org/10.2139/ssrn.904398 at page 2, where he asserts that "Terrorism is not a recent phenomenon. Although terrorism is presumably a complex and multi-causal phenomenon lying between the nexus of war and peace, scholarly research on the causes of international terrorism has always been hampered by a clear, objective definition of the event and the absence of databases chronicling such events over time in a detailed, reliable and consistent manner."

5 **Dr Ebere Richard Adigbuo**, *The New ECOWAS Counter Terrorism Strategy and Arms Trade Treaty, Journal of International Affairs and Global Strategy* Vol.25, 2014, 46-54, at page 46, available at http://www.iiste.org,

risk of an unjustified repression of 'freedom fighters.' These approaches, although apparently complimentary, have proved to be irreconcilable in practice.[6]

The situation is further complicated by the fact that most countries do not even have a single definition of terrorism, but have multiple definitions by various organs of government.[7] Take the United States for instance, a nation that claims to be a leader in the fight against terror, one would expect that it would offer leadership and direction in the search for a universal legal definition of terrorism. On the contrary, the United States, through its various agencies of government, has offered a myriad of definitions, further complicating the study and understanding of the concept.[8]

The obvious difficulty in fashioning a universal definition notwithstanding, there is need to find a universally accepted working definition. The consequence of not finding one is too grave. The gravity is amply captured by **Hardy** and **Williams** in the following words:

---

6 **Eugenia Dumitriu**, *The E.U.'s Definition of Terrorism: The Council Framework Decision on Combating Terrorism*, German Law Journal, Vol. 05 no. 05 page 585, available at http://www.germanlawjournal.com/index. php?pageID=11&artID=435 ; **Sudha Setty**, What's In A Name? How Nations Define Terrorism Ten Years After 9/11, U. Pa. J. Int'l L, Vol. 33:1 [2011]

7 See **Abimbola, J.O., and Adesote, S.A.**, *Domestic Terrorism And Boko Haram Insurgency In Nigeria, Issues And Trends: A Historical Discourse*, Journal of Arts and Contemporary Society, Volume 4, September 2012, 11-29, at pages 14 et seq, available at http://www.cenresinpub.org

8 See the various ways terrorism is defined under the U. S. Law at http://www. state.gov/documents/.../65464.pd.; http://www.dhs.gov/.../dhs_crc...; http://www. justice.gov/.../II/.../u_myths.htm; http://www.nij.gov/topics/.../terrorism/.../welcome.a...; http://www.dictionary.thefreedictionary.com/terrorism.

"The purpose of defining acts of terrorism in domestic legislation, therefore, is not only to proscribe a 'new' type of criminal conduct but also to outline the scope of an effective inter-governmental strategy for countering the threat of international terrorism. Put simply, it will be difficult for states to work together to counter the threat of international terrorism if they cannot agree on the threat that they are trying to counter."[9]

The selfishness and self-preservation modes of regimes have made it impossible to reach common ground on a single universally accepted definition of terrorism. Governments are wont to craft an expansive or imprecise definition of the term to afford it wider latitude in having tools to silence political opposition and to punish dissent. A wide and imprecise definition also allows autocratic governments the use of heavy handed tactics to address a purely domestic law enforcement matter as if it were a terrorism issue. It shields government actions from oversight and from human rights abuse inquiry. So, a precise definition of terrorism becomes all the more crucial, given the propensity of governments to abuse

---

9 **Hardy, Keiran and Williams, George,** *What is Terrorism? Assessing Domestic Legal Definitions* (February 7, 2013) UNSW Law Research Paper No. 2013-16; UCLA Journal of International Law and Foreign Affairs, Vol.16, 2011; UNSW Law Research Paper No. 2013-16, at page 108. Available at SSRN: http://ssrn.com/abstract+2213332; See also page 109 where they argue that "as long as states retain definitions of terrorism that differ from each other in important respects, the international community will struggle to maintain an effective practical campaign against the threat of terrorism. This is especially important in the context of terrorism in contrast to other domestic crimes such as theft or murder because of its uniquely political and transnational nature."

the term. **Prof Setty** cautions that:

> If the international community or any individual
> state is to address the problem of terrorist activity,
> it must first define terrorism's parameters. This
> foundational question is of utmost importance
> in determining who a state or international body
> will consider a terrorist and, therefore, who
> will be subject to the stricter laws, diminished
> rights protections, and harsher penalties that are
> concomitant with the designation of 'terrorism.'[10]

The difficulty of reaching consensus has forced the
United Nations to essentially adopt the common parlance
of "I know terrorism when I see it"[11] in its resolutions
rather than articulate a universal definition. According
to **Professor Sudha Setty**, "soon after the September
11 attacks, the United Nations Security Council took
a bold, novel step in mandating worldwide domestic
lawmaking to combat terrorism, despite the seemingly
central problem that the United Nations has not adopted
a comprehensive definition of terrorism."[12] Despite her
inability to craft a universal definition of terrorism,
the UN has been praised for at least laying the broad
strokes for a concerted push back against terrorism.
Javier Ruperez assesses the contribution of the UN in
the universal fight against international terrorism in the

---

10 **Setty supra,** note 3, at page 7

11 Apologies to the U.S. Supreme Court Justice Potter Stewart who coined a
similar analogy in his bid to define pornography in the seminal case of Jacobellis
v. Ohio, 378 U.S. 184 (1964)

12 Setty Supra, note 3 at page 3

following words:

> [T]he General Assembly has addressed international terrorism by developing a normative framework that identifies terrorism as a problem common to all member states and by encouraging concerted governmental action to develop more specific national and international instruments to address it. The solutions proposed, always within the framework of respect for international law and cooperation between States which is the cornerstone of the Charter, have been gradually strengthened to the point that they have become obligatory as the scope and deadliness of terrorism continue to grow. The package of counter-terrorism measures that the United Nations now imposes on its 191 member states constitutes a strong, solid and reasonable bulwark. Despite initial hesitation and some remaining reticence, the United Nations counter-terrorism policies and doctrines are today a critical point of reference when confronting one of the most serious and visible threats to the security of mankind at the dawn of the twenty-first century.[13]

Having identified the difficulty of, and the controversies around the definition of terrorism, we now turn our discussion to how various international and regional organizations have tried to define terrorism.

---

13 See **Javier Ruperez**, supra, note 10, at page 4

2.2. Definition of Terrorsim by the United Nations and Select Regional Organizations

To aid a better grasp of efforts to reach consensus on what terrorism really is, we turn to the United Nations and a selection of some international and regional organizations to see how they define terrorism. In articulating the various approaches by states and regional bodies to crafting a universal definition of terrorism, **Christian Walter** lays out some of the key elements. According to him:

> Terrorism requires an objective and a subjective element. The objective element is a criminal offence of a certain gravity, mainly the use of physical violence against persons. The possible offences have increasingly been stretched to include the destruction or serious damage to public (or sometimes private) property, including infrastructure facilities. The subjective element requires alternatively, the intention to create a climate of terror and fear within the population, or the intention to coerce (in different degrees according to the different definitions)a government or international organizations.[14]

2.2.A: United Nations Definition of Terrorsim

The United Nations seems to have made a calculated decision to avoid the pitfalls and controversies inherent

---

14 **Christian Walter**, *Defining Terrorism in National and International Law*, at page 21, accessed from http://edoc.mpil.de/conference-on-terrorism/index.cfm

in attempting a universally accepted definition of terrorism. It has chosen instead to enumerate specific activities, actions and incidents it labels terrorism. **Ben Saul's** seminal work "Definition of 'Terrorism' in the UN Security Council: 1985 – 2004"[15] takes an in-depth look at approaches the United Nations has taken in looking at the subject and her unsuccessful attempt at a compromise definition. He also traced the history and evolution of UN attitude to terrorism from the 1980's when most of the violent episodes were attributed more to the then raging Cold War between the West and the Soviet bloc than to terrorism, up to the post 9/11 era with the passing of **Security Council Resolution 1373**. With the direction and encouragement given to them by the UN, member states "went to town" in their attempts to define terrorism and consequently confront the phenomenon. Rather than aid the fight, it appears that in failing, through Resolution 1373, to put boundaries around the issue by offering a definition, the UN has created a monster. **Ben Saul** takes the view that:

> While flexibility in implementation is warranted due to variations in domestic legal systems, this effectively means that each State unilaterally defines terrorism, without any outer legal boundaries set by the international community. Far from urging States to confine overly broad legislation, the CTC has advocated that domestic

---

15 **Ben Sal**, *Definition of "terrorism" in the UN Security Council: 1985 – 2004*, Chinese Journal of International Law (2005), Vol. 4, No. 1, 141 – 166 doi:10.1093/chinesejil/jmi005 downloaded from http://chinesejil.oxfordjournals.org/ on 10/9/2014

terrorism laws be jurisdictionally widened to cover international terrorism, even though some domestic crimes more closely resemble broad national security or public order offences. The absence of a definition also makes it difficult to resolve disputes about whether particular persons or group qualify as terrorists."[16]

Ben Saul is of the view that the UN "...initiated a fight not against terrorism, but 'different terrorisms.'"[17] He argues that "this devolution of discretionary power"[18] to states to create their own definitions "is unprincipled and dangerous."[19] He believes that "...operatively deploying the term without defining it creates uncertainty and allows States to make 'unilateral determinations geared towards their own interests.'"[20]

The closest the Security Council has come to defining terrorism is in its **2004 SC Res 1566 of October 2004.**[21] The Security Council Resolution 1566 describes terrorism at paragraph 3 as:

> ...criminal acts, including against civilians, committed with the intent to cause death or serious bodily injury, or taking of hostages, with the purpose to provoke a state of terror

---

16 Ibid at 158
17 Ibid at 161
18 Ibid

19 Ibid
20 Ibid
21 Ibid at 164

in the general public or in a group of persons or particular persons, intimidate a population or compel a government or an international organization to do or abstain from doing an act, which constitute offences within the scope of and as defined in the international conventions and protocols relating to terrorism ...[22]

This 'definition' has been criticized as not only narrow but "too little, too late."[23]

It does appear that ulterior motives or the aims of the perpetrators of the "terrorist" acts are immaterial to the classification of the act as terrorist. In order words, what makes the activity terrorism in nature is the manner of the act and not the reason for it. Put another way, an act which is terrorist in nature, cannot be given a pass no matter how "justifiable" or noble the motivation behind it. The universal opprobrium against terrorism and terrorist acts is akin to strict liability in domestic laws.

2.2.B: Definition of Terrorism by Select Regional Organizations

I. European Union

The European Union in their 13 June 2002 Council Framework Decision on Combating Terrorism, defines

---

22 UNSC Res 1566 of October 2004

23 **Ben Sal**, supra, note 48

terrorism in Article 1 as an act that:

> may seriously damage a country or an
> international organization where committed
> with the aim of: seriously intimidating a
> population; or unduly compelling a Government
> or international organization to perform or
> abstain from performing any act; or seriously
> destabilizing or destroying the fundamental
> political, constitutional, economic or social
> structures of a country or an international
> organization.[24]

II. The North Atlantic Treaty Organization (NATO)

The North Atlantic Treaty Organization defines
terrorism as "the unlawful use or threatened use of
force or violence against individuals or property in an
attempt to coerce or intimidate governments or societies
to achieve political, religious or ideological objectives."[25]

---

24 Council Framework on Combating Terrorism, Council of the European Union, Brussels, 18 April 2002, Art. 1.; See Defining Terrorism, WP 3, Deliverable 4, October 1, 2008, COT Institute for Safety, Security and Crisis Management, available at www.transnationalterrorism.eu See also Art. 3.2.2 where it is stated that "A terrorist offence, according to the EU's Framework decision, is an offence which may seriously damage a country or an international organization. These offences must be committed with the aim of intimidating people and seriously altering or destroying the political, economic or social structures of a country (murder, bodily injuries, hostage taking, extortion, fabrication of weapons, committing attacks, threatening to commit any of the above, etc.). such offences may be committed by one or more individuals against one or more countries. The Framework Decision defines a terrorist group as a structured organization consisting of more than two persons, established over a period of time and acting in concert. Moreover, instigating, aiding, abetting and attempting to commit terrorist offences will also be punishable (Council of the European Union, 2002)."

25 NATO Glossary of Terms and Definitions, AAP-06 Edition 2012 Version 2

III. The African Union (AU)

The African Union [Umbrella Organization of African Nations] has a rather broad definition of terrorism. Terrorism is defined in the **1999 OAU CONVENTION ON THE PREVENTION AND COMBATING OF TERRORISM** as:

(a) Any act which is a violation of the criminal laws of a State Party and which may endanger the life, physical integrity or freedom of, or cause serious injury or death to, any person, any number or group of persons or causes or may cause damage to public or private property, natural resources, environmental or cultural heritage and is calculated or intended to;

(i) Intimidate, put in fear, force, coerce or induce any government, body, institution, the general public or any segment thereof, to do or abstain from doing any act, or to adopt or abandon a particular standpoint, or to act according to certain principles; or

(ii) Disrupt any public service, the delivery of any essential service to the public or to create a public emergency; or

(iii) Create general insurrection in a State;

(b) any promotion, sponsoring, contribution to, command, aid, incitement, encouragement, attempt, threat, conspiracy, organizing, or procurement of any person, with intent to commit any act referred to in paragraph (a)(i) to (iii).[26]

In an apparent bid to assuage the concerns of member states that are apprehensive of the possibility of a comprehensive definition stripping oppressed peoples of the right to self-determination, the Convention added Article 3. Art. 3 of the Convention excludes from the definition of terrorism "struggles waged by peoples in accordance with the principles of international law for their liberation or self-determination, including armed struggle against colonialism, occupation, aggression and domination by foreign forces..."[27]

2.2.C: How Terrorism is Defined by Nigeria

Since this work is centered on Nigeria, it is prudent to examine how Nigeria defines terrorism. Terrorism is defined in Section 1(2) of the **Terrorism Act of 2011,** as "an act which is deliberately done with malice after thought and which, (b) is intended or can reasonably be regarded as having been intended to (i) unduly compel a government or international organization to perform or to abstain from performing any act (ii) seriously intimidate a populace, (c) involves or causes, as the case may be (I) may cause serious bodily harm or death (II) kidnapping of a person (III) destruction

---

26 OAU Convention On The Prevention And Combating Of Terrorism, 1999

27 Article 3, OAU Convention On The Prevention And Combating Of Terrorism, 1999

of a government or public utility, a transport system, an infrastructure facility, including an information system, a fixed platform located on continental shelf."[28]

We now turn to two key concepts that are central to the controversy around terrorism, and the elusive attempts to define it. They are, respectively, the distinction between a terrorist and a freedom fighter; and the question whether a state or its agents can commit terrorist acts.

2.3: Terrorist or Freedom Fighter?

A major part of the reason for the difficulty in reaching a consensus on a universally acceptable definition of terrorism is the fear that it will subsume legitimate independent movements and legitimate fight for freedom from colonialism and oppressive governments. That is why nations in the Middle East and a good number of nations of the developing world are reluctant to climb onboard a universal definition. And there is genuine reason for their apprehension. **Professor Sudha Setty** highlights the fact that "some nations emphasized the need to except freedom fighting, anti-colonial uprisings, or other related violence from the definition of terrorism."[29] And that "other nations focused on the desire to exclude state-sponsored actions from definitions of terrorism."[30] One will recall that in the recent past, several people and groups that advocated, and in some cases fought,

28 The Terrorism Act, 2011 Laws of the Federal Republic of Nigeria, 2011
29 **Setty supra,** note 3, at page 10
30 Ibid

for the independence of their peoples were tagged terrorists. Some of these notable individuals and groups include Nelson Mandela and his African National Congress [ANC]; Jomo Kenyatta in Kenya and his Uhuru Movement; Julius Nyerere of Tanzania; Kenneth Kaunda of Zambia; Menachem Begin andYitzhak Rabin in Israel; Yasser Arafat and his Palestinian Liberation Organization [PLO]; Robert Mugabe in Zimbabwe [Rhodesia]; Fidel Castro and Raul Castro in Cuba; and Daniel Ortega of Nicaragua. These illustrious men were at various times in history tagged terrorists and hounded for fighting for their peoples' independence and for the freedom of their homelands. They all eventually rose to be leaders of their nations and were accepted into the committee of nations, as heads of state of their various nations. Thus, the coinage of the expression "one man's terrorist is another's freedom fighter." Leading **Alao**, to describe attempts to define terrorism as a "function of individual perception."[31]

For a definition to be universally acceptable therefore, it must take into account the shared concerns of peoples around the world who may have aspirations of having their own country or independent nation and who are genuinely worried about how the means by which they pursue their aspiration will be perceived in the light of the prevailing definition of terrorism. **Eric Chase**

---

31 **Alao, David Oladimeji,** *Boko Haram Insurgency In Nigeria: The Challenges And Lessons*, Singaporean Journal of Business Economics and management Studies vol. 1, No. 4, 2012, at page 4, available at http://www.singaporeanjbem. com/pdfs/SG_VOL_1_(4)/1.pdf

succinctly captures the dilemma thus:

> [D]eveloping a universally accepted definition of terrorism is unlikely – if not impossible – when 'universal' encompasses a stakeholder group, including nation-states, sub-state organizations, individual non-state actors, and scholars. Nation-states, sub-state organizations, and individual non-state actors frequently object to definitions which are perceived to target their *modus operandi*. Indeed, these groups charge that 'terrorists' are merely pursuing just ends with the only means available.[32]

Any attempt at defining terrorism must also take heed of **Professor Blakesley's** warning and avoid the pitfalls that has befallen recent attempts. He believes that "terrorism has been defined in ways that endanger democracy, erode civil liberties, and actually promote terrorism, in that the definitions provides immunity for one's own terroristic conduct."[33] He submits that "the United States and other countries tend to define conduct as terrorism, in ways and at times it finds convenient."[34]

The AU [OAU as it then was] made what seems like a deliberate effort to attempt a clear separation between

---

32 **Eric Chase**, *Defining Terrorism: A Strategic Imperative*, Small Wars Journal, Jan 24 2013 accessed from http://smallwarsjournal.com/print/13722 [last visited on 10/9/2014

33 **Christopher l. Blakesley**, *Ruminations on Terrorism: Expiation and Exposi tion*, 10 New criminal law review 554 (2007) published by William S. Boyd school of Law, University of Nevada Las Vegas, at page 562, accessed from http://ssrn.com/abstract=1151019

34 Ibid

terrorist acts and legitimate efforts of oppressed peoples to pursue self-determination. Article 3 of the **1999 OAU Convention on the Prevention and Combating of Terrorism** provides that "Notwithstanding the provisions of Article 1,[35] the struggle waged by peoples in accordance with the principles of international law for their liberation or self-determination, including armed struggle against colonialism, occupation, aggression and domination by foreign forces shall not be considered as terrorist acts."[36] **Ewi** and **Aning**, herald the AU definition as the first continental legislative instrument to offer an African definition of terrorism. They give a background to, and motivation for, the insertion of Article 3 as follows:

> In order to reconcile the historical ambiguities implicit in the use of the term 'terrorism' in Africa, it differentiated acts of terrorism from the acts committed by people in their struggle for self-determination. This was a significant achievement for a continent that had foreign control and colonialism for centuries and which was still struggling to protect the sovereignty of and territorial integrity of its states. Thus the definition did not emerge from a vacuum but rather from a concrete historical context and the principles enunciated in the charter of the OAU. Based on Africa's unique historical experience, it was therefore necessary to separate the two

---

35 Article 1 defines terrorism and is discussed above

36 Article 3, 1999 OAU Convention On The Prevention And Combating Of Terrorism

concepts, not only for the sake of clarity but also for legal jurisprudence.[37]

It is open to question whether or not Article 3 actually offers the sort of protection it purports to provide for peoples' pursuing self-determination, given the fact that it has a rider that subjects this apparent right to self-determination to the strictures of the UN.

Having recognized that the fear of circumscribing the rights to self-determination partly drives the controversy surrounding the coinage of a broadly acceptable definition of terrorism, we now turn to another driver of the controversy over a universal definition of terrorism.

2.4: Can State Action or State Sanctioned Activity be Defined as a Terrorist Act?

Another thorny aspect of defining terrorism is the question whether state action, especially within its own borders, can be regarded as an act of terrorism. Put differently, can a state commit terrorism against its own people within its own territory? **Christian Walter,** strikes the nail on the head when he asserts that "a look into the historical development of UN action against terrorism reveals that freedom fighters and the question of whether or not the official forces of a State can commit terrorist offences has always rendered debates on

---

37 **Martin Ewi and Kwesi Aning,** *Assessing the role of the African Union in Preventing and Combating Terrorism in Africa,* African Security Review 15.3, at page 37, Institute of Security studies, www.issafrica.org/.../01-oct-2006-assessing-the-role-of-the-africa-unio...

defining terrorism very difficult."[38]   Because legislation is often within the purview of governments, there is a noticeable bias in favour of state action in the definition of terrorism. The thrust of the definition is often times against actions by outside groups while states and their actors are shielded from responsibility. **Udombana** takes the view that "some governments sometimes use terrorist methods as instruments for syndicated crimes or to crush minority or dissident groups."[39]   **David Cortright** worries, and rightly in our view, that "in some cases government officials have used the fight against terrorism as a justification for limiting democratic freedoms and suppressing dissent and minority groups."[40]

Professor Christopher l. Blakesley argues, and we concur, that, "modern definitions of terrorism seek to put one's own state terrorism or terrorism by our own or favoured 'freedom fighters' under erasure, prolonging the problem of terrorism with our hypocrisy."[41] He believes that "to confront terrorism, which is essentially violence against innocents perpetrated for ideological purposes, we need to define it honestly, unmasking the pious fraud that riddles our justifications and excuses for

---

38 **Christian Walter**, *Defining Terrorism in National and International Law*, at page 94, culled from http://edoc.mpil.de/conference-on-terrorism/index.cfm [last visited 10.11.2014]

39 **Udombana** supra, note 1, at page 94

40 **David Cortright**, supra, footnote 2, at page 17

41 **Christopher l. Blakesley**, *Ruminations on Terrorism: Expiation and Exposition*, 10 New criminal law review 554 (2007) at pages 559-560, published by William S. Boyd school of Law, University of Nevada Las Vegas, accessed from http://ssrn.com/abstract=1151019

it."[42] He goes on to offer a "working definition" as "the use of violence against innocent individuals for the purposes of obtaining thereby some military, political, or philosophical end from a third party government or group."[43] **Alao** takes the position that terrorism encompasses both individual, group, non-state and state actions.[44] **Diala Barnabas Chinedu** has an interesting perspective. According to him:

> Terrorism is not new and even though it has been used since the beginning of recorded history it can be relatively hard to define. Terrorism has been described variously as both a tactic and strategy; a crime and a holy duty; a justified reaction to oppression and an inexcusable abomination. [45]

He concludes that in defining terrorism "a lot depends on whose point of view is being represented."[46]

The United Nations recognizes that terrorism could be perpetrated by both state actors and non-state actors as well. The **UN Office of the Special Adviser on Africa** makes reference to that in his articulation of the efforts of the Security Council to police terrorism. He says that:

---

42 Ibid at 560

43 Ibid

44 **Alao, David Oladimeji**, supra, footnote 76

45 **Diala Barnabas Chinedu**, *New Trends In Terrorism In Nigeria: 'Boko Haram Sect'* – *The Villain Of The Piece* [2011], at page 6, available at http://ssrn.com/abstract=1932061

46 Ibid

The Council's actions in the 1990s targeted States and non-state actors alike, in particular, adopting measures under Chapter VII of the UN Charter, imposing targeted sanctions on parties to conflicts and against States accused of sponsoring or aiding terrorism, as well as against individual terrorists, terrorist groups and their supporters and associates.[47]

Daniel E. Agbiboa emphatically maintains that "acts of terrorism can be carried out by states, state actors, non-state actors, groups, or individuals in the pursuit of specific objectives or valued ideals."[48] **Dr. Adigbuo** impliedly recognizes that states can carry out acts of terrorism but attempts, inaccurately in our view, to articulate what he considers non-state terrorism. According to him:

Non-state terrorism refers to those acts of terrorism that are carried out by persons or local groups within the state that are meant to redress domestic grievances. Domestic terrorism has a long history in West Africa. Revolutionary and secessionist groups, marginalized communities struggling for resource control and religious

---

47 United Nations Office of the Special Adviser on Africa , supra, footnote 4, at page 18

48 **Daniel E. Agbiboa**, Is *Might Right? Boko Haram, the Joint Military Task Force, and the Global Jihad,* Journal of Military and Strategic Affairs, Volume 5, No. 3, December 2013, 53-71, at page 54, available at http://www.mercury.ethz.ch/serviceengine/Files/.../CH+3Might+Right.pdf

fundamentalists find themselves in this category.[49]

Dr. Adigbuo's categorization ignores certain realities. Non-state terrorists do not always restrict their activities within a localized space as was seen in the case of Al Qaeda, the Islamic State and even the Boko Haram. Non-state actors do operate outside their own local communities and in other countries. They do not always pursue a purely local agenda. Even the groups listed sometimes work with or are sponsored or supported by state(s) or state officials. In effect, the distinction is not that precise. What matters really is the recognition that terrorism can be carried out by individuals, groups and, yes, even states. This discussion is critical in order to stress the point that how a government or its agencies operate, even in the fight against terrorism, has the potential to open it up to an indictment for terrorism.

2.5: Conclusion

It does appear from a reading of the various attempts at a definition of terrorism that the hallmark of terrorism is that it aims to shock, intimidate, overwhelm or awe the victim(s) and/or other target audience. Terrorism can be classified by the act as well as by the intent of the perpetrator(s). Thus, "Terrorism has been described variously as both a tactic and a strategy; a crime and a holy duty; a justified reaction to oppression and an

---

49 **Dr. Ebere Richard Adigbuo**, *The New ECOWAS Counter Terrorism Strategy and Arms Trade Treaty, Journal of International Affairs and Global Strategy* Vol.25, 2014, 46-54, at page 46, available at http://www.iiste.org

inexcusable abomination. Obviously, a lot depends on whose point of view is being represented."[50]

A journey to finding an acceptable definition of terrorism must begin from the origin of that word. It derives from the Latin word *terrere* or "terror."[51] That word and its elevation to prominence during the French revolution of 1793-1794 speaks volumes of the import of the word.[52] The gravamen of terrorism is obviously to inflict terror, either as an end by itself or as a means to achieving the inflictor's purposes. Thus **Udama** takes the position that "terrorism is by nature political because it involves the acquisition and use of power to advance own interests by forcing others to submit, or agree, to certain demands."[53]

We agree that a consensus on a common notion of terrorism is called for because "without a common agreement on the notion, there can hardly be any common steps to counter terrorism, whether at the

---

50 **Samuel Zumve, Margaret Ingyoroko, Isaac Iorhen Akuva**, *Terrorism In Contemporary Nigeria: A Latent Function Of Official Corruption And State Neglect,* European Scientific Journal March 2013 edition vol.9, No.8, pp 122-140, at page 124, available at http://www.eujournal.org>Home>Archives

51 See **Abimbola, J.O., and Adesote**, S.A., Domestic Terrorism And Boko Haram Insurgency In Nigeria, Issues And Trends: A Historical Discourse, Journal of Arts and Contemporary Society, Volume 4, September 2012, 11-29, at 13, available at http://www.cenresinpub.org

52 See **Christian Akani**, 2011 Terrorism Act in Nigeria: Prospects and Problems, Online International Journal of Arts and Humanities, Volume 2, Issue 8, pp. 218-223, October, 2013, available at http://www.onlineresearchjournals.org/IJAH

53 **Rawlings Akonbede UDAMA**, Understanding Nigeria Terrorism, its Implications to National Peace, Security, Unity and Sustainable Development: A Discuss, IOSR Journal Of Humanities And Social Science (IOSR-JHSS), Volume 8, Issue 5 (Mar. – Apr. 2013), PP 100-115, available at www.Iosrjournals.Org, at page 103; Dr. Ebere Richard Adigbuo, The New ECOWAS Counter Terrorism Strategy and Arms Trade Treaty, Journal of International Affairs and Global Strategy Vol.25, 2014, 46-54, at page 46, available at http://www.iiste.o

domestic or the international level."[54] In fashioning a universal definition we must pay heed to the fact that such a definition must contain "three key elements – violence, fear, and intimidation"[55] and that "each element produces terror in its victim."[56] According to **Rawlings Udama**:

> The essential elements of terrorism ... involves the calculation (intentional) use of unlawful violence to put or produce fear in the public and these acts could be committed by a person, group, and does not exclude the state. It is an adversary acts that influences an audience beyond the immediate victim. The reason and strategy of the terrorists is to draw attention from the populace, organization and states either local or international.[57]

Concerning terrorists, he believes that "they want to obtain the greatest publicity, and most times choose

---

54 Defining Terrorism, WP 3, Deliverable 4, October 1, 2008, COT Institute for Safety, Security and Crisis Management, at page 1,available at www. transnationalterrorism.eu; Dr. Ebere Richard Adigbuo, The New ECOWAS Counter Terrorism Strategy and Arms Trade Treaty, Journal of International Affairs and Global Strategy Vol.25, 2014, 46-54, available at http://www.iiste.org. at page 46 where Dr. Adigbuo insists that "Nations must agree on what terrorism is not." Because, "It is not easy to prevent nations from arming terrorists if these nations do not first agree on who the terrorists are, or on what constitutes terrorism."

55 **Samuel Zumve, Margaret Ingyoroko, Isaac Iorhen Akuva,** *Terrorism In Contemporary Nigeria: A Latent Function Of Official Corruption And State Neglect,* European Scientific Journal March 2013 edition vol.9, No.8, pp 122-140 at page 125, available at http://www.eujournal.org>Home>Archives

56 Ibid

57 **Udama**, footnote 98, at page 102

targets that symbolizes what they opposed."[58] We also agree with **Udama** that "terrorism is a psychological weapon hidden behind an ideological objective either political, economical [sic], or religious demands."[59]

Although careful attempt is needed in defining terrorism to protect peoples' right to self-determination, in practical terms it is extremely difficult to draw that fine line between terror and pursuing self-determination. In our view, at least, governments and their agents can and do commit acts of terror. These are often by way of quelling dissent and in carrying out their so-called counter-terrorism activities.

We finally offer our own definition of terrorism as, the threat or use of force to push a principle, policy, position or point of view, or to force a course of action or conduct, directed at person(s), group(s) or the government.

---

58 Ibid
59 Ibid at page 103

Chapter 3

The Evolution and Growth of Boko Haram

3.1: The Backdrop to Terrorism in Nigeria

The history and the birthing of the Nigerian nation sowed the seeds of the modern Nigerian terrorism. Colonial Great Britain forced together an amalgam of over 250 ethnic peoples and groups, who speak several hundred languages, into an artificial contraption named Nigeria, without consultation with the different groups, and without a clearly articulated basis for the union.[1] These ethnic, cultural and religious groups were forced together and held together by brute force and political machinations that held until the colonial power left the scene. Once Britain was off the scene, the tenuous threads that bound the nation began to fray under the immense stresses and strains of ethnic and religious push and pull. Modern domestic terrorism is but one of

1 **Jibrin Ibrahim** and **Toure Kazah-Toure**, *Ethno-religious Conflicts in Northern Nigeria*, Nordick Africa Institute, 1-5, available at http://www.nai.uu.se/ publications/news/archives/042ibrahimkazah/

the manifestations of this simmering conflict. **Rawlings Udama** describes this scenario in the following passage:

> Nigeria is a complex society with about two hundred and fifty distinct ethnic groups, five hundred different languages and rapid growing population of over 160 million people. Fusing these varied and diverse groups into one unified entity since the amalgamation of 1914 has been a herculean task. The British colonial masters used force to bind the various ethnic nations together. However, after independence in 1960, Nigeria has and continued to experience persistent and intense violence conflicts that has threatened its foundation ... ethnic tensions and civil strife has continued and is fast becoming its second nature, culture or the norms of the society. The centripetal forces that have kept the conglomeration called Nigeria together are fast weakening against the centrifugal forces that might lead to its disintegration.[2]

Terrorism in Nigeria is truly a modern phenomenon. There were violent incidents in the past in Nigeria, such as the pogrom of Igbos in Northern Nigeria in 1966; The Adaka Boro revolt of 1966; the Asaba massacre by the Nigerian armed forces in 1969; and, the Maitasine riots of 1982 in Kano and other Northern cities.[3] An

---

2 **Rawlings Akonbede UdamA**, *Understanding Nigeria Terrorism, its Implications to National Peace, Security, Unity and Sustainable Development: A Discuss*, IOSR Journal Of Humanities And Social Science (IOSR-JHSS), Volume 8, Issue 5 (Mar. – Apr. 2013), PP 100-115, at page 100, available at www.Iosrjournals.Org

3 **Loimeier, Roman** (2012), *Boko Haram: The Development of a Militant Religious Movement in Nigeria, in: Africa* Spectrum, 47, 2-3, 137-155 at pages 140 et seq, available at http://www.africa-spectrum.org

ISS Report on Boko Haram and the challenges it poses to peace, security and unity in Nigeria placed modern domestic terrorism in Nigeria in historical context. The report states that:

> Since gaining independence in 1960, military coups, ethnic and religious tensions have characterized post-independence Nigeria. The end of the civil war (1967-1970) was believed to be an opportunity to unite Nigeria. Yet, in the post-civil war era, Nigeria has been confronted by daunting security challenges including recurrent communal violence that has pitted various communities against one another in the country. After many years of military rule, the reintroduction of multiparty democratic rule in 1999 has coincided or seems to have led to an intensification of ethnic and religious militancy, characterized by acts of terrorism, civil strife and protests.[4]

This book discusses the most potent terrorist episode in modern Nigerian history: the Boko Haram insurgency. **Ogbonnaya** and **Ehigiamusoe** agree that "in Nigeria, the two most recent terrorist challenges to national security have been the Niger Delta militancy and the Boko Haram insurgency. These two terrorist groups have not only challenged the security of the Nigerian state but also its unity, territoriality and sovereignty."[5] **Lt-Gen.**

---

4 ISS Seminar Report, Pretoria: *The Threat of Boko Haram and the Challenges to Peace, Security and Unity in Nigeria,* Held 2 February 2012 in Pretoria, South Africa at page 1, Sourced from http://www.issafrica.org/events/iss-seminar-report-pretoria-the-threat-of-boko-haram-and-the...

5 **Ogbonnaya, Ufiem Maurice, Ehiagiamusoe, Uyi Kizito,** *Niger Delta Militancy, Boko Haram Insurgency and National Security in Nigeria,* Global Security Studies, Summer 2013, Volume 4, Issue 3, available at http://www.academia.edu/.../Niger_Delta_Militancy_Boko_Hara...

Dambazau [rtd] distills the essential characteristics of the two most destructive terrorism episodes bedevilling Nigeria today. He says that:

> The much recently celebrated security challenges are the Niger Delta militancy in the south-south and the Boko Haram insurgency in the north-east. What do they have in common? Both are organized violent rebellion: the former resource-based, and the latter, violent religious extremism; both carry arms leading to various military confrontations; both have separatist agenda as a result of their discontent with the system; and root causes for both are found in extreme poverty, unemployment, and underdevelopment.[6]

Terrorism strikes at the very core of our nation and seeks to tear the nation apart, if not controlled and eventually doused. Udama believes that "the activities of the terrorists over the past years have posed a serious security and developmental challenges (sic) and have threatened the foundation of unity of the country."[7] **Oluwafemi, Adesuyi and Abdulhamid** posit a theory on the root cause of modern terrorism in Nigeria. To them, "Terrorism in Nigeria is a direct upshot of the people's deep disenchantment with their government."[8] They *

---

6 **Abdulrahman Dambazau, Lt. Gen.** [Rtd], *Overcoming Nigeria's Security Challenges*, at page 11, available at http://www.iuokada.edu.ng/.../overcoming%20Nigeria%20Security%20Chall...

7 **Rawlings Akonbede UDAMA**, supra, footnote 2, at page 101

8 **Osho Oluwafemi, Falaye Adeyinka Adesuyi, Shafi'I M. Abdulhamid**, *Combating Terrorism with Cybersecurity: The Nigerian Perspective*, World Journal of Computer Application and Technology 1(4): 103-109, 2013, at page 105, available at http://www.hrpub.org

argue that "the mishandling of national issues has given rise to several dissenting groups along … geographical lines including the Movement for the Emancipation of Niger Delta (MEND) in the South; … and the Jama'atu Ahlus Lid Da'awati Wal Jihad, otherwise known as Boko Haram, in the North."[9] **Ayodeji Bayo Ogunrotifa** employs the Marxist theory of historical materialism in analyzing the environment that encourages the growth and sustenance of terrorism in Nigeria. He asserts that:

> The military clique and the entire ruling class benefitted from the oil boom but it did not develop the productive forces of Nigerian society nor strive to improve the socio-economic well-being of Nigerians. As oil production and revenue rose and accounted for nearly 80 percent of GDP, the Nigerian ruling class neglected other sectors such as agriculture and relied heavy dependence on export of primary products. Despite earning an estimated US $320 billion from the export of crude oil between 1970 and 1999, there was fallen standard of living and rising poverty level as the boom did not have significant improvement in the lives of Nigerians.[10]

Having looked at the background to, and environment that has spawned the homegrown terrorism, we now turn to study the origin and growth of the Boko Haram insurgency.

---

9 Ibid

10 **Ayodeji Bayo Ogunrotifa**, *Class Theory of Terrorism: A Study of Boko Haram Insurgency In Nigeria*, Research on Humanities and Social Sciences, Vol.3, No.1, 2013, 27-60, at page 43, available at http://www.iiste.org

3.2: The Origin and Growth of the Boko Haram Insurgency

There does seem to be a disagreement as to when the Boko Haram sect came into being.[11] Some scholars take the view that the group was formed by Mohammed Yusuf[12] sometime in 2002 in Maiduguri in Borno State, in the extreme northeast of Nigeria.[13] One scholar[14] places the founding of the group around the mid-1990s and credits **Aminu Tashen-Ilimi** as the founder. He asserts that Boko Haram was a "transmutation" of an

---

11 Anyadike, Nkechi O., *Boko Haram and National Security Challenges in Nigeria; Causes and Solutions, Journal of Economic and Sustainable Development,* ISSN 2222-1700 (Paper) ISSN 2222-2855 (Online)Vol.4, No.5, 2013, page 12, available at www.iiste.org ; **Ibrahim Sada Ladan-Baki,** *Corruption And Security Challenges In Developing Countries,* International journal of Politics and Good Governance Volume 5, No. 5.2 Quarter II 2014, 1-19, at pages 10-11; James J.F. Forest, Confronting the Terrorism of Boko Haram in Nigeria, Joint Special Operations University Press, 2012, 1-178, at page 62, available at http://www.jsou.socom.mil

12 **Abimbola and Adesote** say his given name at birth was actually **Mustapha Modu Jon** : Abimbola, J.O., and Adesote, S.A., *Domestic Terrorism And Boko Haram Insurgency In Nigeria,* Issues And Trends: A Historical Discourse, Journal of Arts and Contemporary Society, Volume 4, September 2012, 11-29, at page 17, available at http://www.cenresinpub.org

13 **Daniel Agbiboa,** *The Ongoing Campaign of Terror in Nigeria: Boko Haram versus the State, Stability*: International Journal of Security and Development, Vol 2, No 3 (2013) sourced from http://www.stabilityjournal.org/rt/printerFriendly/st.cl/145 [last accessed 5/2/2014] ; Babjee Pothuraju, Boko Haram's Persistent threat in Nigeria, Backgrounder, March 19, 2012, Institute For Defense Studies & Analyses, New Delhi, India; Roland Marchal, Boko Haram and the resilience of militant Islam in Northern Nigeria, NOREF Report, June 2012, Published by Norwegian Leacebuilsing Resource Centre; **Alao, David Oladimeji,** *Boko-Haram Insurgency In Nigeria: The Challenges And Lessons,* Singaporean Journal of Business Economics and Management Studies Vol.1, No.4, 2012 who takes the position that Boko Haram was founded by Yusuf in 2001; **Diala Barnabas chinaedu,** *New Trends In Terrorism In Nigeria: 'Boko Haram Sect' – The Villain Of The Piece,*[2011], available at http://ssrn.com/abstract=1932061 [Diala actually gave his name as Ustaz Mohammed Yusuf]

14 **Muhammed Kabir Isa,** *Chapter 11: Militant Islamist Groups in Northern Nigeria, available at http://www.mercury.ethz.ch/.../MilitiasRebelsIslamistMilitants Chapter+11.pdf*

earlier group, the *Muhajirun, Hijirah* or *Ahl al-Sunnal wal Jama'ah* group once referred to as the Nigerian Taleban.[15] Still others credit one Muhammed Ali as the first leader and that the group was founded in 1995.[16] According to **Anyadike**:

The obscurity surrounding its true origin perhaps informs why initially, the sect 'had no specific name as its members attracted several descriptions where they operated based on the perception of the local population.'[...] Such names include Taliban and the Yussufiyyah.

The sect soon became formally identified as Ahulsunna wal'jama'ah Hijra – 'Congregation of Followers of the Prophet Involved in the Call to

---

15 See also, **Ibrahim Sada Ladan-Baki**, *Corruption And Security Challenges In Developing Countries, International journal of Politics and Good Governance* Volume 5, No. 5.2 Quarter II 2014, 1-19; **Kyari Mohammed,** The message and methods of Boko Haram, In Boko Haram: Islamism, Politics, Security and the State in Nigeria, edited by Perouse de Montclos, Marc-Antoine, 9-32 at page 13. Eschede, Netherlands: Institut Francais de Recherche en Africaque (IFRA), 2014, available at http://www.infra-nigeria.org/IMG/pdf/boko-haram-islamism-politics-security-nigeria.pdf

16 **Atta Barkindo**, *"Join the Caravan": The Ideology of Political Authority in Islam from Ibn Taymiyya to Boko Haram in North-Eastern Nigeria, Perspectives On Terror*, Vol 7, No 3 (2013), PP 1-10, accessed from http://www.terrorismanalysts.com/pt/index.php/pot/article/view/266/html [last visited on 9/9/2014]; According to Odoemelam Chinedu Christian, Kidafa Ibrahim, Onyebuchi Alexandra Chima and Agu Oluchi Sussan, Influence Of The Boko Haram Security Threat In Nigeria On The Level Of Interest In Mainstream Media News Among Postgraduate Students At The University Of Nigeria, Nsukka, Global Journal of Interdisciplinary Social Science at page 2, available at http://www.gifre.org , "To some other sources, Boko Haram started in 1995 as 'Sahaba' and was initially led by Lawan Abubakar, who later left for the University of Medina in Saudi Arabia for further studies. Late Yusuf Mohammed who was killed in a controversial circumstance in 2009 by men of the Nigerian Polices [sic] force was said to have taken over the leadership after the departure of Abubakar and indoctrinated the sect with his own teaching which he claimed were based on purity and Sharia law."

Islam and Religious struggle.'[17]

Thus leading scholars to conclude that "the history of Boko Haram is as elusive as the group itself and studies on the group remain inconclusive about its origin."[18] The official name of the group is in Arabic, *Jama'atu ahlus-Sunnah Lidda'Awati Wal Jihad*. Translated in English it reads, "People Committed to the Prophet's Teachings for Propagation and Jihad"[19] The sect is however popularly known and referred to as "Boko Haram," which in the local Hausa dialect literally means "Western Education is Sinful." The rejection of secularism by Boko Haram is by itself not that novel or unique. In fact, **Kyari**

---

17 **Anyadike, Nkechi O.**, *Boko Haram and National Security Challenges in Nigeria; Causes and Solutions*, Journal of Economic and Sustainable Development, ISSN 2222-1700 (Paper) ISSN 2222-2855 (Online)Vol.4, No.5, 2013, page 12, available at www.iiste.org , at page 17; See **Abimbola, J.O., and Adesote, S.A.**, *Domestic Terrorism And Boko Haram Insurgency In Nigeria, Issues And Trends: A Historical Discourse*, Journal of Arts and Contemporary Society, Volume 4, September 2012, 11-29, at page 17, available at http://www.cenresinpub.org, where they confirm the controversy over the origin of Boko Haram. They say, "The time that this Islamic militant group emerged in the country is yet unknown. There were series of conflicting reports on their emergence in the northern part of the country. Information at the disposal of the different security agencies pieced together by Sunday Tribune of 12th February 2012 indicated that contrary to the widely-held belief that the Boko Haram started around 2003, the group has been existing since 1995."

18 **Odoemelam Chinedu Christian, Kidafa Ibrahim, Onyebuchi Alexandra Chima and Agu Oluchi Sussan**, *Influence Of The Boko Haram Security Threat In Nigeria On The Level Of Interest In Mainstream Media News Among Postgraduate Students At The University Of Nigeria, Nsukka*, Global Journal of Interdisciplinary Social Science at page 2, available at http://www.gifre.org

19 **Babjee Pothuraju**, *Boko Haram's Persistent threat in Nigeria, Backgrounder*, March 19, 2012, Institute For Defense Studies & Analyses, New Delhi, India, available at http://www.idsa.in/.../ThreatinNigeri...

Mohammed says that "the rejection of secularism and the pursuit of its replacement by Shariah is a current in radical Islam that goes back to the fourteenth century Damascene scholar Ahmad Ibn Taymiyyah."[20]

According to the U.S. House of Representatives, "though not the official moniker, the term Boko Haram is a revealing window into the ideology that drives the organization."[21] **Muhammed Kabir Isa** offers an instructive clarification on the idea of boko as the sect sees it. He says that, "the idea of boko is not just about rejecting Western education per se; it is a judgement of its failure to provide opportunities for better lives and thus became a symbol for Boko Haram movement to capitalize on the shortcomings of yan boko. Subsequently it was coupled with haram (forbidden)."[22] In otherwords, it is a metaphor for the failure of modern democratic society to live up to its ideals and aspirations. **Agbiboa** says that Boko Haram has even rejected the designation, "'Western education is forbidden,'" and instead, the group

---

20 **Kyari Mohammed**, *The message and methods of Boko Haram, In Boko Haram: Islamism, Politics, Security and the State in Nigeria,* edited by Perouse de Montclos, Marc-Antoine, 9-32. Eschede, Netherlands: Institut Francais de Recherche en Africaque (IFRA), 2014, at page 14, available at http://www.infra-nigeria.org/IMG/pdf/boko-haram-islamism-politics-security-nigeria.pdf

21 U.S. House of Representatives Committee on Homeland Security, Boko Haram: Growing Threat to the U.S. Homeland, Published by the Majority Staff of the Committee on September 13, 2013, at page 7, available at http://www.homeland.house.gov/sites/homeland.house.gov/files/documents/09-13-Boko-Haram-Report.pdf

22 *Muhammed Kabir Isa, Militant Islamist Groups in Northern Nigeria,* Chapter 11 of Militias, Rebels and Islamist Militants: Human Insecurity and States Crisis in Africa, pp313-340, at page 333, available at http://www.mercury.ethz.ch/.../MilitiasRebelsIslamistMilitants_Chapter+11.pdf

now prefers the slogan, "Western culture is forbidden."[23]

Scholars therefore do a great disservice by creating the impression that the movement has the shallow objective of a blanket rejection of western education. The movement obviously is about more and way more deeply philosophical than we give it credit. This tendency to underestimate the strength, philosophical underpinning and military strength, of this sect is the reason they continue to be on the ascendency even in the face of a full-blown military attack from the Nigerian armed forces. A foremost scholar of the history of Muslim societies in Africa, **Roman Loimeier**, agrees and says:

> It is equally misleading to view Boko Haram exclusively as a terror organization. Such narrow-minded approach is not particularly useful in fathoming the true character of the movement and understanding why Boko Haram has managed to attract considerable popular support in northern Nigeria despite harsh police and army repression.[24]

Ayodeji Bayo Ogunrotifa credits the disappointment of fundamental Muslims to the "watered-down" implementation

---

23 **Agbiboa, Daniel E**, *Peace at Daggers Drawn? Boko Haram and the State of Emergency in Nigeria*, Studies in Conflict & Terrorism, 37:41-67, 2014, at page 54, available at http://www.researchgate.net/...Peace_at_Daggers_Drawn_Boko_Haram_and_t...

24 **Loimeier, Roman** (2012), *Boko Haram: The Development of a Militant Religious Movement in Nigeria*, in: *Africa Spectrum*, 47, 2-3, 137-155, at page 138, available at http://www.africa-spectrum.org

of Sharia in the northern states in the third republic as the impetus for the formation of the Boko Haram sect. He asserts that "the shoddy way in which sharia law was politically implemented coupled along with dwindling socio-economic situation culminated in the formation of *Jama'atu ahlis Sunna Lidda'awati wal-Jihad* (also known as Boko Haram) in 2002."[25] According to **Ekanem et al**, "ideologically, Boko Haram opposes not only western education, but western culture and modern science."[26] **Nmah** describes Boko Haram as:

[N]otorious for kidnapping, raping, intimidation, and molestation and known to be anti-establishment. For this group, western education is Haram, Hausa word for sin and its adherents are taught that it is their duty, as pure Muslims, to cleanse society of all influences of western education and replace it with Sharia. According to them, they argued that western education is the source of corruption, inequality and must be forbidden.[27]

---

25 Ogunrotifa, supra, footnote 10, at page 47; Abimbola, J.O., and Adesote, S.A., *Domestic Terrorism And Boko Haram Insurgency In Nigeria, Issues And Trends: A Historical Discourse*, Journal of Arts and Contemporary Society, Volume 4, September 2012, 11-29, at page 18, available at http://www.cenresinpub.org

26 **Samuel Asuquo Ekanem**, Jacob Abiodun Dada, Bassey James Ejue, *Boko Haram And Amnesty: A Philo-Legal Appraisal*, International Journal of Humanities and Social Science Vol. 2 No. 4 [Special Issue – February 2012] pp 231 – 244, at page 232, available at http://www.ijhssnet.com/journals/Vol_2_No_4-Special_Issue.../28.pdf

27 **Patrick Nmah**, *Religious Fanaticism, a Threat to National Security: The Case of Boko Haram Sect*, p106, at page 111, available at http://dx.doi.org/10.4314/uja.v13i1.7

Similarly, **Diego Cordano**, writing about Boko Haram says:

This Sunni jihadist group advocates the Islamisation of law and society, to be achieved with the overthrow of Nigeria's government, which they consider to be composed of false and corrupt Muslims, and the creation an Islamic state and sharia courts across the country. The leadership of Boko Haram has supported a version of Islam that makes it forbidden (haram) for Muslims to participate in any social or political activity associated with Western society, such as voting in elections or receiving a secular education.[28]

According to **Agbiboa**, Yusuf was born on 29 January, 1970 in the village of Girgir, in present day Yobe State, in the northeast of Nigeria. He was reputed to be a student of the Islamic Scholar Sheik Gumi who instructed Yusuf on Salafi radicalism.[29] Yusuf's teaching was said to follow

28 **Diego Cordano**, The Evolution of Boko Haram: a growing threat?, Consultancy African Intelligence, Friday June 2014, PP 1-5, available at http://www.consultancyafrica. com/index.php?option=com_content&view=article&id=1695:... [last visited on 8/1/2014]

29 **Daniel Agbiboa**, The Ongoing Campaign of Terror in Nigeria: Boko Haram versus the State, Stability: International Journal of Security and Development, Vol 2, No 3 (2013) sourced from http://www.stabilityjournal.org/rt/printerFriendly/st.cl/145 [last accessed 5/2/2014]; Daniel E. Agbiboa, Is Might Right? Boko Haram, the Joint Military Task Force, and the Global Jihad, Journal of Military and Strategic Affairs, Volume 5, No. 3, December 2013, 53-71, at pages 59-60, See also Ayodeji Bayo Ogunrotifa, Class Theory of Terrorism: A Study of Boko Haram Insurgency In Nigeria, Research on Humanities and Social Sciences, Vol.3, No.1, 2013, 27-60, available at http://www. iiste.org. at page 47 where he asserts that, "Jama'atu Ahlis Sunna Lidda'awati Wal-Jihad (which means People Committed to the Propagation of the Prophet's Teachings and Jihad) was formed by Mohammed Yusuf in 2002. It was later called Yussufiya movement (named after the founder). Yusuf was a secondary school drop-out who went to Chad and Niger Republic to study the Qur'an. While in the two countries, he developed radical views that were abhorrent to Westernization and modernization. Because of the sect's radical and provocative preaching against western education, it was nicknamed Boko Haram. Boko Haram is derived from two words in Hausa language 'Boko' and 'Haram'. The 'boko' means 'book' or 'western education'

the radical path blazed by a 14th century Islamic Scholar, Ibn Taymiyya.[30] **Roman Loimeier** identifies a major influence in Yusuf's studies and teaching. He credits the Saudi Wahhabism for Yusuf's detest for westernization. According to him:

Central to Muhammad Yusuf's argumentation was a text written by a Saudi Arabian Wahhabi-oriented scholar, Abubakar b. 'Abdallah Abu Zayd [...], *titled al-madaris as-'alamiyya al-ajnabiyya al-isti'mariyya: ta'rikhuba wa-makhatiruba* (The Secular, Foreign and Colonial Schools: Their History and Dangers). This text specifically served as the basis for his rejection of a natural science-based (Western and secular) view of the world.[31]

He had built a religious institution in his hometown, including a mosque and school, where he taught children from poor homes who came from all around the region.[32]

---

while 'Haram' means 'forbidden' or 'sinful'. Literally, it means 'western education is forbidden and sinful'"

30 **Anyadike, Nkechi O.**, *Boko Haram and National Security Challenges in Nigeria: Causes and Solutions*, Journal of Economic and Sustainable Development, ISSN 2222-1700 (Paper) ISSN 2222-2855 (Online)Vol.4, No.5, 2013, page 12, available at www. iiste.org . See particularly page 17 where she posits that "Yusuf's notion of 'purity' and teachings were inspired by the works of Ibn Taymiyya, a fourteenth century legal scholar who preached Islamic fundamentalism and is considered a major theorist for radical groups in the middle east."

31 **Loimeier**, Roman, supra, footnote 24, at page 149

32 Ibid; **Samuel Asuquo Ekanem, Jacob Abiodun Dada, Bassey James Ejue**, *Boko Haram And Amnesty: A Philo-Legal Appraisal*, International Journal of Humanities and Social Science Vol. 2 No. 4 [Special Issue – February 2012] pp 231 – 244, at page 233, available at http://www.ijhssnet.com/journals/Vol_2_No_4_Special_Issue.../28. pdf

In 2004,[33] Yusuf extended his religious-educational complex to his native state of Yobe. He set up shop in the village of Kanamma near Nigeria's border with Niger Republic. He named the complex Afghanistan, apparently in solidarity with terrorists that were fighting the United States and their coalition in Afghanistan. **Zumve et al** say that:

> When a young man is poor, illiterate and unemployed, he becomes a clean slate for any kind of brainwashing which according to Karl Max [sic] is more potent when it comes from religion and aided by culture. The reason is very simple. First, these categories of people lack the intellectual power to logically question or critique what they are told.[34]

The sect believe that "evil in the society is as a result of the embrace of Western Civilization, and in order to curb such evil, an Islamic society must be entrenched by destroying modern institutions."[35] They therefore aspire to "replace modern state formation with the traditional

---

33 See ISS Seminar Report, Pretoria: *The Threat of Boko Haram and the Challenges to Peace, Security and Unity in Nigeria*, Held 2 February 2012 in Pretoria, South Africa; Sourced from http://www.issafrica.org/events/iss-seminar-report-pretoria-the-threat-of-boko-haram-and-the... [last visited on 9/9/2014]; Diala Barnabas chinaedu, New Trends In Terrorism In Nigeria: 'Boko Haram Sect' – The Villain Of The Piece,[2011], http://ssrn.com/abstract=1932061

34 **Samuel Zumve, Margaret Ingyoroko, Isaac Iorhen Akuva,** *Terrorism In Contemporary Nigeria: A Latent Function Of Official Corruption And State Neglect,* European Scientific Journal March 2013 edition vol.9, No.8, 122-140, at page 137, available at http://www.eujournal.org/index.php/esj/article/view/882

35 **Patrick Nmah,** supra, footnote 27

Islamic state, because Western values run contrary to Islamic values."[36] **Agbiboa** says that:

> Radical Islamism, …, is a by-product of a number of historical developments, including the social, political, and economic dysfunctionalities of Muslim societies that have blocked these nations from satisfactory development. The shortcomings of these societies created an aperture for extremists to exploit a sense of civilizational humiliation with a re-reading of Islamic history and doctrine that blames and abhors the west.[37]

Roman Loimeier offers another perspective on the environment that bred and nurtured Boko Haram and earlier radical groups and movements in northern Nigeria. He posits that the replacement of Islamic law and theology by western education as the sole vehicle for social and economic mobility in northern Nigeria struck a nerve and that the radicalization that is taking root in northern Nigeria is essentially a push-back by the Islamic order against modernization that has displaced it in the scheme of things in the north. In other words, it is another front in the class struggle between the old system and the new western education based system.

---

36 Ibid at page 122

37 **Daniel E. Agbiboa**, *Is Might Right?*, supra, footnote 29, at page 56

He says:

A sound education in Islamic law and theology has consequently become a sine qua non for participation in public/political debates. The introduction of Western education, as symbolized by the books (Hausa: boko) of British colonial schools, has seriously challenged the hegemonic position of Islamic education and has consequently been seen as both a threat and a symbol of the increasing impact of an alien, colonial, Christian, materialist and corrupt process of Westernization. [38]

3.2.A. Activities of Boko Haram

Although the sect was initially largely non-violent in its activities,[39] they became violent after the extra-judicial killing of hundreds, if not thousands, of their members including their leader, Mohammed Yusuf, in July of 2009.[40] According to **Agbiboa:**

---

38 **Loimeier**, supra, footnote 24, at page 139

39 **Anyadike, Nkechi O.**, *Boko Haram and National Security Challenges in Nigeria; Causes and Solutions*, Journal of Economic and Sustainable Development, ISSN 2222-1700 (Paper) ISSN 2222-2855 (Online)Vol.4, No.5, 2013, page 12, available at www.iiste.org. See page 17 where she confirms the non-violent origin of the sect. She says that "although from the outset, the sect's mission was to impose the Shari'a on Nigeria, the leadership went about its preaching peacefully..."; see Ibrahim Sada Ladan-Baki, Corruption And Security Challenges In Developing Countries, International journal of Politics and Good Governance Volume 5, No. 5.2 Quarter II 2014, 1-19 at page 12 where the author claims that Yusuf was actually against any form of violence saying that it was anti-Islam.

40 ISS Seminar Report, Pretoria: The Threat of Boko Haram and the Challenges to Peace, Security and Unity in Nigeria, Presented by the Conflict Prevention and Risk Analysis & the transnational Threats and International Crime divisions, Pretoria, Thursday, 2nd February 2012, 1-7, at page 5, available at http://www.issafrica.org/events/iss-seminar-report-pretoris-the-threat-of-boko-haram-and-th... [last visited 11/12/2014]; Daniel E. Agbiboa, Is Might Right? Boko Haram, the Joint Military Task Force, and the Global Jihad, Journal of Military and Strategic Affairs, Volume 5, No. 3, December 2013, 53-71, at pages 60-61

For many members, the extrajudicial killing of their founder served to foment pre-existing animosities towards the Nigerian government and its security forces. In the group's bid to avenge the death of its founder, almost every individual and group outside Boko Haram's network was impacted, particularly the Nigerian police and army. Boko Haram's most frequent targets have been police stations, patrols, and individual policemen at home or in public including those who were off-duty or retired.[41]

Kyari Mohammed charges that the sect was goaded into turning violent by the brutality of the Nigerian security forces' crackdown on their sect and its activities. He says:

As the military crackdown intensified, they became desperate and more militant, thereby resorting to more desperate measures, which they had despised in the past, such as burning of school buildings, attacking telecommunications base stations, killing and kidnapping of foreigners, slaughtering as opposed to shooting

---

41 **Agbiboa,** supra, footnote 29, at page 4; The circumstances leading to and how Yusuf was killed was also described by Odoemelam Chinedu Christian, Kidafa Ibrahim, Onyebuchi Alexandra Chima and Agu Oluchi Sussan, *Influence Of The Boko Haram Security Threat In Nigeria On The Level Of Interest In Mainstream Media News Among Postgraduate Students At The University Of Nigeria, Nsukka,* Global Journal of Interdisciplinary Social Science at page 2, available at http:// www.gifre.org in the following words: "To nip the festering crisis in the bud, the late President Umaru Yar'Adua ordered the deployment of the military to contain those government described as dissidents. After initial resistance, Boko Haram fell to the superior fire power of the military, and Yusuf, its leader, was arrested and handed over to the police. Hours later, police executed Yusuf alongside his alleged sponsor, Alhaji Buji Foi, who was the Commissioner for Religious Affairs during the first term of former Governor Ali Modu Sheriff of Borno State."

of opponents, and killing of health officials at routine vaccination clinics, as well as random shooting of pupils and teachers at school.[42]

The activities of the sect thus became a nightmare for both the residents of the affected areas, as well as the security forces that had the responsibility of policing the area. **Odomovo S. Afeno** says that:

[...] the security challenges posed by the group reached a climax in 2009 when the leader of the sect, Yusuf Mohammed and other key members of the group were killed by the police. Following the extra-judicial killing of its leader, the sect regrouped and has continued to perpetrate acts of violence including bomb blasts and suicide attacks against the State.[43]

Babjee Pothuraju paints a picture of the environment that makes it possible for Boko Haram to thrive in

---

42 **Kyari Mohammed**, supra, footnote 20, at page 10

43 **Odomovo S. Afeno**, *The Boko Haram Uprising And Insecurity In Nigeria; Intelligence Failure Or Bad Governance?*, *Conflict Trends* 35, Odomovo S. Afeno, The Boko Haram Uprising And Insecurity In Nigeria; Intelligence Failure Or Bad Governance?, Conflict trends 35, at page 39, available at http://www.academia. edu/.../The_Boko-Haram_Uprising_and_I...; According to the UN Office for the Coordination of Humanitarian Affairs, Analysis; Carrot or Stick? – Nigerians divided over Boko Haram, available at http://www.irinnews.org/printreport. aspx?reportid=95874 [last visited on 12/7/2014], "Boko Haram has morphed. Its original incarnation had its roots in a northern millenarian tradition, a response to the corruption and injustice of both the Nigerian state and the Islamic establishment. After the death of Yusuf, a young cleric who had attracted a significant following, power transferred to the more radical Abubakar Şhekau, and they announced a common cause with the global jihadist movement."

the northeast of Nigeria. He points to the "high levels of poverty, unemployment, corruption and political discrimination in northern Nigeria, combined with population increase,"[44] which "has turned the north into an ideal recruitment ground for Boko Haram, which has exploited the long-term neglect of the north to recruit unemployed and marginalized youth to its cadres."[45]

Boko Haram finances its operations from a number of illegal activities including robberies, abductions, extortion, and from donations from other terrorist organizations. According to the May **2014 START Background Report:**

> Since 2011, AQLIM has provided Boko Haram with financing, including reportedly facilitating donation lines from organizations in Great Britain and Saudi Arabia, trainings and weapons. The two organizations conduct joint operations in Mali and the magnitude of AQLIM's influence on Boko Haram can be seen in their increasingly sophisticated attacks.[46]

Boko Haram uses assault rifles, grenades, rocket propelled grenades, improvised explosive devices,

---

44 Babjee Pothuraju, supra, footnote 19, at page 3

45 Babjee Pothuraju, supra, footnote 19, at pages 3 - 4

46 National Consortium for the Study of Terrorism and Responses to Terrorism, Boko Haram Recent Attacks, Background Report, May 2014, 1-8, at page 3, at page 5, available at http://www.start.umd.edu/pubs/STARTBackgroundReport_BokoHaramRecentAttacks_May2014_O.pdf

car bombs, beheadings, arson and looting, in their operations. Boko Haram eventually added suicide bombers to their arsenal of terror. They use mostly young girls as suicide bombers, since they can easily evade security scrutiny because women, especially young girls, do not fit the usual profiles of terrorists. Using these young girls, they gain access to soft targets, such as markets, schools, public arenas, churches, etc, to effect maximum casualty and damage. Some of the more spectacular suicide bomb attacks have been carried out by women, often children.[47]

Boko Haram continues to wreak havoc on Nigeria and Nigerians. To date, they are reputed to have killed over 35,000 and injured perhaps hundreds of thousands. They have displaced hundreds of thousands of families and driven tens of thousands to neighbouring countries to seek refuge from the violence and carnage. There are no reliable data on, or estimate of, property damage, but anecdotal evidence suggest that property damage is in billions of dollars. The Nigerian government declared a State of emergency for the three northeast states most affected by the Boko Haram activities in May 2013. The states are Borno, Adamawa and Yobe.[48]

---

47 **FRANCE24**, "Female suicide bombers: Boko Haram's weapon of choice, 2015-02-24, available at http://www.france24.com/en/20150224-nigeria-boko-haram-female-...

48 http://www.cnn.com/2013/05/14/world/africa/nigeria-violence/

3.2.B: Boko Haram Transmutes to a Violent Terrorist Organization

In 2009, Yusuf and a large number of his followers and family members, including his father-in-law and financier, Ustaz Buji Foi, were extra-judicially murdered by the police.[49] **Don North** paints the lurid picture of the extrajudicial killing of Yusuf in the following passage:

> A few days later, the police surrounded Yusuf's compound, arrested him and took him to the station. To make sure Yusuf was not released again by his supporters, he was executed. In the days following Yusuf's murder, riots continued and the police killed many of his followers including family members, racking up a death toll of over 1,000. The aftermath of Yusuf's murder was captured on a cell phone video and broadcast over northern Nigeria, assuring his status as a martyr and giving impetus to Boko Haram.[50]

---

49 **Loimeier, Roman** (2012), *Boko Haram: The Development of a Militant Religious Movement in Nigeria, in*: Africa Spectrum, 47, 2-3, 137-155, at pages 150 et seq., available at http://www.africa-spectrum.org; Ibrahim Sada Ladan-Baki, Corruption And Security Challenges In Developing Countries, International journal of Politics and Good Governance Volume 5, No. 5.2 Quarter II 2014, 1-19, at page 12; See detailed account of his capture and eventual extra-judicial execution in James J.F. Forest, Confronting the Terrorism of Boko Haram in Nigeria, Joint Special Operations University Press, 2012, 1-178, at page 64, available at http://www.jsou.socom.mil

50 **Don North**, *Behind the War with Boko Haram*, Consortiumnews.com, November 16, 2014, 1-27, at page 11, available at http://www.consortiumnews.com/2014/11/16/behind-the-war-with-boko-haram/

After Yusuf's death, the leadership of the sect eventually fell to one Abubakar Shekau, a man the authorities had claimed died during the 2009 violent confrontations between the sect and security forces.[51] Yusuf's successor, Abubakar Shekau, is a vicious thug who has turned Boko Haram into an engine of destruction and terror. To underscore the shift in operation from the Yusuf era to the Shakau era, **Don North**, writes that: "Yusuf had initially believed that an Islamic state based on Sharia law could be achieved without violence. His deputy and successor, Abubaker Shekau, argued that success would require an armed struggle and the group increasingly resorted to the murder of their critics and opponents."[52]

As a result of his acts, Mr Shakau has eventually taken his rightful place on the United States list of international terrorists.[53] The United States has a $7 million bounty on his head.[54] The sect has also been designated by the

51 **Anthony Abayomi Adebayo**, *Implications of 'Boko Haram' Terrorism on National Development in Nigeria: A Critical Review*, Mediterranean Journal of Social Sciences, Vol 5 No 16 July 2014, 480 – 489, at page 482; According to the U.S. Council on Foreign Relations: "In July 2009, Boko Haram members refused to follow a motorbike helmet law, leading to heavy-handed police tactics that set off an armed uprising in the northern state of Bauchi and spread into states of Borno, Yobe, and Kano. The incident was suppressed by the army and left more than eight hundred dead. It also led to the televised execution of Yusuf, as well as the deaths of his father-in-law and other sect members, which human rights advocates consider to be extrajudicial killings.": Mohammed Aly Sergie and Toni Johnson, Boko Haram, Council on Foreign Relations, October 7, 2014, available at http://www.cfr.org/global/global.../p32137#!/?...

52 **Don North**, supra, footnote 50, at page 11

53 **Ibrahim Sada Ladan-Baki**, *Corruption And Security Challenges In Developing Countries*, International journal of Politics and Good Governance Volume 5, No. 5.2 Quarter II 2014, 1-19, at page 12; Daniel E. Agbiboa, Is Might Right? Boko Haram, the Joint Military Task Force, and the Global Jihad, Journal of Military and Strategic Affairs, Volume 5, No. 3, December 2013, 53-71, at page 64

54 **Agbiboa, Daniel E**, *Peace at Daggers Drawn? Boko Haram and the State of Emergency in Nigeria, Studies in Conflict & Terrorism*, 37:41-67, 2014, at page 58, available at http://www.researchgate.net/...Peace_at_Daggers_Drawn_Boko_Haram_and_t...

United States and several other foreign governments and international organizations, including the United Nations and the European Union, as a terrorist organization.[55] Their mode of operation includes the use of gunmen on motorbikes, assassination of policemen, politicians, governmental officials, and anyone that criticizes the sect including Muslim clerics.[56] Lately, there does not seem to be any limitation to their range of targets. Anything is fair game.

3.2.C: What is the attraction to Boko Haram?

The question one is tempted to pose is: why do these impressionable young men and women fall for the allure of the Yusufs of this world? The answer apparently relates back to modern revisionist interpretation of Islamic precepts. **Muhammed Kabir Isa** has a ready answer. He says that:

> Muslims have come to define and justify most and any attempts at reviving religion through militant Islamism to fight injustices and

---

55 **The US Department of State, Nigeria Travel Warning,** August 8, 2014, available at http://www.travel.state.gov/content/passports/english/alertswarnings/nigeria... ; EU Press Release of June 2, 2014 titled "The EU lists Boko Haram as a terrorist organization", available at http://www.eeas.europa.eu/legal-content/EN/TXT/PDF/?uri=OJ:L:2014:160:FULL&from=EN ; National Consortium for the Study of Terrorism and Responses to Terrorism, Boko Haram Recent Attacks, Background Report, May 2014, 1-8, at page 2, available at http://www.start.umd.edu/pubs/STARTBackgroundReport_BokoHaramRecentAttacks_May2014_O.pdf

56 **Agbiboa, Daniel Egiegba,** *The Ongoing Campaign of Terror in Nigeria: Boko Haram versus the State, Stability: International Journal of Security and Development,* [S.I.], v. 2, n. 3, p. Art. 52, Oct. 2013. ISSN 2165-2627. Available at: http://www.stabilityjournal.org/article/view/sta.ci/145 [last visited 22 January 2015]

oppression as part of their religious obligations. Ultimately, the belief is that a Charismatic Islamic leader would emerge to oust an existing order of injustice and inequality and establish in its place one that is equal and just, as enshrined by the *Qu'ran* and the *Sunnah* or practices of the Prophet Muhammad.[57]

Agbiboa offers the following thoughts on this query:

[I]t is suggested that in some cases the certainties of the religious viewpoint and the promises of the next world are primary motivating factors in driving insecure, alienated, and marginalized youths to join religious terrorist groups as a means of psychological empowerment. It is further argued that such impressionable, alienated, and disempowered young people are vulnerable to forms of brainwashing and undue influence by recruiters, extremist preachers, or internet materials.[58]

James Forest offers a more practical reason why this vulnerable segment of the society found the Boko Haram

---

57 **Muhammed Kabir Isa**, supra, footnote 22, at page 318

58 **Daniel E. Agbiboa**, *Is Might Right?*, supra, footnote 53, at page 59;? Bruce Hoffman, Inside Terrorism (New York: Columbia University, 2006), 197-228, 288-290, available at http://www.cup.columbia.edu/.../inside-terrorism/97802311269...

message resonant. He says:

> All these socioeconomic changes combined to produce a sense of insecurity and vulnerability among northern Nigerians, and particularly among muslim communities. This, in turn, offers insight into why Boko Haram's ideology has resonated among many, including frustrated university graduates who find legitimacy in their argument that Western society has failed them; their aspirations cannot be met by the system currently in place.[59]

Boko Haram has drawn and continues to draw membership from an inexhaustible pool of unemployed, frustrated and marginalized youth, to swell its ranks.[60] **Udama** argues that "prolonged marginalization and deprivations in the face of plenty has led people to become desperate and willing to die rather than endure the dehumanizing conditions they find themselves"[61]and thus "unemployment and zero opportunities for advancement have resulted in the Boko Haram to easily obtain substantial and growing support base."[62] It then

---

59 **James J.F. Forest,** *Confronting the Terrorism of Boko Haram in Nigeria,* JSOU Report 12-5, Published in 2012 by the Joint Special Operations University in Florida, USA, 1-178, available at http://www.jsou.socom.mil , at page 74

60 **Ibrahim Sada Ladan-Baki,** *Corruption And Security Challenges In Developing Countries, International journal of Politics and Good Governance Volume 5,* No. 5.2 Quarter II 2014, 1-19, at page 11; Loimeier, Roman (2012), Boko Haram: The Development of a Militant Religious Movement in Nigeria, in: Africa Spectrum, 47, 2-3, 137-155, at page 141, available at http://www.africa-spectrum.org

61 **Rawlings Akonbede Udama,** *Understanding Nigeria Terrorism,* supra, footnote 2, at page 108

62 Ibid

means that "terrorism will continue to prosper due to wide spread injustice, oppression, marginalization and extreme poverty among the people."[63]

Nmah claims that Yusuf did not finish secondary school, but travelled to Niger Republic and Chad, to study the Qur'an. Yusuf, in spite of lack of formal education, was "able to attract more than 280,000 members of school drop-outs and university graduates, who were not gainfully employed across Northern Nigeria, as well as in Chad and Niger Republic."[64] These disaffected youth found Yusuf's teaching and rationalizations for their hopeless state very attractive. According to **Nmah**, "they believed that their state of hopelessness was caused by the government that imposed western education and failed to manage the resources of the country to the benefit of all."[65] Besides, they were drawn by the attraction of eternal rewards because, "ideologically, any member who fought and died for the cause of an Islamic/Sharia state by destroying modern state formation and government establishment would automatically gain 'Aljanna' (paradise or heaven)"[66]

---

63 Ibid

64 **Patrick Nmah**, supra, footnote 24, at pages 121-122

65 Ibid at page 122; Zumve, et al posit that, "The group linked the level of poverty in the country especially in the North, its stronghold, to corruption. Corruption to the Boko Haramists is considered a Western value and legacy. The group (Boko Haram) at the onset appeared to have had its operational bases located in the poorest parts of Northern Nigeria. It is in such places where people who have been denied opportunity to go to school and meaningful economic sources of livelihood are making recruitment easier. Poor governance and corruption have provided a rallying cry for Boko Haram." : Samuel Zumve, Margaret Ingyoroko, Isaac Iorhen Akuva, Terrorism In Contemporary Nigeria; A Latent Function Of Official Corruption And State Neglect, European Scientific Journal March 2013 edition vol.9, No.8, 122-140 at page 312

66 Nmah Ibid

Zumve, Ingyoroko and Akuva, link contemporary Nigerian terrorism to official corruption and state neglect. They posit that "economic deprivation, frustration and desperation are the underlying causes of terrorism in Nigeria."[67] They argue that the "social profile of [terrorist groups in Nigeria] is largely indicative of gross disparities of life chances. The ideology behind the formation of Boko Haram terrorist sect and the kidnapping criminal gangs in the Niger Delta region also justifies our proposition."[68] As such, Yusuf was able to attract a large following by providing services, such as feeding and shelter for people. The economic difficulties following the drought in the neighbouring Chad and Niger Republic helped swell the ranks of the sect's membership.[69]

To appreciate why the radical Islamic fundamentalism that gave birth to Boko Haram was able to take root in Northern Nigeria, it is imperative that one understands the philosophical and doctrinal environment in the north at present. According to **Muhammed Kabir Isa:**

Militant Islamists radically reinterpret traditional Islamic concepts, particularly its views of battles or

---

67 **Samuel Zumve, Margaret Ingyoroko, Isaac Iorhen Akuva,** *Terrorism In Contemporary Nigeria; A Latent Function Of Official Corruption And State Neglect,* European Scientific Journal March 2013 edition vol.9, No.8, 122-140, at page 132

68 Ibid

69 **Ibrahim Sada Ladan-Baki,** *Corruption And Security Challenges In Developing Countries,* International journal of Politics and Good Governance Volume 5, No. 5.2 Quarter II 2014, 1-19 at page 13

jihads, when mobilizing the faithful by warning them against 'enemies of Islam' and urging them to defend the faith. The faithful are encouraged to train, organize and actively participate in the actualization of their goals by employing tactics such as temporary withdrawal from society. The faithful can also be urged to target state institutions and symbols that are regarded as secular or state instruments or agencies that are perceived to be tools of oppression and domination.[70]

Ekanem and Ekefre squarely place Boko Haram in the middle of the modern trend of Islamic fundamentalism. They argue that:

Boko Haram is a product of the rigidity and inflexibility of Islamic fundamentalism of the Wahhabi extraction as they continue to react violently to any act or omission viewed as a violation of Sharia or Islamic tenets. This attitude ignores the fact that other religious sects have a corresponding legal right to the same act(s). So, the fundamentalists' effort to maintain a strict and pure Islamic state in a secular country is overtly and covertly a violation of the rights of other people and as such is ignition to religious violence.[71]

---

70 Muhammed Kabir Isa, supra, footnote 22, at page 317

71 **Ekanem, Samuel Asuquo, Ekefre, Ekong Nyong**, *Education and Religious Intolerance in Nigeria: The Need for Essencism as a Philosophy*, Journal of Educational and Social Research, Vol. 3 (2) May 2013, PP 303-310, at page 306

The International Crisis Group, lay a historical backdrop to the environment in Northern Nigeria that incubated Boko Haram. It traces it to the:

[.] end of the 1990s, [when] the far north became politically fractured. Fragmented by the creation of new states, the Hausa-Fulani bloc found itself challenged by increasingly assertive minorities. Torn by controversies over the country's religious identity, there was a rise in tensions between Muslims and Christians. Economic malaise, growing corruption in government, the perversion and decline of social institutions and the rise of criminality all created a sense of disillusionment."[72]

Muhammed Kabir Isa surmises the essential basis and driving force for militant Islamic movement in northern Nigeria that eventually gave rise to the Boko Haram insurgency. He takes the position that, "[t]he rising popularity of militant Islamist movements in northern Nigeria can be attributed to a combination of factors, including increased inequality, injustices, poverty, failed social services, insecurity and legitimacy crisis of the weak authoritarian Nigeria state, as well as failed

---

72 **Ekanem, Samuel Asuquo, Ekefre, Ekong Nyong,** *Education and Religious Intolerance in Nigeria: The Need for Essencism as a Philosophy,* Journal of Educational and Social Research, Vol. 3 (2) May 2013, PP 303-310, at page 306 Northern Nigeria: Background To Conflict, Africa Report No. 168 – 20 December 2010, International Crisis Group, at page 9, available at http://www.academia.edu/.../northern_nigeria_backgr...

structural adjustment programmes."[73] **Oluwafemi et al** attempt an analysis of the driving motivation for these terrorist groups. They assert that "the core activities of these organizations have purely been in response to the inability of society to meet their obligations, which is premised on perceived government's insensitivity to their needs."[74] They conclude that "over the years, terrorism has moved from causes motivated by grievances that were purely socioeconomic to those majorly by religious fundamentalism."[75] Essentially replacing the decline in the activities of the Niger Delta militancy is the upsurge in the Boko Haram insurgency. **Ayodeji Bayo Ogunrotifa** sees the rise of terrorism in Nigeria as just an extension of class warfare[76] between the corrupt ruling class and the oppressed, marginalized and frustrated proletariat. He argues that:

> In a society like Nigeria where: police are corrupt
> and repressive, judiciary are corrupt and not
> independent, infrastructures are crumbling,

---

73 **Muhammad Isa Kabir**, supra, footnote 22, at page 322

74 **Osho Oluwafemi, Falaye Adeyinka Adesuyi, Shafi'I M. Abdulhamid**, *Combating Terrorism with Cybersecurity: The Nigerian Perspective*, World Journal of Computer Application and Technology 1(4): 103-109, 2013, at page 105, available at http://www.hrpub.org

75 Ibid

76 **Ogunrotifa** argues that, "The Boko Haram insurgency ... arose out of long standing grievances with the class structure of the Nigerian capitalist state specifically in the Northern Nigeria where Hausa/Fulani Oligarchic ruling class failed to develop the region, encouraged and entrenched patronage corruption in governance, and place more emphasizes on favoritism in terms of access to qualitative western education by the rich kids at the expense of children from poor background. These symptoms of capitalist under-development in Northern Nigeria heralded long neglect of Almajeri poor street children couple along with widespread poverty and attendant corruption within the entire Nigerian establishment, thus, provides a fertile ground for Boko Haram's ideology to get support from the rank of lumpen class in society who is [sic] frustrated with the current state of affair." Ibid at page 55

politicians have made corruption official and the ruling class created over four decades of grotesquely unequal society vis-à-vis its backward neo-liberal capitalist policies, the alienated members of the lumpen class found solace in sectarian groups like [...] Niger-Delta Militant group, and Boko Haram.[77]

The history of the formation of, and motivation for, Boko Haram notwithstanding, the activities of the sect have become a heavy yoke on the nation and threaten the very survival of the nation. This much was made clear in **ISS Africa's African Security Review**. The report finds that:

The re-emergence of the violent militant group called Boko Haram in 2009 has threatened the survival and cohesiveness of Nigeria as a state. Some are fearful that Nigeria is at the edge of a civil war as Boko Haram has gone on a killing spree, launching rampant and deadly terrorist acts that have claimed the lives of thousands of Nigerians and caused widespread fear across

---

77 **Ayodeji Bayo Ogunrotifa**, supra, footnote 10, at page 48; Zumve, et al, posit that "the dialectics here is that the violent upbringing either by Boko Haram terrorist or militants in the Niger Delta are ultimately due to 'the fallout of frustration with corruption and the attendant social malaise of poverty and unemployment, absolute levels of economic distress or deprivation perpetuated by official corruption'" : Samuel Zumve, Margaret Ingyoroko, Isaac Iorhen Akuva, Terrorism In Contemporary Nigeria; A Latent Function Of Official Corruption And State Neglect, European Scientific Journal March 2013 edition vol.9, No.8, 122-140, at pages 131-132

the country.[78]

Boko Haram at a point was a prominent fixture in the northeast of Nigeria, having captured a large swathe of real estate, which it had christened a Caliphate. **Don North**, writing for Consortiumnews, says:

> Since 2004, the most reliable survey of deaths due to both Nigerian government and Boko Haram operations to date is 25,322. It is estimated Boko Haram now occupies 20 percent of Nigerian territory mostly in the three northwest [sic] states, a land mass the size of Maryland and a population of more than two million. Boko Haram has declared the captured territory part of an Islamic Caliphate with its capital Gwoza, Borno State.[79]

The apparent hypocrisy of Boko Haram is not lost to commentators. **Anthony Abayomi Adebayo** says "the

---

78 ISS Seminar Report, Pretoria: The Threat of Boko Haram and the Challenges to Peace, Security and Unity in Nigeria, Presented by the Conflict Prevention and Risk Analysis & the transnational Threats and International Crime divisions, Pretoria, Thursday, 2nd February 2012, at page 1, available at http://www.issafrica. org/events/iss-seminar-report-pretoris-the-threat-of-boko-haram-and-th..., [last visited 11/12/2014]; Dr. Ebere Richard Adigbuo, The New ECOWAS Counter Terrorism Strategy and Arms Trade Treaty, Journal of International Affairs and Global Strategy Vol.25, 2014, 46-54, at page 47, available at http://www.iiste.org, where he points out that "the political violence carried out by Boko Haram has today claimed thousands of lives in Nigeria and the situation continue to further deteriorate as the group questions the corporate existence of Nigeria."

79 **Don North**, *Behind the War with Boko Haram*, supra, footnote 50, at page 2

group publicly extols its ideology despite the fact that its founder and former leader Muhammad Yusuf was himself a highly educated man who lived a lavish life and drove a Mercedes Benz."[80] They wonder why a sect that rails against western civilization and its allegedly bad influence on Muslims will rely to a large extent on western technology to conduct its activities. They use the internet to disseminate their message and to gather critical information and news. They use cellular phones. They use vehicles and weaponry that are products of western education and technology. They wear western clothes and body armor. They freely use explosive devices parts of which, can be traced to western education and technology. Some of them have University education. Thus, **Udama** snidely points out that:

[T[hough the sect did not see anything good in western education, they have not denounce [sic] using or deprived themselves [sic] from the benefits of the scientific researches and inventions born out of western education such as medicines, automobiles, the assault raffles [sic], communication gadgets, and other information

---

80 **Anthony Abayomi Adebayo**, *Implications of 'Boko Haram' Terrorism on National Development in Nigeria: A Critical Review*, Mediterranean Journal of Social Sciences, Vol 5 No 16 July 2014, 480 – 489, available at http://www.mcser.org/journal/index.php/mjss/article/download/3330/3284 , at page 481; Don North, Behind the War with Boko Haram, Consortiumnews.com, November 16, 2014, 1-27, at page 10, available at http://www.consortiumnews.com/2014/11/16/behind-the-war-with-boko-haram/

technology equipment which they all use.[81]

Don North adds that "although Boko Haram cling to tactics and philosophies not seen since the Middle Ages, their one exception is the production of videos and distribution through Western social media, particularly Facebook YouTube."[82] But, **Roman Loimeier** disagrees with scholars that Yusuf was a hypocrite. He corrects the erroneous impression critics of Yusuf have about his real position on modern technology. According to **Loimeier**:

> His opponents in Nigeria, such as Ja'far Mahmud Adam, were quick to point out Muhammad Yusuf's "hypocrisy" in using "modern means" such as a passport, visa and airplanes (as provided by "corrupt" Nigerian authorities, no less) despite his supposed espousal of anti-modern and ultra-fundamentalist ideas. This statement was rather polemical, though: Muhammad Yusuf and the Boko Haram movement had never taken such a position on modern technology, and had

---

81 **Rawlings Akonbede Udama**, *Understanding Nigeria Terrorism, its Implications to National Peace, Security, Unity and Sustainable Development: A Discuss*, IOSR Journal Of Humanities And Social Science (IOSR-JHSS), Volume 8, Issue 5 (Mar. – Apr. 2013), PP 100-115, available at www.Iosrjournals.Org, at page 106; Muhammed Kabir Isa further underscores that hypocrisy. He says: "ironically, Islamist militant movements regard themselves as pragmatic and modern adaptation of Western-styled organisations that are better suited to deliver the services demanded by large educated cohorts of Muslim youths in northern Nigerian cities. These movements are to adopt Western information technology to advance their cause, reach out to adherents and solicit funds, as well as o connect to other global Islamic movements.": Muhammed Kabir Isa, Chapter : Militant Islamist groups in northern Nigeria, at page 322, available at http://www.mercury.ethz.ch/.../MilitiasRebelsIslamistMilitants_Chapter+11.pdf

82 Don North, Behind the War with Boko Haram, supra, footnote 50, at page 12

in fact claimed that modern technology (by contrast to Western education), meaning mobile phones, television, motorbikes and even modern medicine (as well as AK-47 machine guns), was completely acceptable in Islamic terms.[83]

Although Boko Haram has been forced to give up the contiguous physical territories it controlled, the sect has receded and hidden in plain site amongst the local communities in the entire northeast. From these immersed sites, they routinely strike, causing widespread carnage, death and destruction. Although they have no identifiable territory under their exclusive control, as they once had, they are nonetheless as lethal as they had always been. And they continue to pose an existential threat to the nation.

Having got a bit of a handle on the contextual and theoretical backdrop of domestic terrorism as exemplified by Boko Haram in Nigeria, and having traced the history of the Boko Haram sect, we shall now attempt to have a broader discussion of the factors that triggered the Boko Haram insurgency.

---

83 Loimeier, supra, footnote 49, at page 150?

Chapter 4

Examination of the Factors that Triggered, and Sustain the Boko Haram Insurgency

Boko Haram was ushered into Nigeria by a combination of multiple factors, ranging from the political, economic, social, cultural, legal and religious, among others.[1] A clear articulation and review of these factors will go a long way to assist in finding a solution to this scourge. **Alao** underscores the fact that solution to terrorism must evolve from a clear understanding of factors that cause it. He therefore argues that "acts of terrorism are manifestations of unresolved conflicts and the inability of the government to overcome the challenges are reflections that the root cause(s) of the conflicts are not

---

1 See **Abimbola, J.O., and Adesote, S.A.**, *Domestic Terrorism And Boko Haram Insurgency In Nigeria, Issues And Trends: A Historical Discourse*, Journal of Arts and Contemporary Society, Volume 4, September 2012, 11-29, at 11, available at http://www.cenresinpub.org , where they assert that, "a number of analysts have variously attributed the disturbing trend to political dissatisfaction, ethnic and religious differences, perceived societal neglect and pervasive poverty among the people."

identified and therefore the correct mechanism could not be adopted to manage or resolve it."[2] In otherwords, a misdiagnosis of the drivers of domestic terrorism will lead to a prescription that will not eliminate it. To find a lasting solution to the scourge of domestic terrorism, as typified by the Boko Haram insurgency, we must therefore have a better appreciation of the historical, cultural, economic, political and other contexts in which they take place. To that we now look.

Dr. Adigbuo sees the modern domestic terrorism in Nigeria from the prism of the struggle between the weak and the strong. He takes the position that "terrorism is a tactic of the weak against the powerful"[3] and that "political or social minorities, religious fundamentalists and ethnic movements sometimes turn to acts of terrorism on behalf of their political causes."[4] And that they deploy acts of terrorism such as "kidnapping, hostage-taking, bombing, suicide attacks, and murder"[5] to achieve their objectives. **Ibrahim and Kazah-Toure** add that:

> One of the most important questions informing political mobilisation in Nigeria has been the

---

2 **Alao, David Oladimeji**, *Boko-Haram Insurgency In Nigeria: The Challenges And Lessons,* Singaporean Journal of Business Economics and Management Studies Vol.1, No.4, 2012, at page 2, available at http://www.singaporeanjbem.com/pdfs/SG_VOL_1_(4)/1.pdf

3 **Dr. Ebere Richard Adigbuo**, The New ECOWAS Counter Terrorism Strategy and Arms Trade Treaty, Journal of International Affairs and Global Strategy Vol.25, 2014, 46-54, at page 48, available at http://www.iiste.org

4 Ibid

5 Ibid

conquest of federal power at the centre. The logic of political mobilization has developed along the lines of a zero-sum game. This means that groups are obliged to block the access of others or displace those who already have access if they are to eat from the national cake. That process of a permanent strategy of blockage has amplified the expression of fissiparous tendencies because all those who are not inside are outside.[6]

Addressing the Boko Haram insurgency, **Odomovo S. Afeno** takes the view that "the Boko Haram uprising is not only a security issue."[7] He believes that "the political leadership has failed to transparently use public resources to reduce poverty and prevent all forms of socio-economic and political exclusions as a way of averting human insecurity."[8] Thus, "the Boko Haram uprising is primarily the result of the failure of successive governments in Nigeria to fight corruption, provide public services, create economic opportunities and establish accountable and effective security institutions."[9]

---

6 **Jibrin Ibrahim and Toure Kazah-Toure**, *Ethno-religious conflicts in Northern Nigeria*, Nordick Africa Institute, 1-5, at page 1, available at http://www.nai.uu.se/publications/news/archives/042ibrahimkazah/

7 **Odomovo S. Afeno**, *The Boko Haram Uprising And Insecurity In Nigeria; Intelligence Failure Or Bad Governance?*, Conflict trends 35, at page 40, available at http://www.europal.europa.eu/.../EXPO-AFET_NT(2014...

8 Ibid

9 Ibid; ISS Seminar Report, Pretoria: The Threat of Boko Haram and the Challenges to Peace, Security and Unity in Nigeria, Presented by the Conflict Prevention and Risk Analysis & the transnational Threats and International Crime divisions, Pretoria, Thursday, 2nd February 2012, 1-7, at page 6, available at http://www.issafrica.org/events/iss-seminar-report-pretoris-the-threat-of-boko-haram-and-th... [last visited 11/12/2014]

Udama fears that "the sects' (sic) activities have spread fear across the length and breadth of not only northern Nigeria but the entire country…"[10] and that, "given the ethnic sensitivity of the country, it has pushed further its political polarization and raised the existing suspicion and distrust especially between the north and south."[11] **James Forest** concludes that some of what is discussed in the foregoing paragraphs "are the kinds of grievances and tensions that contribute to an enabling environment for vigilante groups, criminal gangs, thugs, drug smugglers, and radical extremists."[12] **Roman Loimeier** takes the position that "as long as the basic social and economic context does not decisively change – specifically, Nigeria's on-going inability to achieve sustained economic growth as well as some degree of social justice – militant movements such as Boko Haram will rise again."[13]

4.1: Political and Structural Factors

The very "founding" of Nigeria by colonial Great Britain laid a foundation for the various conflicts that Nigeria

---

10 **Udama, Rawlings Akonbede**, *Understanding Nigeria Terrorism, its Implications to National Peace, Security, Unity and Sustainable Development: A Discuss*, IOSR Journal of Humanities And Social Science Volume 8, Issue 5 (Mar. - Apr. 2013), PP 100-115, at page 112, available at http://www.iosrjournals.org

11 Ibid

12 **James J.F. Forest**, *Confronting the Terrorism of Boko Haram in Nigeria*, Joint Special Operations University Press, 2012, 1-178, at page 43, available at http://www.jsou.socom.mil

13 **Loimeier, Roman** (2012), *Boko Haram: The Development of a Militant Religious Movement in Nigeria, in: Africa Spectrum*, 47, 2-3, 137-155, at page 152, available at http://www.africa-spectrum.org

endures today, especially the Boko Haram insurgency. According to **Kyari Mohammed**:

> Colonial policies of divide-and-rule reinforced perceptions of North-South separateness, thereby not only blocking the emergence of a pan-Nigerian movement against colonial rule, but also fossilising the differences and separateness. The emergence and consolidation of a tripodal regional structure and ethno-regional political parties in the late 1940s solidified these positions. These regional identities and policies continue to shape Nigerian politics and governance to this day. [14]

Ours is a defective "federation" that is bursting at the seams with structural issues that call for resolution. Terrorism is a resultant consequence of this defect and no real solution could ever be found without addressing the foundational underpinning of our nation. **Basil Ekot** takes a commendable stab at the heart of the matter. He writes:

> We must note from the outset that these conflicts also arose due to the awkwardness of

---

14 See **Kyari Mohammed**, *The message and methods of Boko Haram, In Boko Haram: Islamism, Politics, Security and the State in Nigeria*, edited by Perouse de Montclos, Marc-Antoine, 9-32 at page 11. Eschede, Netherlands: Institut Francais de Recherche en Africaque (IFRA), 2014, available at http://www.infra-nigeria. org/IMG/pdf/boko-haram-islamism-politics-security-nigeria.pdf

Nigeria federalism. The concentration of power and resources at the centre has been identified as one of the major structural defects of the Nigerian federal system. This concentration has rendered the federating states impotent and powerless, relating to the Federal Government in a dependent manner. In a multi-ethnic society such as Nigeria, such development breeds a sectional monopoly of power and, therefore, lends itself to easy marginalization of others. It further results in suspicion, lack of trust and tension in the body politic.[15]

Structural imbalances in terms of ethnic representation, resource control and revenue allocation, as well as the overbearing centralized control by the federal government, are all at the heart of the matter. The constituent ethnic, cultural and religious groups that make up Nigeria feel cheated by both the manner of amalgamation and the result of amalgamation. The feeling seems to be that opportunity should be given to the constituent parts of the federation to seek out an agreed upon basis for the Nigerian political union. Because of this perceived dislocation, the various ethnic, cultural, linguistic and religious groups are not

---

15 **Basil Ekot**, *Conflict, Religion and Ethnicity in the Post-Colonial Nigerian State*, The Australasian Review of African Studies, Volume 30 Number 2 December 2009, pp 47-67, at page 49, available at http://www.federalism-bulletin.eu/User/index.php?PAGE=Sito_it/boll...

properly vested in the primacy of the Nigerian nation. Rather, their primary allegiance is to their own group. **Agaptus Nwozor** captures this fact in the following passage:

> The various ethnic groups that make up contemporary Nigeria were forcefully banded together and as such were not privy to, nor participated in, negotiating the basis for Nigeria statehood. The externality factor of the union and the internal rigidities prevalent in the operations of the Nigerian state constitutes a threat to its corporate survival.[16]

The presidential system of government that Nigeria operates, seems more of a unitary system than a federating system, since enormous power is concentrated in the central government, with pittances devolving to the federating states and local governments. Given the patronage system that has eaten deep into the Nigerian political class, the Presidential system is a catalyst for a winner take all dash to the finish, for the political elites that dominate the political landscape of Nigeria. **Francis** and **Sardesai** believe that the politicians disburse revenues entrusted to them

---

16 **Agaptus Nwozor**, *Media, Ethnicity and the Challenge of Peace: Exploring the Crisis of State-Building in Nigeria,* The Journal of Pan African Studies, Vol.6, no.9, May 2014, at page 147, available at http://www.jpanafrican.com/docs/vol6no9/6.9-11-Nwozor.pdf

as if it is their personal estate. They charge that:

> Public employment and goods may be viewed
> and used primarily as resources for personal
> or group advancement rather than as a means
> to serve the public good. Political leaders at
> all levels of government are under pressure to
> reward their clients and supporters, and as a
> consequence, the management and allocation
> of resources may follow the lines dictated by
> patronage rather than policy.[17]

The realization by the political class that to the winner lies the huge spoils have made politics and the scramble for political office a fight to the death endeavor. In other words, politicking has become a do or die affair. **Paul Francis et al** aptly describe this state of affair in the following passage:

> Presidential system often play out as zero sum
> game in which the prevailing faction gains
> access to all the benefits during elections. Under
> conditions of high social fragmentation, a
> "winner take all" political system may become
> a source of instability because people's access

---

17 **Francis, P., Sardesai, S,** *Republic of Nigeria: Niger Delta Social and Conflict Analysis*, World Bank's Sustainable Development Department Africa Region Report, May 2008, 1-69, at page 7, available at http://www.sitesresources.world-bank.org/EXTSOCIALDEV/.../Niger_Del...

to public resources may depend upon electoral success. In Nigeria, this model increases the stakes in every election since access to goods and services largely depends on who is in power.[18]

The use of ethnic and religious identities by politicians and the Nigerian elite in their fight for power, influence, and relevance, helps to overheat the polity and has helped fuel modern terrorism. **James Forest** argues, correctly in our view, that:

Nigeria's structural and sociopolitical emphasis on ethnic identity is a core challenge to the future security and prosperity of their country. In essence, local customs and government policies enforce and amplify ethnic divisions instead of national unity. A person's identity is first and foremost a Hausa, Igbo, Yoruba, Ijaw, et cetera – not a "Nigerian." There has been a failure to create a national consciousness, a universal patriotism across Nigeria.[19]

According to **Dr. Agaptus Nwozor**, "the continuing dependence of the Nigerian elite on state power as its main source of accumulation places high premium on

---

18 **Paul Francis, Deidre Lapin, Paula Rossiasco**, *"Securing Development And Peace In The Niger Delta: A Social and Conflict Analysis for Change"*, Study prepared for publication by the Woodrow Wilson International Center for Scholars, Africa Program and Project on Leadership and Building State Capacity, 1-160, at page 37, available at http://www.wilsoncenter.org/sites/default/files/AFR_110929_Niger%20Delta_0113.pdf

19 **James Forest,** supra, note 12, at page 42

it wherein they would go to any length to safeguard it, including mobilizing the masses and exploiting ethnic and religious prejudices."[20] Thus, he concludes, "this distortion of the federalist principle and the recourse of the elite to religious and ethnic prejudices to advance their political agenda have had the effect of eroding peace in the polity."[21] **Lt. Gen. Dambazau [Rtd.],** makes the point that "there are scholars who hold the view that ethnic rivalry and distrust are a consequence of colonial strategy of divide and rule,"[22] but he adds that this is "a situation that persists as a strategy for politicians for the mobilization of political support and votes during elections."[23]

James J.F. Forest charges that "in Nigeria, the powerful make decisions based on what they believe is required for their political survival and the economic security of their family, clan, and close associates."[24] Therefore, "because of this system of patronage and personal largesse, a political culture has developed in which the government is not seen as a means to serve the people and the state, but rather, the means to wealth."[25] Employment and

---

20 **Agaptus Nwozor**, supra, note 16, at page 151.

21 Ibid

22 **Abdulrahman Dambazau, Lt. Gen. [Rtd]**, *Overcoming Nigeria's Security Challenges*, at page 4, available at http://www.iuokada.edu.ng/.../Overcoming%20Nigerias%20Security%20Chall.

23 Ibid

24 **James Forest**, supra, footnote 12, e at page 32

25 Ibid at page 33

distribution of infrastructure and social amenities are neither based on merit nor motivated by need. Rather, the driving factor is the spreading of patronage and political largesse to supporters. According to **Ibrahim and Toure**:

> The Nigerian political elite has been involved in an intense struggle to have access to what has been called the national cake. In that process, patterns of political domination are constantly being transformed. It is this constantly changing pattern of domination that is producing the fears and anxieties that underlie increasing conflict and intolerance.[26]

This has often resulted in the creation of over-bloated bureaucracies to sustain this patronage system. Leading **Paul Francis et al** to conclude that, "these practices in Nigeria have led to an extremely bloated public sector with widespread duplication of agencies and responsibilities. Much of the budget is consumed in supporting the costs of the bureaucracy itself rather than the services it ostensibly exists to provide."[27] **Ibrahim Sada Ladan-Baki** highlights the destructive impact of creating more and more bureaucratic layers in Nigeria's body politic and the drain it causes on the resources that should be better directed to providing essential social

---

26 **Ibrahim & Toure**, supra, note 6, at page 2

27 **Paul Francis**, et al., supra, note 18, at page 32

services. He identifies the continuing unviability of the constituent parts of the federating units resulting from the creation of more and more levels of bureaucracy. He asserts that, "in essence, the more the exercise to presumably create new states and local government areas, the less powerful and viable the component units of the federal structure, and the more the corruption networks in the system. National development suffers while personal enrichment increases."[28]

It does then appear that the federal government's motivation for creating these additional levels of bureaucracy was not to bring government to the grassroots, rather a ploy to continue to emasculate the constituent states and thus continue to ensure their dependence on the federal government. In essence, making the federal set-up more of a unitary than federating unit. **Paul Francis et al** reach the same conclusion in the following passage:

In fact, the creation of states and LGAs is the outcome of two simultaneous but opposing processes. One tendency is to satisfy the demands of local and ethnic (or sub-ethnic) minorities by granting them their own administrative units; the second consolidates the strength of the federal government by keeping the growing

---

28 **Ibrahim Sada Ladan-Baki**, *Corruption And Security Challenges In Developing Countries*, International journal of Politics and Good Governance Volume 5, No. 5.2 Quarter II 2014, 1-19, at page 9

number of states and LGAs relatively weak.[29]

The structural imbalance between the weaker states in relation to the increasingly stronger and more domineering federal government has heightened regional and ethno-religious competition and attendant violent conflicts.

Mention must also be made of dubious politicians, ethnic and religious leaders, that use terror to fan the embers of political, ethnic and religious tensions, to further their personal selfish ambitions. Their activities add fuel to the already explosive situation in the north-east of Nigeria. The tensions that are stoked coupled with the thugs that are trained and deployed by these politicians eventually metamorphose into armed criminals and terrorists. Rogue politicians are wont to recruit idle and unemployed youth as their political thugs and enforcers, only to dump them after the elections. These abandoned vicious thugs now turn their guns and other dangerous weapons on innocent civilians and in many cases join terror groups in the Northeast theatre.[30] Therefore, a significant part of the blame must go to politicians for the terrorist fires that are burning rampant in the north-east

---

29 **Paul Francis, et al.**, supra, note 18, at pages 24 - 27

30 **Kimiebi Imomotimi Ebienfa** (2011): *Militancy in the Niger Delta and the Emergent categories*, Review of African Political economy, 38:130, 637-643, available at http://www.kimiebi.blogspot.com/2012/.../militancy-in-niger-delta-and-emergent.html

of Nigeria. To solve this terrorist scourge, politicians must be alive to their responsibilities to both their local communities and their country, as citizens and leaders. The practice of stoking divisions and grooming vicious thugs to advance their selfish political interests must cease, for there to be any chance of getting a handle on terrorism in Nigeria.

This factor is further exacerbated by the fact that successive Nigerian governments have failed in their duties to Nigeria and Nigerians, and this has resulted in the loss of respect, trust, and confidence by Nigerians in their government. Thus, the resort, in most cases, to self help in dealing with societal issues. Speaking of the Boko Haram insurgency, **Kyari Mohammed** says "the inability of the state to guarantee the security of citizens – in fact, their failure to defend even their own installations and officers – not only emboldened sect members but had the effect of remobilising passive members into action."[31] **Lt. Gen. Abdulrahman Dambazau [Rtd.]** addresses the responsibility of the Nigerian government to protect Nigerians in their persons and properties and articulates the historical and constitutional obligation of government to Nigerians in the following passage:

> Before we suggest how to overcome the security challenges in Nigeria, we must begin by acknowledging the fact that it is the sole

---

31 **Kyari Mohammed**, supra, note 14, at page 25

responsibility of a government to guarantee the security of its citizens, and also as a matter of fact it is this responsibility that gives any government its legitimacy. In the case of Nigeria, the responsibility to protect is clearly spelt out in Sec 14(2)(b) of the 1999 Constitution which states that "the security and welfare of the people shall be the primary purpose of government." This is the basis for the social contract in which we as citizens of Nigeria surrender some of our freedoms in addition to submitting ourselves to the authority relating to governance in order for us to enjoy the full protection of our remaining rights. These rights which include those of life; dignity of human persons; personal liberty; fair hearing; private and family life; freedom of thought, conscience and religion; freedom of expression; peaceful assembly and association; freedom of movement; and freedom from discrimination, are enshrined in sections 33 to 43 of our Constitution. These rights are fundamental to the social contract between government and the citizens, and failure to guarantee them by the former not only means a violation of the "agreement," but also a threat to the security of a nation.[32]

In summary, bad governance is the hallmark of the Nigerian political elite. Bad governance is the complaint of

---

32 **Dambazau**, supra, note 22, at pages 3-4

terrorists. The Nigerian political elite govern the country as if it is their private estate. There is no consideration of the needs of the governed and there is zero accountability. No real headway can therefore be made in countering terror without addressing the structural imbalance that is discussed above, and especially bad governance.

4.2: Corruption

Corruption is, without a doubt, the thorniest issue that confronts Nigeria today. In Nigeria, corruption is no longer an exception to the rule or an aberration. Corruption is the rule and has pervaded the entire strata of society. It is not an exaggeration to assert that almost everything that ails the country today has some link to corruption. Nigerians of every stripe are thoroughly fed up with corruption and they are frustrated by the failure of leadership to rein in institutional corruption. Corruption is one of the top three triggers of terrorism in Nigeria.

The U.S. House of Representatives takes the view that, "the consensus among most observers is that the level of corruption in Nigeria weakens the government's legitimacy, and must be tackled to restore public confidence in Nigeria's government."[33] **James J.F. Forest** shines light on the central role corruption plays in fueling

---

33 U.S. House of Representatives Committee on Homeland Security, Boko Haram: Growing Threat to the U.S. Homeland, Published by the Majority Staff of the Committee on September 13, 2013, at page 32, available at http://www.homeland. house.gov/sites/homeland.house.gov/files/documents/09-13-Boko-Haram-Report.pdf

terrorism. He argues that:

> When a government fails to adhere to
> the conventional social contract between
> government and the governed, its citizens
> become disenchanted and seek the power to
> force change. This, in turn, has resulted in a
> variety of revolutionary movements throughout
> history. Corrupt governments seek to maintain
> and increase their power over others and over
> resources by any means necessary, while the
> powerless see the corruption and look for ways to
> combat it – even through violent acts of terrorism,
> as that may be perceived as their only form of
> recourse. In the African context, corruption has
> indeed been a common underlying factor in
> various forms of political violence, and is cited
> often by Boko Haram as one of the motivating
> causes for their campaign of terror.[34]

Many Nigerians, particularly a teeming population of
unemployed, frustrated and hopelessly marginalized
youths have become increasingly frustrated with
the stranglehold corruption has on the political
leadership and the unwillingness or inability of the
ruling elites to meaningfully tackle corruption. **Ibaba**
refers to what he terms "primitive accumulation"
of wealth and identifies it as the bane of the political elite

---

34 **James Forest**, supra, note 12, at page 6

in Nigeria. He says that:

> The privatization of the state defines the character of the Nigerian state. In Nigeria, politics is largely seen as a means of accumulation of wealth; and because the state is the object of political competition and medium for the allocation of resources, it has been effectively used to achieve the goal of primitive accumulation of wealth. The result is the privatization of the state by the custodians of power at all levels of governance (federal, state and local), and its consequent utilization for the pursuit of individual, sectional and ethnic interests; as against the pursuit of the common interests or the public good . . . the backlash is the result of the dilemma of choosing between the promotion of private or public interests. In most cases, the State promotes the private interest, and this has made it to be overtly partisan.[35]

Given that the only meaningful access to wealth in Nigeria is largely through acquisition of political power, the restive youth are quickly being drawn to marginal and violent groups as a sure bet to gaining access to political power and thus economic power as well. **Ayodeji Bayo Ogunrotifa** does not pull punches in laying the blame of this sorry state of affairs on the corrupt elite. He

---

35 **Ibaba S. Ibaba**, *Alienation and Militancy in the Niger Delta: Hostage Taking and the dilemma of the Nigerian State*, page 11, at page 21, available at http://www.ajol.info/index.php/ajcr/article/viewFile/39424/59588

charges that:

Rather than resolving the socio-economic problems bedeviling the country, the civilian regime from local, state and national level added an appalling insult upon injury and implemented avalanche of anti-people policies such as privatization, retrenchment of workers, partial removal of subsidy, education commercialization and others. Bribery and corruption became more entrenched and institutionalized as the access to state power become access to amass ill-gotten wealth.[36]

Diala laments that "the wealth of the nation keeps revolving around those at the helm of affairs of government without thinking of how the poor survives. Billions and Trillions have been wasted over the years by short sighted self-serving government on personal aggrandizement."[37] Thus, he concludes, "this extreme

---

36 **Ayodeji Bayo Ogunrotifa**, *Class Theory of Terrorism: A Study of Boko Haram Insurgency In Nigeria*, Research on Humanities and Social Sciences, Vol.3, No.1, 2013, 27-60, at page 47, available at http://www.iiste.org

37 **Diala Barnabas Chinaedu**, *New Trends In Terrorism In Nigeria: 'Boko Haram Sect' – The Villain Of The Piece* [2011], at page 11, available at http://ssrn.com/abstract=1932061, where he charges that "those in power amass ill-gotten wealth stolen from the nation's resources as there [sic] personal property, thereby plunging the nation into a deep mess of which terrorism has become part of the consequences."; Paul Francis, Deidre Lapin, Paula Rossiasco, Development And Peace In The Niger Delta: A Social and Conflict Analysis for Change", Study prepared for publication by the Woodrow Wilson International Center for Scholars, Africa Program and Project on Leadership and Building State Capacity, 1-160, at page 31, available at http://www.wilsoncenter.org/sites/default/files/AFR_110929_Niger%20Delta_0113.pdf, where they argue that "a characteristic that distinguishes the Nigerian political economy from an idealized model of pluralist politics and public administration is the lack of a strict division between the public and private spheres […] In such a system, public employment and goods are seen primarily as resources for personal or group advancement rather than a means to serve the public good."

social and economic inequality therefore, propels the poor in joining any insurgent group to destroy any exiting government including the innocent civilians who eventually become victims."[38] The crippling poverty and astronomical level of unemployment, especially among the youths in north-east Nigeria, is chiefly blamed for the rather large pool of recruits for the terrorist group and this is linked directly to corruption. The political leadership, both at the federal and state levels, rather than apply public funds towards addressing infrastructural and social amenities requirements of their citizens, embezzle these funds thus leaving the hapless masses to suffer untold hardship. This problem is on full display at the security and defence ministries where for the past several years, billions of dollars of defense and security budgetary allocations have been embezzled or misused resulting in Nigeria's security forces routinely being routed by the Boko Haram sect in almost every military engagement.

Corruption is a real drag on Nigerians, especially the poor and the disadvantaged, and it militates against good governance and blocks the responsible allocation and application of public funds. Corruption is the reason the government is failing in its responsibility to provide needed social amenities and public infrastructure.

---

38 **Diala**, Ibid

Nwanegbo and Odigbo rightly surmise that:

Corruption is bad not because money and benefits change hands, and not because of the motives of participants, but because it privatizes valuable aspects of public life, bypassing processes of representation, debate, and choice [...]. It has been described in the academic circles as cancer militating against Nigeria's development; corruption is deeply threatening the fabric of the Nigerian society [...]. Corruption hampers economic growth, disproportionately burdens the poor and undermines the effectiveness of investment and aid.[39]

4.3: Economic Factors

Poverty, unemployment, and a dearth of economic opportunities are probably some of the most cited reasons for the insurgency, and the attraction of and growth in the ranks of the Boko Haram sect. According to **Sam Ogege**:

The poor development status of Nigeria no doubt breeds atmosphere of frustrated expectations and foster widespread indignation on the part of those that are trapped in the vortex circle of abject poverty. The condition of hopelessness

---

39 **Nwanegbo, C. Jaja, Odigbo, Jude,** *Security and National Development in Nigeria: The Threat of Boko Haram,* International Journal of Humanities and Social Science Vol. 3 No. 4 [Special Issue – February 2013, 285-291, at page 289

is further aggravated by impotent poverty eradication programmes and conspiratorial neglect by the Nigerian state. In the face of this predicament, individuals and groups respond differently depending on situational factor and capacity. These responses are crystallized and find expression in various shades of anti-social behaviours including armed robbery, kidnapping, insurgency among others.[40]

Boko Haram devises an alluring propaganda that, rightly, blames the government for the desperate plight of the youths, whilst promising them a better life and a more promising future in terrorism and violent crimes. According to **Kyari Mohammed**:

Mohammed Yusuf's evangelism began in the form of a Muslim social movement: catering for orphans, widows, and the vulnerable. The excluded, especially the almajirai (itinerant students) who had flocked in large numbers to the urban areas owing to rural destitution, became a ready pool for recruitment and mobilisation. In difficult times, the vulnerable and excluded can be easily mobilised.[41]

---

40 Ogege, Sam Omadjohwoefe, *Insecurity and Sustainable Development: The Boko Haram Debacle in Nigeria*, American International Journal of Social Science, Vol. 2 No.7; October 2013, 82-88, at page 82, available at http://www.aijss-net.com/journals/Vol_2_No_7_October_2013/10.pdf

41 **Kyari Mohammed**, supra, note 14, at page 23

In the absence of any hopes for sustenance and social mobility, these desperate youths are joining this terrorist group in droves. **Diala** agrees that:

> [T]he issue of youth unemployment is seen as a factor that has engendered terrorism. Thus, the startling youth unemployment in Nigeria has negative implications on nation's stability. There is a common saying that goes thus, 'an idle man is the work shop of the devil' What this means is that anyone who is not engaged in any productive venture would end up being influenced into doing ugly acts.[42]

Diala's assertion hit the nail right on the head. The inability of the government to address the economic issues of poverty and lack of opportunity is a fodder for the terrorists and violent criminals. **Zumve et al** make a persuasive case for state neglect and the dearth of economic opportunities as the driving force for the growth of terrorism and the supply of terrorist foot soldiers. They argue that:

> For people living hand-to-mouth, life is a series of struggles often ending in tragedy, anger, resentment, and despair are volatile combinations in the minds of young men and women who see little hope of escaping their situation. For

---

42 **Diala,** supra, note 37, at page 13

recruiters of terrorist organizations, these young minds can be manipulated to pick up arms. By stoking latent frustrations at the injustice of poverty and promising a sense of community, brotherhood, and commitment to a higher cause, a recruiter can more easily convince a teenager to become a suicide bomber or a kidnapper. [43]

Diala adds that "one of the major reasons for terrorism in Nigeria is … the level of crippling poverty."[44] He charges that "when hardships of life give existence little meaning, then people are bound to treat life with levity." [45]This is why some people have opted for terrorism as a means of income even at the expense of their lives and that of their fellow human beings.[46]

Unemployment among the teeming youth population in Northern Nigeria is a fodder for Boko Haram. **Anthony Abayomi Adebayo** identifies the central role youth

---

43 **Samuel Zumve, Margaret Ingyoroko, Isaac Iorhen Akuva,** *Terrorism In Contemporary Nigeria: A Latent Function Of Official Corruption And State Neglect,* European Scientific Journal March 2013 edition vol.9, No.8, pp 122-140, at pages 133-134, available at http://www.eujournal.org/index.php/esj/article/view/882

44 **Diala**, supra, note 37, at page 11

45 Ibid

46 Ibid; **Paul Francis, Deidre Lapin, Paula Rossiasco,** *"Securing Development And Peace In The Niger Delta: A Social and Conflict Analysis for Change",* Study prepared for publication by the Woodrow Wilson International Center for Scholars, Africa Program and Project on Leadership and Building State Capacity, 1-160, at page 30, available at http://www.wilsoncenter.org/sites/default/files/ AFR_110929_Niger%20Delta_0113.pdf, where they argue that, "lack of available and appropriate work limits the possibilities for young people to move out of poverty. Limited employment also reduces the opportunity cost of turning to violent forms of struggle and criminal activities [...] Thus unemployment, particularly of youth, has helped to drive and sustain high levels of violence and criminality throughout the delta region."

unemployment plays in swelling the ranks of the Boko Haram sect in the northeast of Nigeria. He argues that:

> Youth unemployment poses a great threat to the country's stability and development, and if not checkmated on time, it may lead to disastrous consequences for the nation. Desperation can drive the unemployed youths into living outside the law in order to survive and as a means of expressing dissatisfaction at the apparent neglect of their very existence. This situation has afforded the Boko Haram sect the luxury of easy recruitment of young people into their fold.[47]

The United States House of Representatives has also come away with the impression that extreme poverty in northern Nigeria is the chief driver of radicalism and terrorism in the region. The large pool of unemployed, extremely poor and frustrated youth are easy pickings for Boko Haram, Ansaru and other terrorist groups in northern Nigeria. According to them:

> Boko Haram draws its domestic support largely from a population of northern Muslim Nigerians predisposed to tolerate Boko Haram or perhaps even support the group as a challenge

---

47 **Anthony Abayomi Adebayo,** *Implications of 'Boko Haram' Terrorism on National Development in Nigeria: A Critical Review,* Mediterranean Journal of Social Sciences, Vol 5 No 16 July 2014, 480 – 489, at page 483, available at http://www.academia.edu/.../BOKO_HARAM_INSURGENCY_I...

to the federal state that has so badly failed to serve their interests. Even Nigeria's official figures demonstrate the severity of the problem. According to Nigeria's National Bureau of Statistics, "relative poverty was most apparent in Muslim dominated northern states ... [almost] 70% of Nigerians in 2010 were living in 'absolute poverty.'" The trend leads experts to believe that the inequality in Nigeria is promoting widespread support of Boko Haram as the group has actively capitalized on these grievances in a conscious attempt to market themselves, using a number of tactics to attract support.[48]

Consequently, "Boko Haram therefore provides a platform for unemployed youth and disgruntled persons to attack a system they believe is largely responsible for their plight."[49] **Zumve et al** add that:

There is a colony of lumpen proletariat majority of whom are not in regular employment who gain their subsistence mainly from crime. These colonies of destitute who are desolate become major reservoir of foot soldiers for the Boko Haram sect. The grunts that blow themselves up along with innocents around them are drawn

---

48 U.S. House of Representatives Committee on Homeland Security, supra, note 33, at page 29

49 **Odomovo S. Afeno**, *The Boko Haram Uprising And Insecurity In Nigeria; Intelligence Failure Or Bad Governance?*, Conflict trends 35, available at http://www.europal.europa.eu/.../EXPO-AFET_NT(2014...

from this pool of poor underclass, idle youths with few prospects for employment. Significantly, the North-west and Northeast recorded the highest poverty rates in the country in 2010, with 77.7% and 76% respectively.[50]

It is clear that unemployment and lack of economic opportunities are at the heart of the Boko Haram insurgency. Addressing youth unemployment and the creation of economic opportunities should therefore be a mainstay in any strategy to confront terrorism in Nigeria.

4.4: The Dearth of Critical Infrastructures and Abject Lack of Social Amenities

Absence of critical public infrastructure, social amenities and social services such as water, electricity, good roads, public transportation, schools, medical centers, medical service, etc., are also cited by the Boko Haram sect for their decision to take up arms against the Nigerian state. **Muhammed Kabir Isa** argues that the militancy and insurgency that Nigeria faces today is the result of failure of leadership to offer real and sustained leadership. He believes that "militancy, extremism, radicalism and fundamentalist means or ideologies are used to fill alternative spaces that the state has either failed to provide or closed; or they are a reaction against

---

50 **Zumve**, et al., supra, note 43, at page 133

alienation from modern institutions of governance that fail to deliver social services and other benefits to the people."[51] **Zumve et al** add that:

> Contemporary terrorism in Nigeria is a latent function of prolonged failure of the Nigerian State to deliver purposeful good governance. When the Federal, state and Local Governments steal all the money allocated for building schools, hospitals, industries, etc, the greater percentage of the citizenry especially the youths are denied good education, employment and good health. These youths are therefore affected socially, psychologically and economically. Frustrations, dejection and hopelessness remain a day to day occurrence in their lives [...] They can easily be brainwashed and indoctrinated with false doctrines and co-opted into illegal societies.[52]

The absence of modern social amenities such as schools, hospitals, good roads, water, electricity, etc which is clearly attributable to corruption and bad governance drives violence and terrorism. In the face of the lack of access to modern conveniences and no hope for social and economic mobility, Nigerian youths are being driven to violent crimes and terrorism.

---

51 **Muhammed Kabir Isa,** *Chapter 11: Militant Islamist Groups in Northern Nigeria,* at page 336, available at http://www.mercury.ethz.ch/.../MilitiasRebelsIslamistMilitants_Chapter+11.pdf

52 **Zumve, et al.,** supra, note 43, at pages 123-124

4.5: Religious Factors

Religious fundamentalism, and the influence of radical Islamic teachers, are major driving forces in the Boko Haram insurgency. This Islamic fundamentalism has its modern origin in the reinterpretation of Salafism and derives inspiration from the Iranian Revolution of 1979. It eventually drifted south to North Africa and thence to West and East Africa. It has found fertile ground in Somalia, the Sudan, Mali, Niger, Chad and Nigeria and is making inroads into Northern Cameroon. It was embraced by Muhammed Yusuf, the acclaimed founder of Boko Haram and thus became the philosophical basis of their beliefs, teaching, and operation. **Kyari Mohammed** traces the path of this social cancer. He says:

The 1979 Iranian Revolution, which overthrew the Pahlavi dynasty and established an Islamic republic in its place in spite of US resistance, became another major source of Islamic radicalisation. It created the impression and instilled in many Muslim youths the possibility and practicability of using Islam as a vehicle for political and social transformation. The 1980s witnessed a proliferation of Iranian revolutionary literature in Nigeria which inspired the Islamic Movement.[53]

---

53 **Kyari Mohammed**, supra, note 14, at page 22

Their radical interpretation of Prophet Mohammed's teachings has pitted them not only against "unbelievers" and peoples of other faiths, but even against fellow Muslims who do not subscribe to their radical interpretation of the Quran. Their aversion to religious dissent and religious plurality is at the heart of their brutality towards non-adherents. That is what makes their activities in Nigeria so frightening. This Iranian revolution inspired radical interpretation of the Quran was driven a mile further by the anger felt by this radical fringe because of the perceived tepid application of the Sharia legal system that was adopted by a large section of the states in northern Nigeria in the 2000s. According to **Kyari Mohammed**:

> The introduction of Sharia, with a full range of criminal law punishments, in Zamfara State and its whirlwind adoption by eleven other northern Nigerian states since 2000 accelerated the pace of radicalisation. The protagonists of Shariah created the impression that it would lead to a qualitative improvement in the lives of the inhabitants of Sharia states. However, the operation of Shariah as an adjunct to, and its subordination to, the secular constitution was anathema to radical Islamists, who now demanded a full complement of Shariah law as against the Zamfara model, which Boko Haram ridiculed and rejected. The inability of the

Shariah states to implement the law in full led to the rejection of the Zamfara model of Shariah by Boko Haram, who insisted on a full Shariah or nothing.[54]

To solve the Boko Haram question, the growth of this radical interpretation of the Quran has to be addressed if there is to be any chance of resolution. Theological re-education and sensitization are crucial pieces of any strategy to stem violent Islamic radicalism in Nigeria. **Rose C. Uzoma** takes the view that:

Religious pluralism in Nigeria has prevented national and social cohesion and threatened Nigeria's social stability by pitting different religious groups against one another. The Nigerian government has not fully implemented the [Nigerian] constitution's promise of religious freedom, resulting in feelings of insecurity, especially for Christians in the north, and a deepening divide between Christians and Muslims.[55]

Basil Ekot identifies religion as a driving force for conflict in Nigeria today. His point is that "religion can

---

54 Ibid at pages 22-3

55 **Rose C. Uzoma**, *Religious Pluralism, Cultural Differences, And Social Stability In Nigeria*, Brigham Young University Law Review [SUMMER 2004] 651-664, at page 663, available at http://www.digitalcommons.law.byu.edu/cg, /viewcontent. cgi?article=2197

be both an integrative and divisive factor in any society [and that] when the divisive elements of religion are not properly handled and brought under strict control, they create tensions and unrest in a society."[56] He concludes that "there is no doubt the issue of religion in Nigeria has become divisive rather than integrative. Religion has neither helped to preserve social order nor even to lower individual anxiety."[57] **Udama** posits that "religious ideological indoctrination and its manipulation have played immense role in conflicts or civil unrest in Nigeria."[58] **Ekanem** and **Ekefre** blame the potent mix of a large pool of uneducated and impressionable youth with their susceptibility to religious indoctrination for the increasing growth of the insurgency in the north. They maintain that:

A deep reflection on the history of the northern part of Nigeria reveals very high level of illiteracy. This illiteracy of the majority of the northern masses exposed them to the manipulation of the few elites that employed religion and ethnicity as a tool for socio-political, economic and governance advantage.[59]

---

56 **Basil Ekot,** supra, note 15, at page 53

57 Ibid at pp 53-54

58 **Udama,** supra, note 10, at page 109

59 **Ekanem, Samuel Asuquo, Ekefre, Ekong Nyong,** *Education and Religious Intolerance in Nigeria: The Need for Essencism as a Philosophy,* Journal of Educational and Social Research, Vol. 3 (2) May 2013, PP 303-310, at page 306, available at http://www.mcser-org.ervinhatibi.com/journal/index.php/jesr/article/.../168/159

The impact of the burgeoning almajiri children in the North cannot be discounted in discussing the environment that fuels the Boko Haram Insurgency in the north. The confluence of the Boko Haram and the almajiris was the fuel for the insurgency. This convergence was aptly summed up by the **International Crisis Group** in the following passage:

> With urbanization, more and more children are sent to schools far from their families, and millions of Almajiri children are required to beg for alms (almajiranchi) for their upkeep. While this system is ostensibly designed to prepare them for some of the hardships they may encounter later in life, in a context of urbanisation and increasing poverty, it is open to abuse and may foster criminality. In cities like Kano and Kaduna, many of the alms-begging street children have graduated into Yanda-ba, adolescent groups that once served to socialize teenagers into adulthood but have now, in many cases, transformed into gangs. In 2005, the National Council for the Welfare of Destitute estimated there were 7 million Almajirai children in northern Nigeria, mostly in the far northern states.[60]

---

60 Northern Nigeria: Background To Conflict, Africa Report No. 168 – 20 December 2010, International Crisis Group, at page 10, available at http://www.academia.edu/.../NORTHERN_NIGERIA_BACKGR...

These lost children are increasingly being sucked in by the false and malicious propaganda of terrorists, masking as Islamic scholars. These uneducated, unemployed, restive youths, are a recruiting bonanza for the Boko Haram insurgents.

4.6: Cultural Factors

The multi-ethnic, multi-cultural and multi-religious nature of Nigeria is raising existential challenges to the nation. According to **Salawu**:

> With over four hundred (400) ethnic groups, belonging to several religious sects, Nigeria since independence has remained a multi-ethnic nation state, which has been grappling and trying to cope with the problem of ethnicity on the one hand, and the problem of ethno-religious conflicts on the other. This is because over the years the phenomena of ethnicity and religious intolerance have led to incessant recurrence of ethno-religious conflicts, which have given birth to many ethnic militias...[61]

The debasing of religion and cultures of the north may have been a driving force, at least for the Boko Haram

---

61 **B. Salawu**, *Ethno-Religious Conflicts in Nigeria: Casual Analysis and Proposals for New Management Strategies*, European Journal of social Sciences – Volume 13, Number 3 (2010), at page 345, available at http://www.eisf.eu/.../0071-Salawu-2010-Nigeria-ethno-religious-confli...

Insurgency. **Anyadike** surmises that:

> Boko Haram is an Islamic sect that believes politics in northern Nigeria has been hijacked by a group of corrupt and false Muslims; and also that westernization has bread [sic] corruption in the Nigerian polity and therefore wants to wage war against westernization of all sorts in the country by creating a theocratic state ruled by Shari'a law.[62]

Addressing these deep-seated institutionalized ethnic, cultural, religious and linguistic divisions must be a medium and long term strategy of the Nigerian government, if there is to be any hope of eliminating terrorism and violence, as an avenue of dispute resolution in Nigeria.

The irresponsible and reckless actions of journalists and the mass media [including internet "activists"] have been cited as fueling terrorism, albeit unwittingly. The **International Crisis Group** believes that:

> The mass media has also contributed: sensational newspaper headlines have provoked or aggravated violence on several occasions. The circulation of rumour, whether through media or more informally, frequently serves to spread

---

62 **Anyadike, Nkechi O.**, *Boko Haram and National Security Challenges in Nigeria; Causes and Solutions*, Journal of Economic and Sustainable Development, ISSN 2222-1700 (Paper) ISSN 2222-2855 (Online)Vol.4, No.5, 2013, page 12, at page 22, available at www.iiste.org

and sustain violence. A notable example occurred on the eve of Nigeria's hosting of the Miss World beauty pageant in November 2002, when Thisday made what were considered insulting remarks linking the Prophet Mohammed to the event. Over 200 people were killed in subsequent rioting in Kaduna. In other cases, the media have carried outright hate speech directed to religious groups.[63]

Dr. Agaptus Nwozor joins the chorus of those indicting the media for exacerbating the ethnic and religious conflicts, rather than playing a constructive role. He charges that:

> Rather than project and elevate the media as the conscience of the society, the elite have deployed it as part of the ensembles of their welfare. Worse still, the media organizations operate from the parochial prism of ethnicity and religion, thus compounding the dilemma of cultivating the national ethos that can be a promoter of peace.[64]

Don North also highlights the destructive part the Nigerian media play in fanning and sustaining terrorism in Nigeria. He says:

> Much of Nigeria's news media is itself divided along ethnic lines and, outside of a handful of

---

63 *Northern Nigeria: Background To Conflict*, supra, note 60, at page 21
64 **Agaptus Nwozor**, supra, note 16, at page 156

responsible news outlets, is addicted to lurid allegations and dark conspiracy theories. Some even portray Boko Haram as a government plot to destroy the largely Muslim north, while others suspect northern politicians are secretly supporting the insurgents to discredit President Jonathan, a southerner and Christian.[65]

David Anderson, QC sounds a note of warning about the self-fulfilling prophetic nature of "terrorism." He cautions against glamourizing terror and taking advantage of the hysteria surrounding "terrorism." He says that:

> Terrorism can make the careers of political leaders, prosecutors, journalists, lawyers and activists. It swells the budgets of military and intelligence services, publishers, universities and film studios. The police officer transferred to a counter-terrorism unit walks that bit taller... All these people are by the mere use of the T-word taken out of the normal vocabulary of crime, government, commerce or academe into a mental space that is inhabited by Robespierre, Irish dynamiters, Russian anarchists, Olympic hostage-takers, muhajahideen, desert emirs and

---

65 **Don North,** *Behind the War with Boko Haram,* Consortiumnews.com, November 16, 2014, 1-27, at page 9, available at http://www.consortiumnews. com/2014/11/16/behind-the-war-with-boko-haram/

on the other side of the fence, Special Branch, undercover agents, Navy seals and drones. All have a shared interest in the problem being a serious and frightening one. Mutually reinforcing relationships are legion – not least between the terrorists themselves, who rely on publicity to promote fear, and the media which knows from experience that there is no better word than terror with which to invigorate the front page.[66]

4.7: Flawed Counter-Terrorism Strategy

Nigerian government's response to Boko Haram is the deployment of brute force in a bid to regain control and extend the elites' corrupt dominance of the political space. The coercive and repressive strategy being increasingly adopted by the government to tackle dissent and snuff out legitimate agitations have led to the upping of the ante of violence by the marginalized groups and thus further feeding the frenzy and vicious cycle of violence. According to **Kyari Mohammed**, "the military Joint Task Force – Operation Restore Order (JTF) functioned like an army of occupation. Unable to distinguish Boko Haram members from unarmed civilians, they resorted to taking vengeance on the whole civilian population. This had the effect of alienating them from the community."[67]

---

66 **Anderson, David**, *Shielding the Compass; How to Fight Terrorism Without Defeating the law, 1-19, at page 3*, (June 15, 2013) , Available at SSRN: http://www.ssrn.com/abstract=2292950
67 **Kyari Mohammed**, supra, note 14, at page 25

David Cortright makes the case that repressive measures actually breed extremism among the repressed people. He argues that "overtly repressive measures could also exacerbate the conditions that give rise to political extremism."[68] And that "empirical research has found a strong correlation between the denial of political freedom and the rise of terrorism."[69] His thesis is that "measures of political repression are a statistically significant indicator of the likelihood of terrorist recruitment."[70] He sees a truism in the fact that "people without opportunity to voice their opinions and organize politically often turn to violence as the only way of expressing their grievances."[71] He believes that "many of those who become political militants are motivated not by a hatred of freedom, but by an extreme yearning for it."[72]

Udombana hands a serious indictment on those responsible for conducting the war on terror for their abusive practices. He charges that "the war on terrorism has made so many inroads into the rule of law and human rights as to render both concepts almost

---

68 **David Cortrigh**t, *A critical Evaluation of the UN Counter-Terrorism Program: Accomplishments and Challenges, A Crime and Global Paper presented at: Global Enforcement Regimes, Transnational Organized Crime, International Terrorism and money Laundering*, held at the Transnational Institute (TNI) in Amsterdam, 28-29 April 2005, at page 17, available at http://www.tni.org/crime

69 Ibid

70 Ibid

71 Cortright supra, note 68, at page 18

72 **Cortright** supra, note 68, at page 18

meaningless."[73] He believes that "the use of torture and extralegal imprisonment creates a breach in the rule of law, accelerates the race to the bottom in human rights, and ties anti-terrorism policies in knots."[74] **Sarah Margon** of the Human Rights Watch, addressing the increasing violent nature of the Boko Haram insurgency as a result of the vicious response of security forces in the northeast of Nigeria, charges that:

> The tactics of the government security forces are barely more palatable than those of the militants themselves. Nigerian security forces are known for raiding local communities, executing men in front of their families, arbitrarily arresting and beating people, burning residential property and stealing money while searching homes. Nigerian authorities also routinely hold suspects incommunicado without charge or trial in secret detention facilities and abuse and torture them. Unsurprisingly, due process rights for detainees are often absent.[75]

This hardnosed strategy, with its attendant senseless brutality and blanket human rights abuses by the security

---

73 **Nsongarua J. Udombana**, *Battling Rights: International Law And Africa's War On Terrorism*, 13 Afr. Y.B. Int'l L. 67 2005, at page 70, available at http://www.ssrn. com/abstract=1806304

74 Ibid

75 **Sarah Margon,** , *How Do You Beat Boko Haram With An Army That's Almost As Evil?*, May 14, 2014, Human Rights Watch, available at http://www.hrw.org/ print/news/2014/05/14/how-do-you-beat-boko-haram-army-thats-almo... [last visited 5/29/2014]

forces, has thus hardened the resolve of the terrorists and has begun to win them sympathizers, especially among the victims of police and army brutality.[76] Anecdotal evidence suggest that in many cases, the villages facing the threat of the Boko Haram attacks are more scared of the security forces than even the terrorists.[77] According to the **UN Office for the Coordination of Humanitarian Affairs**:

The security forces' Joint Task force (JTF) has also failed to win the wholehearted support of those they are deployed to protect. "It's just collective punishment for everybody," a doctor in the northeastern city of Maiduguri, where Boko Haram began in 2002, told IRIN. "whenever there is an incident [the soldiers] cordon the area and start beating people …With time it will be the whole society against the military." A frustrated state prosecutor added: "Even if you flash your identity card at JTF you are told, 'You lawyers, you are the brains behind our problems'. Colleagues have been made to do frog-jumps; there is so much intimidation and disrespect."[78]

---

76 **James J.F. Forest**, *Confronting the Terrorism of Boko Haram in Nigeria, Joint Special Operations*, University Press, 2012, 1-178, at pages 91-92, available at http://www.jsou.socom.mil

77 See **Kyari Mohammed**, *The message and methods of Boko Haram, In Boko Haram: Islamism, Politics, Security and the State in Nigeria*, edited by Perouse de Montclos, Marc-Antoine, 9-32 at pages 26 et seq. Eschede, Netherlands: Institut Francais de Recherche en Africaque (IFRA), 2014, available at http://www.infra-nigeria.org/IMG/pdf/boko-haram-islamism-politics-security-nigeria.pdf

78 UN Office for the Coordination of Humanitarian Affairs, Analysis; Carrot or Stick? – Nigerians divided over Boko Haram, available at http://www.irinnews.org/printreport.aspx?reportid=95874 [last visited on 12/7/2014]

Villagers and entire neighbourhoods have been known to have been deserted after a terrorist attack, not because of the attack, but for fear of the scorched earth response of the security forces. According to **Roland Marchal:**

> One clear aspect of Boko Haram's appeal is its struggle with the Police and army. Complaints and cases citing the brutality and corruption within Nigeria's security services elicit little, if any, reaction from the political elites, reinforcing a sense of helplessness among an often-victimised general population. Mohammed Yusuf's killing at the hands of the police (as well as hundreds of Boko Haram members) is a crucial driver in the current wave of assassinations and attacks carried out by Boko Haram against security personnel and infrastructure.[79]

Rather than offering a solution, the counter-terrorism strategy of Nigeria's security agencies seems to be adding fuel to the fire of terrorism, by hardening terrorists, and alienating and thus driving victims of terrorism into the folds of the terrorists. **J. Shola Omotola** offers an indictment of the security services' take no prisoner approach to the fight of terrorism. He regrets that:

> . . . the military-like fashion in which the war against terror has been fought has compromised

---

79 **Roland Marchal**, *Boko Haram and the resilience of militant Islam in Northern Nigeria*, NOREF Report, June 2012, Published by Norwegian Leacebuilsing Resource Centre, at page 4, available at http://www.peacebuilding.no/.../ dc58a110fb362470133354efb8fee228.pdf

and complicated the security situation. As people's rights are flagrantly violated in the course of prosecuting the war, new sources of security threats develop. People will respond to the violation of their rights in some way, most likely in a violent manner, especially when they have explored available sources of local remedy without respite.[80]

Omotola counsels the use of strategies that address the root causes of terrorism as much more productive than brutal force alone.[81]

One can safely argue that if Muhammed Yusuf, some members of his family and scores of Boko Haram members, were not extra-judicially murdered by the Nigerian police in July 2009, Nigeria probably could have been dealing with a radically different Boko Haram from the one presently led by Abubakar Shekau. A conflict that could have been resolved through dialogue, and failing that, by trial in court, was so bungled that it bred a destructive insurgency that has now plunged Nigeria into an existential fight. **The Human Rights Watch** has this to say about the unfortunate events of July 2009:

In 2009, Nigerian police forces fighting Boko

---

80 **J. Shola Omotola**, *Assessing The Counter-Terrorism Measures In Africa: Implications For Human Rights And National Security*, Conflict Trends, Issue 2 (2008), at page 43, African Centre for the Constructive Resolution of Disputes (ACCORD), Umhlanga Rocks, South Africa, available at http://www.mercury.ethz.ch/serviceengine/Files/ISN/101869/.../chapter+7.pdf

81 Ibid

Haram in the northern city of Maiduguri lost about 30 officers in a violent firefight. The next day, they executed many of the men they had rounded up and detained as suspected Boko Haram fighters. The retaliatory killings often happened right outside police headquarters in full view of the public. Bodies piled up outside the buildings while the executions continued.[82]

Victims are being literally forced to choose between a rock and hard place. The excessive militarization of government response to the Boko Harm insurgency, has exacerbated the problem rather than control it. This problem is aptly articulated by **Odomovo S. Afeno** in his seminal work on the Nigerian government's response to terrorism. He says the "government is increasingly putting too much emphasis on the maintenance of physical security typified by the presence of military, police and intelligence agents, and paying little attention to human development issues which are essential for sustainable national security."[83] He accuses the government of using "excessive force to arrest, detain and possibly even kill anyone who happens to be in the wrong place at the wrong time, thereby exacerbating a situation which they are meant to alleviate."[84] **Paul Francis et al** underscore the total disconnect the

---

82 **Sarah Margon**, supra, footnote 75

83 **Afeno**, supra, note 7, at page 40

84 Ibid

brutal counter-terrorism activities of the government has created between the Nigerian government and citizens of Nigeria. According to them, "the relationship between citizens and security forces is one of suspicion, mistrust and, in some cases, fear. A history of abuses committed toward civilians by security forces has created a perception that their mandate is not to protect citizens but to safeguard powerful interests, including their own." [85]

There is little doubt that the unbridled abuse of human, constitutional and civil rights of both suspected terrorists and innocent victims by the Nigerian security agencies, including the various Joint Military Task Forces formed in the Northeast of the country, fuel terrorism. A case in point is the extra-judicial killing of Muhammed Yusuf, some members of his family and hundreds of his followers in 2009, following clashes between the sect and security agents. According to **Agbiboa:**

> [T]he ultra-violent turn BH took should also be traced back to the extrajudicial killing of its leader, Mohammed Yusuf, and the ongoing arbitrary arrest, torture, and killing of its members by state security forces. Until 2009 BH was seen as radical but not ultra-violent. The killing of the group's founder under police custody provoked a staunch reaction from BH members who primarily want to settle their

---

85 **Paul Francis, et al.**, supra, note 18, at page 33

scores with the police and army. In a video that was released in June 2010, Abubakar Shakau – the group's current leader – vowed to avenge the deaths of its members.[86]

Kyari Mohammed concludes that the Nigerian "security agencies have completely lost the hearts and minds in this war through high-handedness and brutality". [87]

A first step in turning the corner in the fight against terrorism in Nigeria is a total overhaul of Nigeria's counter-terrorism operation to de-emphasize coercive action and emphasize a strategy that includes addressing some of the underlying environment that forced Nigerians to take up arms against the state and their fellow citizens. Nigeria clearly cannot kill it's way out of this quagmire.

4.8: Legal Factors

The absence of alternative legal/political channels to address legitimate concerns by aggrieved sections of the society have left them with criminality, violence and terrorism as the only available outlets.[88] **Adekunbi**

86 **Daniel E. Agbiboa**, *Is Might Right? Boko Haram, the Joint Military Task Force, and the Global Jihad,* Journal of Military and Strategic Affairs, Volume 5, No. 3, December 2013, 53-71, at pages 64-65, available at http://www.inss.org.il/index.aspx?id=4538&articleid=6649

87 **Kyari Mohammed**, supra, note 14, at page 28

88 **Paul Francis, Deidre Lapin, Paula Rossiasco**, *Securing Development And Peace In The Niger Delta: A Social and Conflict Analysis for Change,* Study prepared for publication by the Woodrow Wilson International Center for Scholars Africa Program and Project on Leadership and Building State Capacity, 1-160, at page 51, available at http://www.wilsoncenter.org/sites/default/files/AFR_110929_Niger%20Delta_0113.pdf

Odusanya takes the position that "Boko Haram, the Niger-Delta militants [...] and others despite their varied approaches, provide platforms for those disillusioned with Nigeria's narrow political system to express their grievances."[89] **Abimbola and Adesote** add that:

> The issue here is that our brothers and sisters who have taken to domestic terrorism, in the Niger Delta region through the formation of various youth militias and that of Boko Haram in the northern part of the country are saying that since nobody wants to listen and engage them, perhaps, violent [sic] as a means of expressing their grievances may [sic] the best option.[90]

The judiciary in Nigeria is notoriously corrupt and hopelessly dependent on the executive branch of government to be effective in protecting individual and group interests.[91] The feeling among Nigerians that the court offers no real avenue for judicial redress against injustice and unfairness, real or imagined, makes terrorism and violent criminality attractive options to disaffected individuals and groups. **Paul Francis et al** take the position that "in the absence of legal recourse,

---

89 **Adekunbi Olukemi Johnson Odusanya**, *The Challenge Of Democratic Governance In The African Region: The Nigerian Experience*, OIDA international Journal of Sustainable Development 06:06 (2013), 11-22, at page 18, available at http://www.ssrn.com/link/OIDA-Intl-Journal-Sustainable-dev.html

90 **Abimbola, J.O., and Adesote, S.A.**, *Domestic Terrorism And Boko Haram Insurgency In Nigeria, Issues And Trends: A Historical Discourse*, Journal of Arts and Contemporary Society, Volume 4, September 2012, 11-29, at page 23, available at http://www.cenresinpub.org

91 **Paul Francis, Deidre Lapin, Paula Rossiasco**, supra, note 88

some aggrieved communities have concluded that there are few alternatives to the use of force in asserting their legitimate rights."[92]

In order to make any kind of inroad in the fight against terrorism, a real effort must be made to address the institutional rot in the judicial branch of government. The judiciary must be strengthened and made truly independent of the other branches of government to enhance its ability to "speak truth to authority" and thus be a real beacon of freedom from oppression and shelter for the aggrieved. If Nigerians see that they have a legitimate shot at obtaining redress for whatever grievance they harbour against the government in a court of law, violence and terror will cease to be viable options.

It is, therefore, apparent that a defective political structure and the inability of the political elite to rein in corruption coupled with absence of viable peaceful avenues to vent dissent, drives terrorism in Nigeria.

4.9: Porous Borders, Smuggling and Arms Proliferation

One of the critical and enduring factors that enables terrorism in Nigeria is her porous borders and her inability to police cross-border traffic of people, materials, arms, drugs and funds. Nigeria's borders with Niger Republic, Chad and Northern Cameroon are vast and hardly manned. The communities that

---

92 Ibid at pages 34-35

straddle the borders have intermarried, traded with and interacted with each other for centuries, even before the arrival of Europeans on the scene. The **U.S. House of Representatives** recognizes that, "because of Nigeria's porous borders and frequent movement between intertwined tribal communities [sic] Nigeria and neighboring states, '...there is evidence to suggest that these tribal relationships facilitate weapons trafficking and other cross-border smuggling transactions.'"[93] The cultural, social, religious and commercial relationships developed by these communities continue till date and thus have been leveraged by Boko Haram to facilitate cross-border movement of members, military supplies and funding. Membership of Boko Haram is drawn from communities in all these countries and they move freely throughout the entire sub-region. **Dambazau** paints a vivid picture of this problem in the following passage:

> Nigeria's borders covering a little over 4000 km are porous and easily accessible not only through the 90 legal entry points, but also additional 1,497 illegal routes. . . With our porous borders criminal groups and insurgents easily smuggle weapons into the country: from Niger Delta where they trade illegally bunkered oil for arms, some of which are sold to criminals in the south east who then terrorize communities with

---

93 U.S. House of Representatives Committee on Homeland Security, supra, note 33, at page 10

armed banditry and kidnapping; from the north east, especially weapons from Libya, Chad and Somalia, which the Boko Haram insurgents find useful in terrorizing communities; and through the Seme border in the south west.[94]

Coupled with Nigeria's porous borders are the proliferation of small arms and light weaponry. All these have been blamed for the upsurge in terrorist activities in the country. According to **Dr Adigbuo** "whether as a result of civil wars or terrorist activities the abundant supply of small arms, ammunition, light weapons and explosives has played a crucial role."[95] It is clear that any attempt to stem terrorism in Nigeria must take into account the issue of her porous borders with its attendant cross-border smuggling of fighters, supplies, illicit drugs and funds.

In conclusion, the modern domestic terrorism that Nigeria presently battles has been nurtured by the deplorable environment created by a number of factors. A proper analysis and appreciation of these factors are a *sine qua non* for finding a lasting solution to the scourge of domestic terrorism. We, therefore, agree with **Salawu** that:

It is important to note ... that the failure of the Nigerian leaders to establish good governments, forge national integration and promote what

---

94 **Dambazau**, supra, note 22, at page 10

95 **Dr. Ebere Richard Adigbuo**, supra, note 3, at page 48;

can be called real economic progress, through deliberate and articulated policies, has led to mass poverty and unemployment. This has resulted into communal, ethnic, religious and class conflicts that have now characterized the Nigerian nation. Poverty and unemployment have therefore served as nursery bed for many ethno-religious conflicts in Nigeria because the country now has a reservoir of poor people who warmongers as mercenary fighters. What this means theoretically is that poverty and unemployment increase the number of people who are prepared to kill or be killed for a given course at token benefit. This explains why all ethno-religious crises that ever occurred in Nigeria have a large turnout of people (including the under-aged) as fighters.[96]

To **Zumve et al** "terrorism in Nigeria is the ultimate price that we (as a society) face for producing a colony of depraved, deprived and frustrated youths as a consequence of Official Corruption and a dysfunctional Nigeria state."[97] It is hard to fault their conclusion. **James J.F. Forest** artfully summarizes the factors that breed and sustain terrorism in Nigeria in the following passage:

---

96 **B. Salawu**, *Ethno-Religious Conflicts in Nigeria: Causal Analysis and Proposals for New Management Strategies*, European Journal of social Sciences – Volume 13, Number 3 (2010), at page 348, available at http://www.eisf.eu/.../0071-Salawu-2010-Nigeria-ethno-religious-confli...

97 **Zumve, et al.**, supra, note 43, at page 124

The cumulative effect of this toxic brew of grievances [referring to all the factors discussed in this chapter] is dejection and marginalization. With the combination of bad governance, centralization of power and wealth, political intrigue, crumbling (or nonexistent) infrastructure, regional disparities and many more problems that cannot be addressed here due to space limitations, it is no wonder that many observers have argued that Nigeria offers the kinds of conditions in which revolutionaries and extremists have found fertile ground for recruiting and launching violent movements. But exacerbating these conditions even further is the prominent role that the system of institutionalized ethnic identity - a key factor in many instances of political violence worldwide - plays in the political and social lives of Nigerians.[98]

A description of the drivers of terrorism in Nigeria does not come with any more clarity than the foregoing words.

Having looked at the triggers of the Boko Haram insurgency, we now turn to a discussion of the impact of the sect's militant insurgency in Nigeria.

---

98 **James Forest**, supra, note 12, at page 39

Chapter 5

Examination and Evaluation of the Impact of Boko Haram Activities in Nigeria

Terrorism has dealt Nigeria some debilitating body blows. It is no exaggeration for one to assert that the Boko Haram insurgency poses an existential threat to the nation. Indeed, Boko Haram attacks "appear to be strategically targeted at Nigeria's ethno-religious fault line, as well as national security forces, in a bid to hurt the nation's stability."[1] **Udama** says that:

Political, religious or ethnic-based instability within a country has the potential to imperil peace, unity, economic and social development in Nigeria. Though the terrorist groups are mostly based in the north fighting for an unidentified cause at present, its potentials to disrupt the entire

---

1 **Agbiboa, Daniel E**, *Peace at Daggers Drawn? Boko Haram and the State of Emergency in Nigeria*, Studies in Conflict & Terrorism, 37:41-67, 2014, at page 54, available at http://www.researchgate.net/...Peace_at_Daggers_Drawn_Boko_Haram_and_t...

country are high. For instance, the activities of terrorist [sic] have paralysed almost all sections of the country. It had breached peace, threatened the unity and impeded economic progress and development of Nigeria.[2]

Oladunjoye and **Omemu** try to articulate some of the impacts of the Boko Haram terrorism in Nigeria in the following passage:

Since the advent of a new dimension to terrorism in Nigeria, it is clear that the fabric of Nigeria [sic] economic foundation has really been shaken. The impact of the activities of the dreaded Boko Haram has brought physical, psychological and economic damage to the [sic] Nigeria's fragile economy. There is a sharp drop in the [sic] commercial activities in the North as foreign investors are gradually diverting from Nigeria due to the increasing security crisis.[3]

---

2 **Udama, Rawlings Akonbede**, *Understanding Nigeria Terrorism, its Implications to National Peace, Security, Unity and Sustainable Development: A Discuss*, IOSR Journal of Humanities And Social Science Volume 8, Issue 5 (Mar. - Apr. 2013), PP 100-115, at page 112, available at http://www.researchgate.net/.../269751730_Understanding_Nigeria...; Anthony Abayomi Adebayo articulates some of the cost of crime and terrorism on affected societies. He says: 'The cost of crime are tangible and intangible, economic or social, direct or indirect, physical or psychological, individual or community. In fact, it is from the cost that the consequences of crime are derived. The cost of crime can be incurred as a result of actual experience of criminal activities, when there is physical injury, when properties are stolen, damaged or destroyed. As a consequence of the prevalence of crime in society, the demographic composition may be altered through mass movement of people from crime-prone areas to areas perceived to be relatively crime-free. This can also lead to brain-drain and other socio-economic problems." : Anthony Abayomi Adebayo, Implications of 'Boko Haram' Terrorism on National Development in Nigeria: A Critical Review, Mediterranean Journal of Social Sciences, Vol 5 No 16 July 2014, 480-489 at page 483

3 **Oladunjoye, Patrick, Omemu, Felix**, *Effect Of Boko Haram On School Attendance In Northern Nigeria*, British journal of Education Vol.1, No.2 pp 1-9, at page 8, December 2013, Published by European Centre for Research Training and Development UK (available at www.ea-journals.org)

I.S. Popoola draws attention to the fact that Boko Haram and its activities in the northeast pose a serious threat to the corporate existence of Nigeria, because of its mirroring of the events leading up to the infamous Nigerian civil war of 1967-70. He asserts that "the directive by the sect demanding southerners to relocate to their states also poses a serious threat to the corporate existence of Nigeria. Political observers recalled that such calls were the prelude to the Nigerian civil war of 1967."[4] It is, therefore, apparent that Boko Haram is threatening the very existence of Nigeria and that if unchecked, terrorism will cause a complete disintegration of the country.

We now look at how Boko Haram has impacted and is impacting specific sections and sectors of Nigeria.

5.1: Political Impact

The political instability that is brought about by Boko Haram has pushed Nigeria to the tip of implosion. The Boko Haram insurgency in northern Nigeria, in particular, is tearing at the very heart of Nigeria's fragile union. According to the **ISS Seminar Report**:

> The re-emergence of the violent militant group called Boko Haram in 2009 has threatened the survival and the cohesiveness of Nigeria as a state. Some are fearful that Nigeria is at the edge

---

4 **I.S. Popoola,** *Press and Terrorism in Nigeria: A Discourse on Boko Haram,* Global Media Journal, African Edition 2012 Vol 6 (1) PP 43-66, at page 61, available at http://www.globalmedia.journals.ac.za

of a civil war as Boko Haram has gone on a killing spree, launching rampant and deadly terrorist acts that have claimed the lives of thousands of Nigerians and caused widespread fear across the country.[5]

Terrorism challenges the authority of the state to protect its citizens and denigrates the esteem of the government and its security forces in the minds of the citizens. In other words, it emasculates the state and calls into question its ability to fulfil its primary mandate to the citizens. According to **Oladimeji** and **Oresanwo**, "the other aim of terror is to shake the authority of state by degrading the public institutions, security forces and other public officers in the eyes of public opinion."[6]

Deep-seated hatred, mistrust and suspicion that is simmering amongst the different ethnic and religious segments of the country is being exploited by these terrorists to increase their ranks and lend support to their nefarious causes. Boko Haram pursues a secondary agenda of fermenting a destabilizing sectarian conflict in the country. According to **James J.F. Forest,** the "spate of

5 **ISS Seminar Report, Pretoria:** *The Threat of Boko Haram and the Challenges to Peace, Security and Unity in Nigeria*, Held 2 February 2012 in Pretoria, South Africa, at page 1, Sourced from http://www.issafrica.org/events/iss-seminar-report-pretoria-the-threat-of-boko-haram-and-the... [last visited on 9/9/2014]

6 **Oladimeji, Moruff Sanjo, Oresanwo, Adeniyi Marcus,** *"Effects of Terrorism on the International Business in Nigeria"* International Journal of Humanities and Social Science, Vol. 4, No. 7(1); May 2014, 247-255, at page 249, available at http://www.ijhssnet.com/journals/Vol_4_No_7_1_May_2014/30.pdf

attacks against churches from December 2011 through February 2012 are seen by many as but the latest attempt to provoke Christians into retaliatory attacks against Muslims, part of an overall effort to spark widespread sectarian conflict in order to destabilize the government."[7] **Kyari Mohammed** also highlights the politicization of the Boko Haram insurgency along ethnic, religious and regional lines by unscrupulous political and religious leaders. He says:

> Like most issues in Nigeria, the Boko Haram insurgency has been politicised along ethnic, regional, and religious lines. The recent withdrawal of the Catholic Church from CAN may not be unconnected with the open partisanship and inflammatory statements of CAN President Ayo Oritsejeafor, who has fanned the embers of hatred rather than seeking solutions. The Catholic Church gave as its reasons for withdrawal the "polarizing statements of some Christian leaders" and the need to "promote Christian unity and peaceful coexistence with Christians and non-christians alike," an obvious reference to the quarrelsome leadership of Oritsajeafor.[8]

---

7 **James J.F. Forest,** *Confronting the Terrorism of Boko Haram in Nigeria,* Joint Special Operations University Press, 2012, 1-178, at page 2, available at http://www.jsou.socom.mil

8 Kyari Mohammed, *"The message and methods of Boko Haram",* In *Boko Haram: Islamism,* Politics, Security and the State in Nigeria, edited by Perouse de Montclos, Marc-Antoine, 9-32. Eschede, Netherlands: Institut Francais de Recherche en Africaque (IFRA), 2014, at page 21, available at http://www.infra-nigeria.org/IMG/pdf/boko-haram-islamism-politics-security-nigeria.pdf

The **U.S. Department of Justice** warns that "attacks on Christians and their churches serve to fuel existing religious tensions and create further displacement" because "attacks on Christians often lead to reprisals."[9] They fear that "continued attacks on Christians and churches, regardless of whether they are the primary or exclusive targets, could lead to more religion-based conflicts, further destabilizing large parts of the country."[10] **START's May 2014 Background Report**, says "Boko Haram's major attacks on churches and religious figures have at times been followed by rioting and retaliatory attacks against Muslim targets, exacerbating religious polarization of the Nigerian population."[11]

A glaring example of the profound nature of the negative impact of the Boko Haram insurgency in Nigeria is the unprecedented postponement of the scheduled Nigeria's presidential election from 14 February 2015 to 28 March 2015. The major reason advanced for the said postponement was the insecurity brought about by the Boko Haram activities in the northeast of Nigeria.[12] Anecdotal evidence suggests that the routing of the

---

9 **Hanibal Goitom**, *Nigeria: Boko Haram*, Report for the U.S. Department of Justice, July 2014, The Library of Congress, 1-11, available at http://www.justice.gov/.../nigeria/2014-010..

10 Ibid at page 7

11 *National Consortium for the Study of Terrorism and Responses to Terrorism, Boko Haram Recent Attacks*, BACKGROUND REPORT, May 2014, 1-8, at page 3, available at http://www.start.umd.edu/pubs/STARTBackgroundReport_Boko-HaramRecentAttacks_May2014_O.pdf

12 CBC NEWS, Nigeria postpones vote to March 18 over Boko Haram, Feb 07, 2015, available at http://www.cbc.ca/news/world/nigeria-postpones-vote-to-march-18-over-boko-haram-violence-1.2949099

ruling Peoples Democratic Party [PDP] by the main opposition All Progressive Congress [APC] in the 28 March 2015 presidential election is linked for the most part to the inability of the Jonathan Administration to rein in the Boko Haram sect in northeast Nigeria.

5.2: Budgetary Impact:

Terrorism has had a grave impact on the Nigerian government's budget. The heightened security situation has resulted in a budget skewed in favour of defence and law enforcement, thus derogating from other human and social services needs of the nation. **Oladimeji** and **Oresanwo** say that:

> Nigeria's federal government plans to spend a considerable 20% of its 2012 budget on security – equivalent to the share the US spent on security following the 11 September terrorist attacks, in 2001. In 2013 it was increased to 27.11 but in 2014, N845 billion ($5.29 billion) was provided for recurrent and service vote for security in Nigeria.[13]

These are huge budgetary allocations and have huge negative impact on the ability of the government to address the requirements of other critical sectors. It is also a huge diversion of funds that could have been

---

13 **Oladimeji, Moruff Sanjo, Oresanwo, Adeniyi Marcus,** supra, footnote 6, at page 250

deployed to making capital investment in terms of critical infrastructure such as electricity, transportation and education. Even more disheartening is the fact that given the recurring embarrassing losses by the security forces in military confrontation with Boko Haram, and the revelations of elements in the military, of lack of equipment for men on the front lines, that majority of these budgetary allocations have either been embezzled and/or grossly mismanaged. **Alao et al** stress that, "In an attempt to address insecurity, there is the tendency for governments to increase its spending on security, while resources could be diverted from socio-economic development programmes that could transform the nation and provide conduit pipe for fraud and misappropriation of fund in the name of security coverage."[14]

According to the **UN Office for the Coordination of Humanitarian Affairs**, the Nigerian government in 2012 budgeted an unprecedented US $6 billion in defence and security vote.[15] **Anthony Abayomi Adebayo** supplies a key example of how the fighting of terrorism diverts critically needed resources to law enforcement instead of other social needs. He says "the budget of N921.91 billion earmarked to combat terrorism in Nigeria in the year

---

14 **Alao, David Oladimeji, Atere, Clement Olusegun, Alao, Oluwafisayo,** *Boko Haram Insurgency In Nigeria: The Challenges And Lessons,* Singaporean Journal of Business Economics and Management Studies, Vol.1, No.4, 2012, 1-15, at page 9, available at http://www.singaporeanjbem.com/pdfs/SG_VOL_1_(4)/1.pdf
15 UN Office for the Coordination of Humanitarian Affairs, Analysis; Carrot or Stick? – Nigerians divided over Boko Haram, available at http://www.irinnews.org/printreport.aspx?reportid=95874 [last visited on 12/7/2014],

2012 alone, could have been deployed to development programmes that the nation desperately need."[16] **Patrick Nmah** poses a very pertinent question. He says:

> What is sometimes a subject of controversy is how much should be allocated to defense in view of the fact that there are other pressing national needs such as the provision of free education, medical services, employment, good network of roads, energy, and essential civilian consumer goods, which require also substantial amount of resources to be committed to their provision. The insurgent Boko Haram and its like have given rise to the question of how much to be provided for defense in recent time.[17]

Nmah concludes that "many states of the world have incurred lots of loses in their over-all economic growth and development arising from the ugly incidence of terrorism. Terrorism has impacted negatively on national economies through increase in military and security spending."[18]

Nigeria's security and anti-terrorism budget has quadrupled in the last several years as a result of her anti-

---

16 **Anthony Abayomi Adebayo**, *Implications of 'Boko Haram' Terrorism on National Development in Nigeria: A Critical Review*, Mediterranean Journal of Social Sciences, Vol 5 No 16 July 2014, 480 – 489, at page 484, available at http://www.mcser.org.journal/index.php/mjss/article/download/3330/3284

17 **Patrick Nmah**, *Religious Fanaticism, a Threat to National Security: The Case of Boko Haram Sect*, p106, at page 108, Published in http://dx.doi.org/10.4314/uja.v13i1.7

18 Ibid at page 110

terrorism activities. The security and defence budget far outstrip the entire budgets for education, health, social services, agriculture and economic development combined. **Oladimeji** and **Oresanwo** speaking of the impact of diverting so much of the nation's budget to security and counter terrorism in lieu of allocating enough funds to other critical sectors, agree with analysts that "government's huge security spend [sic] has an opportunity cost – it implies less spending on power infrastructure, education and healthcare, which combined have been allocated a smaller budget than security in 2012."[19] **Ogege** adds:

> The Boko Haram's insecurity problems has caused a greater percentage of internal resources and attention to be devoted only to the security sector. With the enormous resources at its disposal, leadership in Nigeria is confronted with the problem of focusing its expenditure priorities on security in disfavor of viable human capital development and other growth and productivity promoting sectors. This no doubt, poses a serious challenge to a dynamic framework for the provision of job options and the elimination of poverty, which of course constitutes the hallmark of sustainable development. This is made worse as leadership is preoccupied by

---

19 **Oladimeji, Moruff Sanjo, Oresanwo, Adeniyi Marcus**, supra, note 6, at page 250

waging and bent on winning the war against terrorism through huge budgetary allocations to the security sector.[20]

The sad irony of it all is that with the budget skewed inordinately in favour of huge allocations to security and counterterrorism, the underlying problems of unemployment, dearth of critical infrastructure and essential social services are left unaddressed further driving more people into the fold of the terrorists. The result of this budgetary imbalance is the creation of a vicious cycle. People are frustrated by the absence of these essential attributes of life and they take up terrorism and violence to voice their frustration. The government diverts its scarce resources to fight the violence and by so doing ignores what drove people to terrorism in the first place. That in turn prompts more frustration and more violence. And so the cycle repeats *ad infinitum*.

5.3: Impact on the Economy

With the increasing ferocity of the Boko Haram insurgency in northern Nigeria, capital flight from Nigeria to other nations with relative peace is on the rise. The violence and attendant palpable fear in the local communities that are directly victimized, have caused serious disruptions to economic activities in

---

20 **Ogege, Sam Omadjohwoefe**, *Insecurity and sustainable Development: The Boko Haram Debacle in Nigeria*, American International Journal of Social Science Vol. 2 No. 7; October 2013, 82-88, at page 87, available at http://www.aijssnet. com/journals/Vol_2_No_7_October_2013/10.pdf

those communities. According to **Ogege**:

> People are no longer free to go about their
> economic activities for fear of being killed.
> This is made worse as several thousands of
> people have migrated swiftly to the southern
> part of Nigeria. The overall implications for
> sustainable development is that the economy is
> fast deteriorating. The murderous campaigns
> and vicious onslaughts on individuals and
> institutions provide an highly unfavourable
> business environment for internal and foreign
> investors. Foreign investment is a major factor
> in the achievement of sustainable development
> [...] Nigeria can no longer avail itself of this
> opportunity due to unfavourable business
> environment of insecurity created by the violent
> activities of Boko Haram.[21]

Economic disruptions brought about by the Boko
Haram insurgency have caused palpable fear and thus
forced the disruption of activities such as the closing of
schools, airports, roads, streets, entire neighborhoods,
markets and government offices. **Oladunjoye** and
Omemu charge that there is increasing loss of qualified
manpower in the northeast as a result of the Boko Haram
insurgency.[22] They posit that "with the massive killing

---

21 Ibid at pages 86-87

22 Oladunjoye, Patrick, Omemu, Felix, Effect Of Boko Haram On School
Attendance In Northern Nigeria, British journal of Education Vol.1, No.2 pp
1-9, December 2013, Published by European Centre for Research Training and
Development UK (available at www.ea-journals.org)

of youth coppers serving in the [sic] Northern Nigeria in 2010 most corpers especially southerners reject postings to the north thereby affecting the manpower needs of the people."[23] And, of course, the cultural exchange between the peoples of the regions of the country, which the National Youth Service Corp scheme was meant to foster, is a big loser also.

The inability to attract foreign investments and business to Nigeria can be directly linked to insecurity resulting from the Boko Haram insurgency. Addressing the negative impact of terrorism on Nigeria's economy, **Akpan et al** assert that "it complicates the already unattractive Nigerian economy in view of its cost. It reduces the chances of Foreign Direct Investment and hinders greater productivity."[24] **Anthony Abayomi Adebayo** adds that "Boko Haram insurgency and terrorism is a bad signal to foreign investors"[25] and that since "the issue of investment is also about the issue of security, no investor will come to invest in Nigeria with the current security challenge."[26] **Oladimeji** and

---

23 Ibid at page 9

24 **Patrick L. Akpan, Ebele Mary Onwuka, Chinedu Onyeizugbe,** *Terrorist Activities And Economic Development In Nigeria: An Early Warning Signal,* OIDA International Journal of Sustainable Development 05: 04 (2012), 69-78 , at page 72, available at http://www.papers.ssrn.com/.../SSRN_ID2173041_co...

25 **Anthony Abayomi Adebayo,** supra, note 16, at page 484

26 Ibid; see also page 481 where he argues that: "In rich as well as poor countries, terrorism exerts a heavy toll on national economies. It is inevitable that the economic impact would be more felt in unsophisticated mono-cultural low-income economies than they would be felt in highly advanced, diversified industrial economies. There-fore, the continued rise in insecurity in the country, if not checked, may result in greater investor apathy for the country and resulting in low inflow of Foreign Direct Investment (FDI), and would make institutional investors look for other stable econ-omies to invest their money. On the state of the country, when people feel insecure, their appetite to invest, to buy or rent from the product of investment reduces; and that is why all over the world, any country that radiates an environment of insecurity naturally repels investment initiatives from both the international community and its own local investors."

Oresanwo say that:

> The atmosphere of distrust that terrorists bring
> forth increase the business running costs. The
> almost unpredictability of the terrorists events
> render the business plans useless. The tension
> and the pressure that terror brings in the society
> change the production and consumption patterns
> in the country and the shopping, transportation
> and tourism preferences of people.[27]

The Boko Haram insurgency has had a negative impact
on food production of the north-eastern states. The
insurgency has dealt and continues to deal devastating
blows on the economies of the states in the north-east
region of Nigeria. It is also impacting food supplies
in the country, given the fact that the affected areas
are in the critical cattle herding, food and grain
producing region. **Udama** recognizes this fact and
regrets that Boko Haram:

> [H]as succeeded in creating fear and terror that
> has hunted everybody and the productivity of the
> people has been stalled. Most economic activities
> have come to a halt due to uncertainty in the
> country. It has paralysed economic activities
> in the northern parts of the country were [sic]
> these activities incidents are prevalent, thereby

---

27 **Oladimeji, Moruff Sanjo, Oresanwo, Adeniyi Marcus,** supra, note 6, at
page 248

worsening the already bad situation. It has also disrupted economic activities because people fear to go to the markets to transact business because they do not know where the next attempt will be. The northern part of the country that used to be a major food supply [sic] to the entire country has been fled by people living in the region. This has had adverse effect on food supply and prices as well. Northern Nigeria that is trying desperately to industrialised [sic]but with a dangerous group such as Boko Haram, investors either foreign or local cannot invest in an unstable environment.[28]

Adebayo paints a rather gory picture of the devastation Boko Haram insurgency has wreaked on the economy of northern Nigeria. He raises the spectre of investors and businesses fleeing the violence in the north and heading south, and in some cases overseas. He says people are leaving the north in droves for safer climes to do business. This has a disastrous impact on the economy of northern Nigeria and is negatively impactful on the lives of Nigerians in the north. According to him:

> For most of the north, the ongoing insurgency has had a significant negative impact on the regional economy. Lebanese and Indian expatriates who have established businesses in Kano going back

---

28 **Udama, Rawlings Akonbede**, supra, note 2, at pages 112-3

decades have relocated to Abuja and the south. A good number have left the country altogether. Hotels, banks and other business sectors have witnessed significant reductions in their activities. The border towns that have thrived on trade with neighbouring countries have also seen their businesses curtailed because of increasing restrictions on cross-border traffic. In Kano alone, an estimated 126 industries have recently closed down. [...] Another trend is the massive movement of southerners from the north, many of them SME operators and professionals.[29]

Although no accurate statistics are available to say for sure, one scholar suggests that terrorism has a direct impact on financial markets. **Karolyi** attempts an articulation of impact of terrorism on Financial Markets. He argues that:

The immediate impact of terrorist attacks on financial and commodity markets are predictable in that they lead to increases in investors' risk aversion. The market reactions are also consistent with the expected economic impact of terrorism in the intermediate and longer term: by reducing confidence and increasing the risk aversion of consumers and firms, by lowering consumption and real investment activity, by

---

29 **Anthony Abayomi Adebayo**, supra, note 16, at page 484

triggering economic slowdown if not outright recession, and by spilling over to other stock markets, fixed income market yields, currency and even other commodity markets. There is also the potential impact of psychological fear of terrorism on economic behavior.[30]

Karolyi, therefore, surmises that:

Prices of individual stocks reflect investors' hopes and fears about the future, and taken in aggregate, stock price movements can generate a tidal wave of activity. Because of their liquidity, terrorist attacks and other unforeseen disastrous occurrences can have serious implications for stocks and bonds. Decisions to buy and sell can quickly, easily and inexpensively, be reversed. When information becomes available about a cataclysmic event, like terrorist attack, investors often flee the market in search of safer financial instruments and panic selling can ensue.[31]

Terrorism has also impacted key sectors such as tourism, transportation, communication and power generation in Nigeria. According to **Ogege:**

---

30 **Karolyi, George Andrew,** *The Consequences of Terrorism for Financial Markets: What Do We Know?*, (May 7, 2006, at page 1, available at SSRN: http://ssrn.com/abstract=904398 or http://dx.doi.org/10.2139/ssrn.904398

31 Ibid at page 3

Another way in which insecurity negatively affects sustainable development is in the sphere of tourism. Tourism is a viable sector with sufficient economic, socio-cultural benefits. However, for a country to reap these benefits, a country must be free of security threats. Security constitutes a sensitive aspect of tourism. Nigeria has abundant tourist centres. However, they have made negligible contribution to sustainable development due to the security challenges perpetuated by the incessant bombings by Boko Haram.[32]

The hospitality and tourism industry in Abuja was dealt a serious blow when the US Department of State alerted US and Western citizens in Abuja of impending terror attacks on major hotels in the city. The alert was said to be based on reliable information about a potential attack.[33] This led to reduction in patronage as patrons stayed away from prominent hotels like the Transcorp Hilton and Sheraton, amongst others. The reputational damage and loss of business sustained by these hotels have been huge. **Adeyinka Ajayi** says that:

The impact of terrorism and crisis however, can

---

32 **Ogege, Sam Omadjohwoefe**, supra, note 20, at page 87

33 See "US Embassy Warns of Possible Terror Attacks on Luxury Hotels in Abuja", sourced on 4/27/2015 from http://www.lindablog.siteblogs.net/2015/02/28/us-embassy-warns-of-possible-terror-attacks-on-luxury-hotels-in-abuja/
See also James J.F. Forest, supra, note 7,

be more severe on developing economies and emerging tourist destinations. This is because competition for global tourism business is keen, and developing a world class tourist destination requires huge investment in infrastructural facilities and security outfits. This huge financial commitment nevertheless, a sudden eruption of crisis or terrorist act is capable of driving away tourists and slowing down economic growth.[34]

Because Abuja is relatively safer than the far north, it continues to maintain a certain level of business in this sector. However, cities such as Maiduguri in the north-east and Kano in the north-west have not been that lucky. They have seen a huge plunge in their hospitality and hotel business sectors. **Alao, Atere** and **Alao** catalogue the fall out of terrorism on Nigeria's economy in the following passage:

The implications of multi-dimensional conflicts in Nigeria as well as the fall out of Boko Haram insurgence have left behind an inestimable damage to every facet of life in Nigeria. There is no gaining [sic] saying that it has slowed down the national growth and development since no investors would prefer to invest in a crisis ridden

---

34 **Adeyinka Peters Ajayi**, *The Economic Impact Of Crisis And Militancy On Tourism Destination Development In Niger-Delta*, Asian Journal of Management sciences and education Vol. 1. No. 1, page 127 at page 129, April 2012, sourced from www.leena-luna.co.jp

nation. It further compounded the problems associated with the relocation of Multinational Companies to safer territories in Africa like Ghana due to infrastructural decay. One of the noticeable effect has been the tendency to worsen unemployment and lead to youth restiveness, thereby making crime a profitable venture and attractive. It has also led to near collapse of tourism industry as the nation loses huge foreign currency that could have accrued from this sector.[35]

Even the aviation sector and associated businesses are feeling the pain of this insecurity.[36] A good example is the international carrier, Royal Dutch Airlines [KLM] that for a period of time, had to stop parking their planes at Abuja, but instead dropped off passengers at the Nnamdi Azikiwe international Airport in Abuja and then flew their empty planes and crew to spend the night in Accra, Ghana, only to return the following day to pick up passengers travelling back to Holland. The impact is not only the blight on Nigeria's reputation, but more substantially, the Nigerian hotels that could have made money housing the crew as well as the funds that could

---

35 **Adeyinka Peters Ajayi,** ibid, , at pages 8-9

36 See FinIntell Magazine of January 21, 2013, "Delta Airline Exit From Abuja – The Business Implications" sourced on 4/27/2015 from http://www. myfinancialintellignce.com/transport/delta-airline-exit-abuja---business-implications/2013-01-21

have been made from selling aviation fuel to the carrier were lost. We must also point out that restaurants, bars and clubs, supermarkets, gift shops and other businesses that could have benefitted from the patronage of the airline crew were all losers.

5.4: Infrastructure and Property Damage

Next to the 'body count' of the dead and wounded, the greatest loss is by the internally displaced and those that have taken refuge across the Nigerian border. And after the enormous economic losses and costs brought on by the insurgency, comes infrastructural and property damage. Nigeria is notoriously bereft of much needed infrastructure and social amenities, such as electricity, portable water, schools, medical clinics and medical services, roads, etc. The little existing infrastructure is increasingly becoming targets for terror attacks. According to **Oladimeji** and **Oresanwo**, "the cost of terror attack and insecurity in Nigeria has slow [sic] down its infrastructure development."[37] Social disruption and destruction of critical social infrastructures such as schools, government buildings, prisons, police stations and army barracks, churches and mosques, and critical technology installations such as cellular phone masts, are some of the consequences of terrorism. **Adebayo** says that "the tragedy is that the collapse of local economies and the erosion of social capital reinforce a downward

---

37 **Oladimeji, Moruff Sanjo, Oresanwo, Adeniyi Marcus,** supra, note 6, at page 249

spiral of further impoverishment, which in itself sows the seeds of further conflict."[38] The Boko Haram sect has attacked, destroyed and damaged schools, clinics, churches, government buildings, prisons, police stations and barracks, army barracks and military installations. Precious military vehicles and lethal equipment including aircraft, tanks, troop carriers, etc., have either been stolen or destroyed.[39]

In addition, business, public and private properties have been destroyed or damaged by the activities of the Boko Haram insurgency in the north. Whole towns, villages, hamlets and neighbourhoods have been razed by either the marauding sect or the Nigerian security forces in reprisal attacks in reaction to Boko Haram activities. Dozens of cellular towers have been destroyed by the sect, resulting in the loss of vital phone services for inhabitants of swathes of remote areas of the far north.[40] Businesses have been burnt either by Boko Haram, or by security services in retaliation against locals they suspect to be sympathizers of the sect. Thousands of vehicles have been destroyed in these episodes. Thousands of homes have fallen victim to the cycle of violence and mayhem.

---

38 **Anthony Abayomi Adebayo**, supra, note 16, at page 484

39 **U.S. Department of State, Bureau of Counterterrorism**, Country Reports on Terrorism 2013, 1-21, at page 13, available at http://www.state.gov/j/ct/rls/crt/2013/224820.htm

40 **National Consortium for the Study of Terrorism and Responses to Terrorism**, *Boko Haram Recent Attacks*, Start Background ReportMay 2014, 1-8, at page 7, available at http://www.start.umd.edu/pubs/STARTBackgroundReport_Boko-HaramRecentAttacks_May2014_O.pdf

Although Nigeria is notorious for her lack of record keeping and collation of critical data, anecdotal evidence suggest that the governments, at all levels, federal, state and local, as well as corporations, businesses and private individuals have lost and continue to lose, tens of billions of dollars to the Boko Haram menace.

5.5: Impact on Education

The sustained campaign against western style schools by Boko Haram, and the loss of precious school infrastructure, equipment and teaching staff in the north, is a big blow to the efforts of government to bring education and social mobility to this disadvantaged region of the country. Education is a key sector that has borne the brunt of the Boko Haram insurgency in the north-east of Nigeria. Because of the much publicized aversion of the sect to western education, western model schools and institutions in the north-east have been on the cross-hairs of the Boko Haram military assaults and explosives device campaign. According to **START's May 2014 Background Report**:

> Boko Haram's name and ideology indicate antipathy towards western educational norms. Despite this, Boko Haram did not initially target schools, with only three attacks recorded prior to 2012. In 2012, Boko Haram started targeting schools on a regular basis, with 47 attacks that

year resulting in 77 fatalities. While attacks on schools decreased in 2013, perhaps due to frequent school closures in its areas of operations, Boko Haram carried out 14 attacks on schools in which 119 people died. In February 2014, Boko Haram attacked a boarding school in Yobe state, killing 29 male students and driving the girls away with admonition to get married.[41]

Scores of schools have been attacked and hundreds of school children have been killed, injured or abducted by Boko Haram throughout the region. The most notable example is the abduction of close to three hundred school girls from a secondary school in Chibok, Borno State.[42] Teachers and school administrators have also been victims of Boko Haram. School buildings and properties are familiar arson targets for Boko Haram. The result is a mass decline in school enrolment and attendance in the region and elsewhere in northern Nigeria.[43] **Oladunjoye** and **Omemu** calculated the cost of terrorism on education and educational facilities in the country and came to the conclusion that "Education is worst hit by the Boko Haram activities."[44] Continuing, they found that "[t]he constant threat posed by Boko

41 National Consortium for the Study of Terrorism and Responses to Terrorism, supra, note 11, at page 4

42 **Adam Nossiter**, *Boko Haram Abducted Nigerian Girls One Year Ago*, The New York Times, April 14, 2015, available at http://www.nytimes.com/2015/04/15/world/africa/nigeria-boko-haram-chibok-kidnapped-girls.html

43 **The Economist**, *"Boko Haram's impact on Nigeria: Education in crisis*, May 9th, 2014, available at http://www.economist.com/blogs/baobab/2014/05/boko-harams-impact-nigeria

44 **Oladunjoye, Patrick, Omemu, Felix**, supra, note 3, at page 4

Haram which started in 2009 [...] undermines efforts at improving education in the region. These groups have carried out several attacks and issued threats to schools in the North in some of these attacks, teachers were killed or injured and structures razed."[45] They have no doubt that "Boko Haram has dealt a fatal blow on the enrolment of pupils and students to schools in the [sic] Northern Nigeria. Parents and pupils live in perpetual fear of attacks and this may have direct effect on school attendance."[46]

Additionally, **Oladunjoye** and **Omemu** assert that because of the activities of Boko Haram "most primary school children [in the Northeast] have permanently dropped out of school either as a result of the death of their parents or as a result of the fear of sporadic attacks."[47] **Ekanem et al** raise the grave impact of terrorism on education in Nigeria and, particularly on the National Youth Service Scheme. According to them, "Students have been forced to flee their schools. Indeed so grave is the problem that some Governors have vowed never to allow Nigerian students from their states to go back to the northern part of Nigeria where the presence of the group [Boko Haram] is growing exponentially."[48]

---

45 Ibid

46 Ibid at page 5

47 Ibid at page 9

48 Samuel Asuquo Ekanem, Jacob Abiodun Dada, Bassey James Ejue, Boko Haram And Amnesty: A Philo-Legal Appraisal, International Journal of Humanities and Social Science Vol. 2 No. 4 [Special Issue – February 2012] pp 231 – 244, at page 232, available at http://www.ijhssnet.com/journals/vol_2_No_4_Special_Issue.../28.pdf

They conclude that:

> [T]he activities of Boko Haram have affected the postings of students of Southern extraction on national youth service to the north. Parents are strongly resisting the posting of their children as corpers to the north. This, in itself is a fatal blow to the noble objective of the scheme as a unifying strategy. Indeed, the unity of Nigeria is seriously threatened by Boko Haram.[49]

5.6: Negative impact on Nigeria's Image on the International Scene

The ever increasing violence and daring aggression of the Boko Haram terrorists are bringing unwelcomed negative attention to Nigeria around the world. **Alao et al** point out the debilitating damage terrorism is doing to Nigeria's image overseas. According to them:

> Another dimension of the Boko Haram insurgency is the effect on the corporate image of Nigeria within committee of nations. [...] For a decade, efforts were made without success to rebrand the shattered image of Nigeria. There is no amount of image laundering that can influence the impression of the international community if negative news on a daily basis

---

49 Ibid at page 232

emanate from the nation.[50]

Travel Advisories issued by foreign nations for their citizens travelling to or planning to travel to Nigeria is increasingly painting Nigeria in very bad light. On 8 August 2014, the United States Department of State warned United States citizens and permanent residents about the risk of travelling to Nigeria stating that the security situation in Nigeria was fluid and unpredictable.[51] They were advised to avoid travelling to three states in the Northeast of Nigeria, to wit, Borno, Adamawa and Yobe states. The travel advisory specifically warned that:

> Kidnappings remain a security concern throughout the country. Since the beginning of 2013, there have been multiple reports of kidnappings involving U.S. citizens. Kidnapping of foreign nationals and attacks against Nigerian police forces in Lagos State and the Niger Delta region continue to effect personal security for those travelling in these areas. Criminals or militants have abducted foreign nationals, including U.S. citizens, from off-shore and land-based oil facilities and maritime vessels, residential compounds, and public roadways. Ansaru, an offshoot of Boko Haram, has specifically targeted foreigners in the north for

---

50 **Alao, David Oladimeji, Atere, Clement Olusegun, Alao, Oluwafisayo,** supra, note 14, at page 9

51 The US Department of State, Nigeria Travel Warning, August 8, 2014, 1-3, available at http://www.travel.state.gov/content/passports/english/alertswarnings/nigeria...

kidnap in the past few years with lethal outcomes.[52]

This has been worsened by the fact that the UN at a point had placed an indefinite embargo on all official travels to Nigeria.[53] **Adebayo** says that:

> In the wake of the crisis in the country, many international agencies and countries began to issue travel warnings to their citizens about the dangers involved in travelling and doing business in some parts of the country. Precisely, the United States warned American citizens of the risks of coming to Nigeria, with particular emphasis to Akwa Ibom, Bayelsa, Delta, Rivers, Abia, Edo, Imo, Jos, Bauchi, Gombe, Yobe and Borno states; and the gulf of Guinea […], and this has grave consequences for the development of the country.[54]

#BRING BACK OUR GIRLS: Perhaps one of the most negative worldwide publicity the image of Nigeria has had to suffer was the online twitter campaign mounted (with good intentions) to bring attention to and thus facilitate the return of over 200 innocent school girls abducted by the Boko Haram group from a high school in Chibok in Borno State of north-east Nigeria.[55] The movement led

---

52 Ibid at page 2

53 **Popoola, I.S.**, *Press and Terrorism in Nigeria: A Discourse on Boko Haram*, 43-66 at page 58, Global Media Journal African Edition 2012 Vol 6(1), available at http://www.globalmedia.journals.ac.za

54 **Anthony Abayomi Adebayo**, supra, note 16, at page 484

55 **Don North**, *Behind the War with Boko Haram*, Consortiumnews.com, November 16, 2014, 1-27, at page 3, available at http://www.consortiumnews.com/2014/11/16/behind-the-war-with-boko-haram/

by a foremost proponent for education and social justice, Dr. Oby Ezekwesili, was so prevalent and the impact so resounding that it attracted the support of thousands of prominent figures around the world, including the United States First Lady, Michelle Obama, and several political, movie, music and business icons around the world, including the Nobel Peace Prize winner, Malala Yousafzai. Such a horrific image of innocent girls being driven into the bush at night and possibly facing rape and all kinds of physical, emotional, and sexual abuse, sent shock waves down the spines of millions of people around the world. The damage such a depraved activity has done to Nigeria's image is incalculable. **Diego Cordano** writes that, "The recent kidnapping of over 250 girls has attracted extensive international attention and has spawned a social media campaign known on Twitter by the slogan #BringBackOurGirls."[56] Following this unfortunate incident in May 2014, Nigeria attracted the most negative attention from the international media with almost every media outlet in the world carrying news of the abduction. CNN, BBC, Aljazeera, CCTV, ITV, etc ran series of coverage on terrorism in Nigeria. Even up to the moment, international news media and online outlets, carry daily reports on the activities of the Boko Haram sect in Nigeria. It does appear as if the

---

56 **Diego Cordano**, *The Evolution of Boko Haram: a growing threat?*, *Consultancy African Intelligence*, Friday June 2014, PP 1-5, at page 1, available at http://www.consultancyafrica.com/index.php?option=com_content&view=article&id=1695:...

only news that makes it out of Nigeria is either about terrorism, corruption, or fraud.

The Boko Haram insurgency has spawned a transnational problem. Their activities are not restricted to Nigeria. They are increasingly making cross-border raids and attacks on targets in Chad and particularly in northern Cameroon. Leading **Nathaniel Manni** to conclude that, "Boko haram presents a very real threat to both African and Global security. The group has continued to conduct increasingly deadly attacks within Nigeria and may be developing transnational ambitions as evidenced by statements from the group's leadership."[57] The **United States Department of State**, in its reports on terrorism in Africa, cites the targeted killings of Cameroonians and Nigerians living in Cameroon in the villages of Kouseri and Kolofata; the kidnapping of a French family of 7 in the far north of Cameroon, who were later released in Nigeria after ransom was paid; and the kidnapping of a French priest near the northern Cameroon town of Koza and his later release in Nigeria.[58] The U.S. House of Representatives, cites both the abduction of the French family in Cameroon and the assassination in Nigeria, on October 20, 2012, of the mayor of a Cameroonian border town, by Boko Haram and say that, "these

---

57 **Nathaniel Manni,** *"Boko Haram: A Threat to Africa and Global Security"*, Global Security Studies, Fall 2012, Volume 3, Issue 4, PP 44-54, at page 51, available at http://www.globalsecuritystudies.com/Manni%20BH%20FINAL.pdf

58 U.S. Department of State, Bureau of Counterterrorism, Country Reports on Terrorism 2013, 1-21, at page 3, available at http://www.state.gov/j/ct/rls/crt/2013/224820.htm

developments clearly provide Boko Haram with an international footprint that goes beyond local politics."[59] **Diego Cordano** underscores the trans-border nature of the Boko Haram threat. He writes that:

> Boko Haram has also developed critical links with communities located in the border areas for the purposes of refuge, training, transit and recruitment. For example, Cameroon has become an important centre for recruitment, given the relatively poor majority Muslim northern part of the country and a wealthier majority Christian south. Boko Haram has certainly been able to obtain sophisticated arms and weapons thanks to smuggling operations within and across Nigeria's borders. For example, man-portable air-defence systems have entered Nigeria through Tuareg smuggling networks in Niger, possibly linked to AQIM. The long and porous borders between Nigeria and Cameroon, Niger, and Chad, often in mountainous areas or in the jungle, have facilitated this activity. [...] In addition, it is worth observing that the movement's presence in Cameroon, Chad, and Niger is increasing, and these countries have all felt the impact of Boko Haram's activities, especially with regard to local

---

59 U.S. House of Representatives Committee on Homeland Security, Boko Haram: Growing Threat to the U.S. Homeland, September 13, 2013, 1-39, at page 9, Prepared by the Majority Staff of the Committee on Homeland Security, available at http://www.homeland.house.gov/sites/homeland.house.gov/files/documents/09-13-Boko-Haram-Report.pdf

economies. [...] In this respect, Boko Haram seems to increasingly turn from being a localized problem to a national and regional threat.[60]

Don North underscores the grave threat Boko Haram poses to countries in the sub-region including Chad, Niger and Cameroon. He says:

The danger presented by Boko Haram extends far beyond Nigeria, which although a troubled state is the most populous and wealthiest in Africa. Boko Haram may have regional ambitions. A consolidation of its successes in Nigeria's three northeastern states would give Boko Haram a strategic springboard to invade neighboring Niger, Cameroon and Chad – weak states that would have difficulty surviving a serious siege.[61]

Don North's prediction seems prophetic, given that Boko Haram had early in 2015 started mounting cross-border assaults on towns and villages in Cameroon leading the President of that country to cry out for foreign help.[62] Chad has also joined the effort to battle Boko Haram. According to **Dos Santos**, "Cameroon ... is used by Boko Haram as an operational base and to kidnap westerners for ransom, from which to acquire weapons and attract

---

60 **Diego Cordano**, supra, note 56, at page 3

61 **Don North**, supra, note 55, at page 10

62 Reuters, Cameroon appeals for international military aid to fight Boko Haram, Friday January 9, 2015, available at http://www.reuters.com/assets/print?aid=USKBNOKI18920150109

members or secure the release of detained militants."[63]

Boko Haram has in essence placed Nigeria squarely in the center of the world's terrorism map.

5.7: Humanitarian Catastrophe, Internally Displaced Persons, and Refugees

An under-reported impact of the Boko Haram insurgency, is the huge humanitarian catastrophe their activities have brought upon Nigeria. So also is the huge population of Nigerians that have been internally displaced, and many of those who have taken refuge in neighbouring nations.[64] **Amnesty International** say that "more than a million people are displaced inside Nigeria and hundreds of thousands have fled across its borders into Chad, Cameroon and Nigeria [sic]."[65] According to **Gustavo Placido Dos Santos** (quoting the United Nations Office for the Co-ordination of Humanitarian Assistance), "since 2013 Boko Haram's attacks have displaced around 300,000 people. Most have fled to other states, the remainder seeking refuge in neighbouring countries. Recently, the government relief agency, the

---

63 **Gustavo Placido Dos Santos**, *Boko Haram: Time for an Alternative Approach*, Portuguese Institute of International Relations and Security, IPRIS Viewpoints, April 2014, 1-3, at page 2, available at http://www.opendemocracy.net/

64 **Hanibal Goitom**, *Nigeria: Boko Haram, Report for the U.S. Department of Justice*, July 2014, 1-11, at page 9, available at http://www.justice.gov/.../nigeria/2014-010...

65 **Ibrahim Abdulaziz and Haruna Umar**, Amnesty: *Nigeria massacre deadliest in history of Boko Haram*, AP January 9, 2015, available at http://www.news.yahoo.com/7-kids-reunite-parents-lost-nigeria-islamic-uprising-094251667.html?soc_src=mediacontentsharebuttons&soc_trk=ma

National Emergency Management Agency, declared a humanitarian crisis affecting more than three million people."[66] **The Human Rights Watch** says that:

> Nearly 300,000 people in Borno, Yobe, and Adamawa states – 70 percent of them women and children – have fled their homes since early 2013, according to the United Nations Office for the Coordination of Humanitarian Assistance (UNOCHA). The Office of the United Nations High Commissioner for Refugees (UNHCR) puts the figure on internally displaced people in Nigeria at more than 470,000. Most are staying with families in other parts of Nigeria, and another 60,000 or so have sought refuge in neighboring Cameroon, Chad, and Niger since May 2013, according to UNHCR.[67]

The activities of Boko Haram in the north-east have led to forced relocation and a huge pool of internally displaced people in northern Nigeria. It has forced migrations and relocation of peoples and businesses from the north-east tip of the country towards north-central and southern Nigeria.[68] Hundreds of thousands of refugees have moved to neighbouring countries such as

---

66 **Gustavo Placido Dos Santos**, supra, note 63

67 *Human Rights Watch, Nigeria: Boko Haram Attacks Cause Humanitarian Crisis* [1], March 14, 2014, 1-4, at page 1, available at http://www.hrw.org/print/news/2014/03/14/nigeria-boko-haram-attacks-cause-humanitarian-crisis

68 **Don North**, supra, note 55,

Chad, Niger and Cameroon, in search of protection and shelter. Hundreds of thousands of internally displaced persons roam the streets of major cities of the north-east, including Maiduguri, Yola, Damaturu and elsewhere.[69] The **US Department of Justice** says:

> Six of these states in the northeast (Adamawa, Bauchi, Borno, Gombe, Taraba, and Yobe) have been the hardest hit, with close to six hundred fifty thousand residents being internally displaced. Borno State, home for over two hundred fifty thousand of the internally displaced persons, of which one hundred thousand are in the capital, Maiduguri, the birth place of Boko Haram, has fared the worst.[70]

Oladunjoye and **Omemu** underscore the social disruptions brought about by the Boko Haram insurgency as follows:

> The list of the various attacks by this sect – Boko Haram in 2013 is endless. They have unleashed fear and terror in the minds of the people staying in these parts of the country[71] thereby affecting every aspects of their social and economic

---

69 Ibid at page 8

70 **Hanibal Goitom,** *Nigeria: Boko Haram, Report for the U.S. Department of Justice*, July 2014, The Library of Congress, 1-11, at page 4, available at http://www.justice.gov/.../nigeria/2014-010...

71 Referring to the northeast Nigeria

life. Such insecurity have [sic] led to massive migration from such troubled areas to other parts of the country which is believed to be less vulnerable to Boko Haram attack.[72]

According to **Ekanem et al**:

[T]he activities of Boko Haram have created a situation of insecurity, instability, increase in crime and has worsened the welfare and quality of life on Nigerians. This can be attested to by the mass movement of residents from other states of the federation out of the North Eastern part of the country, especially Maiduguri, which is the capital of Borno State. This situation has made it impossible for the citizens in that part of Nigeria to carry on their legitimate businesses.[73]

The spectacular Boko Haram attack on Baga, Borno State, on the banks of Lake Chad, was unprecedented in its brutality and drove tens of thousands of inhabitants through the lake into neighbouring Chad. The entire town and the surrounding villages and hamlets were completely razed by the marauding sect. Close to 2000 lives were reportedly lost and thousands injured.[74] Up till this moment some of these refugees are still living in

---

72 **Oladunjoye, et al**, supra, note 3, at page 3

73 **Samuel Asuquo Ekanem, Jacob Abiodun Dada, Bassey James Ejue**, supra, note 48, at page 231

74 **Jeremy Bender and Armin Rosen**, *Boko Haram Just Pulled Off One Of The Deadliest Terrorist Attacks In History*, Business Insider, January 9, 2015, available at http://www.businessinsider.com/boko-harams-deadliest-terrorist-attack-2015-1

makeshift tents and huts out in the Chadian desert.

5.8: Loss of Human Rights, and Constitutional Protection:

An impact that is also often ignored by scholars in the discussion of impacts and effects of terrorism is the increasing loss of human rights and constitutional protections, by both innocent victims and alleged terrorists, in equal measures. Efforts to counter terrorism often result in the passing of draconian anti-terrorism legislation that essentially spread a wide drag-net that is often capable of sweeping in all and every possible activity. In addition, counter-terrorism activities by law enforcement and armed forces result in large scale ignoring of constitutional safeguards and even blatant abuse and deprivation of human rights. Human rights abuses, both by the terrorists and the security forces, which are all inordinately borne by hapless innocent civilians, is a direct result of the activities of terrorists in the country. According to **Udama**:

> The civil rights of individuals and even their more basic civil liberties as guaranteed by the Constitution has been jeopardised. While the Islamic sects unleash terror on the people, the activities of the security agents have become deplorable as well hence the abuses of people's liberty have become the order of the day. They

have deployed an unconventional and extra-judicial method of shoot at sight which is usually adopted by the government to tackle widespread public disturbances and terrible crimes. The security agents stop people at will, restrict people's movement by the day and especially at night and kill anyone at the least suspicion.[75]

By matching the ruthless crudity and unbridled violence of the terrorist groups, the Nigerian security forces have indirectly handed the terrorists victory. The Nigerian security forces are unwittingly doing the bidding of terrorists by making the lives of hapless victims unbearable through their ruthless and callous counter-terrorism strategies of indiscriminate extra-judicial killings, maiming and prolonged detention of victims, and alleged terrorists, as well as the criminal looting of properties and burning of homes and businesses. By engaging the terrorists in the act of brutality and depraved indifference to the lives, liberty and constitutional rights of victims and alleged terrorists alike, the Nigerian security forces have lost the moral high-ground that is critical for winning the hearts and minds of the citizenry in any anti-terrorism strategy. If the activities of government mirrors, and in some cases exceeds that of terrorists, how can the government win the trust and support of its citizens? **A.F. Ahokegh** says that the "local people felt more intimidated by the soldiers deployed

---

75 **Udama, Rawlings Akonbede**, supra, note 2, at page 112

to fight Boko Haram than they did of Boko Haram"[76] and that "this sentiment was compounded by the violent and indiscriminate responses of the security forces, which frequently caused the destruction of property and the loss of innocent lives."[77]

There have been reports of indiscriminate arrests, shootings, maiming and detention of civilians by security forces and burning of victims' homes, businesses, vehicles and looting of their personal properties, including cash, electronics and cellphones.[78] There has even been reports of rape of women and young girls by these marauding security forces, in the name of counter-terrorism. Curiously, in spite of hundreds of tactical operations by the Joint Task Force and other security outfits, and the blanket arrest of thousands of people, there is scant evidence of prosecution of terrorist suspects. As such, observers conclude that most of the arrested suspects are being extra judicially executed without proper investigation, charges, and conviction in criminal courts.[79] Some are allegedly being held indefinitely at undisclosed locations and without access to lawyers

---

76 **A. F. Ahokegh**, *Boko Haram: A 21st Century Challenge In Nigeria*, European Scientific Journal, September edition vol.8. No.21, 46-55, 52, available at http://www.eujournal.org>Home>Vol8,No21(2012)>Ahokegh

77 Ibid

78 **Human Rights Watch**, *"Nigeria: At Least 1,000 Civilians Dead Since January"* March 26, 2015, available at http://www.hrw.org/news/2015/03/26/nigeria-least-1000-civilians-dead-january-o

79 **Amnesty International**, *"Nigeria: Gruesome footage implicates military in war crimes"*, 5 August 2014, available at http://www.amnesty.org/en/articles/news/2014/08/nigeria-gruesome-footage-implicates-military-war-crimes/

and their families. **Professor Amos N. Guiora** ably articulates this slide down the slippery slope. He asserts that:

> Counterterrorism – like terrorism – is a reality. Nations have the absolute obligation and right to protect innocent civilians against those seeking to harm them. However, implementation of counterterrorism obligations must be tempered by due process. The essence of democracy is granting – and protecting- civil and political rights of attacker and attacked alike. Failure to provide due process to individuals suspected of involvement in terrorism leads to a society dangerously approaching a slippery slope from which there is no return. While controversial and, perhaps, unappetizing the true test of democracy is protecting those seeking to attack it.[80]

David Anderson, QC is wary of the increasing inclination to pass draconian legislation against "terrorism" and the highhanded nature of anti-terrorism activities that are directed at seemingly regular criminal activities that can be better handled by regular law enforcement. Although he concedes the serious nature of terrorism and the need to have extraordinary

---

80 **Professor Amos N. Guiora**, *Due Process and Counterterrorism*, at page 1, available at http://www.ssrn.com/abstract=1680009

responses to it, he worries that reactions to terrorism have driven policy-makers towards paranoia. He argues that:

> [T]here are great dangers in such generalized approach. To take an understanding of terrorism that is derived from history or social science, and allow it to serve as a justification for any number of specific legal powers, is a dangerous course. However serious or unique the problem of "terrorism," it does not follow merely from its seriousness or uniqueness that special powers are necessary to combat it. If special powers are to be justified, it must be by reference to the particular demands of policing and prosecuting terrorism.[81]

Don North says that "because of the scorched-earth policies and human rights violations, the Nigerian army and police are often feared as much as Boko Haram."[82] The brutality of the Nigerian security forces and their blanket victimization of both suspected terrorists and innocent victims have been discussed in chapter 3 and elsewhere in this work. Suffice it to stress that innocent Nigerians as well as suspected terrorists continue to be literally under the jack boot of the security forces in the

---

81 **Anderson, David,** *Shielding the Compass; How to Fight Terrorism Without Defeating the law* (June 15, 2013), at pages 5-6 , available at SSRN: http://www.ssrn. com/abstract=2292950 [last visited September 23, 2014]

82 **Don North**, *Behind the War with Boko Haram*, Consortiumnews.com, November 16, 2014, 1-27, at page 8, available at http://www.consortiumnews. com/2014/11/16/behind-the-war-with-boko-haram/

north-east.[83]   There have been reported cases of mass executions of suspected terrorists, alleged sympathizers and indeed innocent onlookers, in several incidents in the north-east.[84]   As a matter of fact, the gruesome public extrajudicial executions of sect members and suspected sect members on the heels of the July 2009 violent confrontation between the sect and security forces in several cities in the north that culminated in the much publicized public execution of Muhammad Yusuf, the sect's founder, is still fresh in the public's mind.

Another curious thing that should irk the imagination of scholars of Nigerian counter-terrorism activities in the north-east is the whereabouts of thousands of people that have been scooped up by security agencies in the course of the operations against Boko Haram. Nobody seems to be asking questions why no one has been brought into court with charges of terrorism in spite of the fact that there is no evidence that these people have been released. This clearly supplies the indication that most of these people have either been executed or are still being detained at undisclosed places for undisclosed charges. There is also no indication that the ones detained have had access to legal representation or even to members of

---

83 The U.S. State Department, *"Nigeria 2013 Human Rights Report"*, available at http://www.state.gov/documents/organization/220358.pdf
84 Human Rights Watch, *"Nigeria: At Least 1,000 Civilians Dead Since January"* March 26, 2015, available at http://www.hrw.org/news/2015/03/26/nigeria-least-1000-civilians-dead-january-o; Amnesty International, "Nigeria: Gruesome footage implicates military in war crimes", 5 August 2014, available at http://www.amnesty.org/en/articles/news/2014/08/nigeria-gruesome-footage-implicates-military-war-crimes/

their families. That should be a cause for concern.

5.9: The Body Count

The greatest price Nigeria and Nigerians are paying for the Boko Haram insurgency is the loss of lives, both victims and alleged terrorists. For the past dozen years or so, over thirty-five thousand lives have been lost to terrorism in northern Nigeria. According to **START's May 2014 Background Report:**

> In Nigeria, Boko Haram was responsible for more than 80 percent of all terrorist attacks between 1970 and 2013 for which perpetrator group was identified, despite their relatively recent onset of violence in 2009. Likewise, deaths from Boko Haram's attacks represented nearly 70 percent of all fatalities from terrorist attacks in Nigeria during this time period.[85]

The **U.S. Council on Foreign Relations** assesses the human impact of the Boko Haram insurgency. It says, "Boko Haram, a diffused Islamist sect, has attacked Nigeria's police and military, politicians, schools, religious buildings, public institutions, and civilians with increasing regularity since 2009. More than five

---

85   Paul Francis, Deidre Lapin, Paula Rossiasco, *Securing Development And Peace In The Niger Delta: A Social and Conflict Analysis for Change,* Study prepared for publication by the Woodrow Wilson International Center for Scholars Africa Program and Project on Leadership and Building State Capacity, 1-160, at page 51, available at http://www.wilsoncenter.org/sites/default/files/AFR_110929_Niger%20Delta_0113.pdf

thousand people have been killed in Boko Haram-related violence, and three hundred thousand have been displaced."[86] **Diego Cordano** adds that "overall, more than 4,000 people are estimated to have been killed in more than 600 Boko Haram attacks, making Boko Haram one of the deadliest terrorist groups in the world."[87] According to **Amnesty International,** "the 5-year insurgency killed more than 10,000 people last year [2014] alone."[88] The loss of lives is now a daily occurrence in northern Nigeria as a result of the Boko Haram insurgency. **Adebayo** counts the human cost in the following passage:

> The HWR report with its scary figures revealed that, in 2011 alone, 'Boko Haram' struck 115 times and killed 550 people. Within the first three weeks of the year 2012, the sect killed 250 people with the deadliest being the coordinated bombings in the ancient city of Kano, which claimed 185 lives. A few weeks later, another 12 people were killed in a shoot-out between the Joint Task Force (JTF) and members of the sect in Maiduguri, Borno State. On Sunday, February 26, suicide bombers hit a Church in Jos, killing four persons, with another four in a reprisal

---

86 **Mohammed Aly Sergie** and **Toni Johnson,** *Boko Haram,* Council on Foreign Relations, October 7, 2014, available at http://www.cfr.org>Nigeria

87 **Diego Cordano,** supra, note 56, at page 1

88 **Ibrahim Abdulaziz and Haruna Umar,** *Amnesty: Nigeria massacre deadliest in history of Boko Haram,* AP January 9, 2015, available at http://www.news.yahoo.com/7-kids-reunite-parents-lost-nigeria-islamic-uprising-094251667.html?soc_src=mediacontentsharebuttons&soc_trk=ma

attack, and destroying 38 vehicles. In the night of the same day, gunmen attacked Shuwa Police Station in Madagali local government area of Adamawa State, killing three policemen on guard. The number continues to add on a daily basis.[89]

According to the **FATF REPORT**:

[T] United States' 2011 Country Report on Terrorism indicated Africa experienced 978 attacks in 2011, an 11.5% increase over 2010. This is attributable in large part to the more frequent attacks of the Nigeria-based terrorist group Boko Haram, which conducted 136 attacks in 2011 – up from 31 in 2010." In 2012, Boko Haram conducted 364 terrorist attacks, which killed 1132 people.[90]

Lt. Gen. Dambazau, [Rtd.] tries to size the cost of conflict on human lives in Nigeria. He says that "people have been killed, injured or displaced; properties destroyed; businesses closed and investors scared away; and communities are split along ethno-religious lines."[91] The

---

89 **Anthony Abayomi Adebayo,** supra, note 16, at page 484-5

90 **FATF Report,** *Terrorist Financing In West Africa*, October 2013, paragraph 1.1, available at http://www.fatfa-gafi.org/.../...

91 **Abdulrahman Dambazau, Lt. Gen. [Rtd]**, *Overcoming Nigeria's Security Challenges*, at page 5, available at http://www.iuokada.edu.ng/.../Overcoming%20 Nigerias%20Security%20Chall...

death toll continues daily in the north-east. It has actually got worse since Chad, Niger and Cameroon joined the military effort to checkmate Boko Haram activities in the regions bordering Nigeria. The Nigerian armed forces have also stepped up their security activities in the area. With the renewed ferocious offensive mounted by Nigeria's military forces against Boko Haram in the far north-east, human casualties and property damage continue to mount. The stepped up offensive is forcing the sect to adopt even more horrific and desperate tactics, particularly increased suicide bombings.

Given the huge negative impact the activities of Boko Haram is having on Nigeria, and the heavy toll it is visiting on innocent hapless victims, it is auspicious to prescribe ways and means to curtail the carnage.

Chapter 6

Prescription for
Eliminating Boko Haram

Nigeria took decades of political, economic, social and institutional missteps and mishaps, to dig herself into the existential hole it finds herself today. It will therefore take a concerted and multi-faceted effort to dig herself out of it. This is what **Dambazau** terms "a multidimensional approach."[1] **Sarah Margon** of the **Human Rights Watch**, blames the Nigerian government for its failure to adequately confront the Boko Haram question with the right combination of approaches. She says:

> There is no question that the Nigerian government has failed to adequately address the problem of Boko Haram, primarily because it is relying solely on a hard-nosed, military approach instead of crafting a more wide-ranging strategy to address some of the catalysts of Boko Haram's

---

1 **Abdulrahman Dambazau, Lt. Gen. [Rtd]**, *Overcoming Nigeria's Security Challenges*, at page 11, available at http://www.iuokada.edu.ng/.../Overcoming%20 Nigerias%20Security%20Chall...

existence: rampant corruption, widespread poverty and systemic impunity for abuses.[2]

Solution to Nigeria's domestic terrorism scourge can be found in the soup of options served up by a cross-section of scholars and pundits. Even the United States government recognizes that Nigerian security forces cannot kill terrorism and violence out of Nigeria. The causes must be addressed concurrently with coercive activities. The **United States Department of State** reports in its **2013 Terrorism Reports on Africa**, that "the United States called on the Nigerian government to employ a more comprehensive strategy to address Boko Haram that combines security efforts with political and development efforts to reduce Boko Haram's appeal, address the legitimate concerns of the people of northern Nigeria, and protect the rights of all of Nigeria's citizens."[3] **Babjee Pothuraju** offers a roadmap for confronting Nigeria's most prominent domestic terrorist challenge, the Boko Haram insurgency. His idea is practically in lock step with the position of the **U.S. State Department** cited above. He takes the position that:

---

2 **Sarah Margon**, *How Do You Beat Boko Haram With an Army That's Almost as Evil?*, May 14, 2014, Human Rights Watch, available at http://www.hrw.org/print/news/2014/05/14/how-do-you-beat-boko-haram-army-thats-almo... [last visited 5/29/2014]

3 U.S. Department of State, Bureau of Counterterrorism, Country Reports on Terrorism 2013, 1-21, at page 13, available at http://www.state.gov/j/ct/rls/crt/2013/224820.htm

While Boko Haram is essentially treated as a security issue, Nigeria needs to find effective ways of addressing the root causes for its emergence; these lie in socio-economic and political developments in the country. Therefore, some kind of federal intervention is needed, especially in education and healthcare, and greater pressure needs to be exerted on the northern elites to develop the region. The government needs to advance employment programmes to deal with social and political grievances in the north. It also needs to ensure that Nigeria's vast natural and political resources are used to fuel growth and development for the benefit of all, rather than consumed in a 'downward spiral of corruption, internal conflict, and violence.'[4]

Odomovo S. Afeno advocates a kitchen sink approach to confronting terrorism in Nigeria. He believes that any efforts aimed at solving the scourge of terrorism in Nigeria "should involve a combination of political, economic and security strategies that can produce realistic and timely improvement in the standard of living of the citizenry."[5] He lays out specific steps thus:

---

4 **Babjee Pothuraju**, *Boko Haram's Persistent threat in Nigeria*, Backgrounder, March 19, 2012, Institute For Defense Studies & Analyses, New Delhi, India, at page 8, available at http:/www.mercury.ethz.ch/.../Files/ISN/ThreatinNigeria_Babjepothuraju.pdf

5 **Odomovo S. Afeno**, *The Boko Haram Uprising And Insecurity In Nigeria; Intelligence Failure Or Bad Governance?*, Conflict trends 35, at page 41, available at http://www.academia.edu/.../The_Boko_Haram_Uprising_and_I...

Crucial national issues such as widespread corruption, poverty, unemployment and all forms of socio-political and economic exclusions should be addressed through effective poverty alleviation and human development programmes. In addition, security and intelligence agencies should be empowered in areas of counter-insurgency and improved capabilities for proactive response, as well as the promotion of inter-agency collaboration in the form of information sharing in order to effectively curtail both existing and emerging national and human security threats."[6]

Zumve et al offer their own recipe on how to tackle the Boko Haram terrorism in Nigeria. They make the following suggestions:

For Nigeria to successfully tackle the menace of terrorism, a major step must be taken; that is, the revitalization of Nigeria's economy. A vibrant economy will create job opportunities for the youths and change their lives in the positive direction. Such programs like the Amnesty granted the Niger Delta militants, can be extended to the North, especially the North-East to rehabilitate the army of desperate and depraved youths. The government should put in

6 Ibid

place more precise measures to deal with corrupt bureaucrats and politicians. There should be a shift from rhetoric to practical ways of punishing identified corrupt public officials and sponsors of terrorism.[7]

Ayodeji Bayo Ogunrotifa suggests a class approach to the analysis of the causes of domestic terrorism and insists that a solution can only be fashioned by first addressing the class structural imbalance in Nigeria. His argument is that:

[P]olicy recommendation from class perspective ... seeks to address what causes antagonism and tension among classes, why do members of the lumpen class form or join sectarian groups and engage in individual terrorism, and how can lumpen class be discouraged from engaging in individual terrorism or forming/joining sectarian groups that believe in the use of individual terrorism? The answers to these underlie the policy direction the class perspective might take in addressing problems posed by individual terrorism.[8]

Daniel Agbiboa discusses two competing approaches

---

7 **Samuel Zumve, Margaret Ingyoroko, Isaac Iorhen Akuva**, *Terrorism In Contemporary Nigeria: A Latent Function Of Official Corruption And State Neglect*, European Scientific Journal March 2013 edition vol.9, No.8, pp 122-140, at page 138, available at http://www.eujournal.org/index.php/esj/article/view/882

8 Ayodeji Bayo Ogunrotifa, *Class Theory of Terrorism: A Study of Boko Haram Insurgency In Nigeria*, Research on Humanities and Social Sciences, Vol.3, No.1, 2013, 27-60, available at http://www.iiste.org

to fighting terrorism, the coercive and the conciliation approaches. He argues that the coercive approach is counter-productive since it creates a vicious cycle of violence. According to him:

> With regard to how states can deal with terrorist groups, two competing counter-terrorism approaches may be gleaned from existing literature: coercive and conciliation. The crux of the debate is whether states should use harsh policies to punish terrorists and thus deter future acts, or focus on root causes and reduce incentives to use terrorism. Phrased alternatively: Do coercive policies deter terrorism, or do they create a vicious cycle of violence?[9]

Ekanem and **Ekefre** advocate education as the key to engendering change from and conversion out of violence and terror. They recognize that 'the present situation is capable of derailing the democratic structure and it posed a mortal danger to the unity of the country.' They urge that:

> The solution to this danger lies in Education and a philosophy of education that will recover the very head, the heart and hand of the very people that champion this conflict and redirect

---

9 **Daniel E. Agbiboa**, *Is Might Right? Boko Haram, the Joint Military Task Force, and the Global Jihad*, Journal of Military and Strategic Affairs, Volume 5, No. 3, December 2013, 53-71, at pages 54-55, available at http://www.mercury.ethz.ch/serviceengine/Files/.../CH+3+Might+Right.pdf

them toward reinventing their understanding and conception of religion, while locating the role of man in natural design. This approach will move the diagnosis of religious conflicts in Nigeria from the underlying socio-political, economic and governance factors and focus to a more holistic and practical means of providing a lasting solution to this problem.[10]

Frey and **Luechinger** advocate the use of opportunity costs to terrorists and potential terrorists as the basis for any anti-terrorism strategy. They "argue that an effective way to fight terrorism is to raise the opportunity costs to terrorists."[11] According to them:

This differs fundamentally from traditional deterrence policy which seeks to raise the material cost to potential terrorists. Indeed, the two approaches imply quite different policies. The opportunity costs faced by potential terrorists consist in the utility they could gain by not engaging in terrorism. These are the activities they can undertake outside of terrorism. Higher opportunity costs reduce the

---

10 **Ekanem, Samuel Asuquo, Ekefre, Ekong Nyong**, *Education and Religious Intolerance in Nigeria: The Need for Essencism as a Philosophy*, Journal of Educational and Social Research, Vol. 3 (2) May 2013, PP 303-310, at page 305, available at http://www.mcser-org.ervinhatibi.com/journal/index.php/jesr/article/.../168/159

11 **Bruno S. Frey and Simon Luechinger**, *How to Fight Terrorism: Alternatives to Deterrence*, December 2002, working Paper No. 137, institute for Empirical Research in Economics, University of Zurich Working Paper Series, PP 1-23, at page 8, available at http://www.iew.unzh.ch/wp/

willingness of a (potential) terrorist to commit terrorist activities. An increase in the opportunity cost or, equivalently, a reduction in the costs of all other activities, therefore reduces the amount of terrorism.[12]

Daniel Agbiboa also pushes an approach that seeks to address the underlying causes of terrorism as opposed to use of brute force as the sole response to terrorism. He argues that, "conciliatory approach holds that states should address the root causes of terrorism, thereby decreasing the legitimacy of terrorist's claims and the traction for its cause. States use conciliation to resolve a crisis or to forestall future crisis by negotiating with terrorists."[13] **Abimbola** and **Adesote** caution that:

If the government is not proactive towards addressing the challenge of domestic terrorism, most importantly with the trends and dimensions with which the dreaded Islamic sect popularly known as Boko Haram is carrying out its nefarious activities in the country, it is likely the country [sic] experience another civil war which may invariably lead to disintegration.[14]

Nathaniel Manni offers a strategy to solve the Boko

---

12 Ibid

13 **Daniel E. Agbiboa**, *Is Might Right?*, supra, note 9, at page 55

14 **Abimbola, J.O., and Adesote, S.A.**, *Domestic Terrorism And Boko Haram Insurgency In Nigeria, Issues And Trends*: A Historical Discourse, Journal of Arts and Contemporary Society, Volume 4, September 2012, 11-29, at page 28, available at http://www.cenresinpub.org

Haram menace in northern Nigeria. He believes that:

> To effectively combat the growing threat of Boko
> Haram, the Nigerian government must take
> multiple steps to eliminate the factors that have
> fueled the group's existence. These steps would
> include; eliminating widespread government
> corruption, improving human rights, working
> with the international community in developing
> effective CT policy, improving the relationship
> between Christians and Muslims within Nigeria,
> and fighting poverty and hunger within the
> country. Taking these steps will eliminate the
> key factors that have both contributed to the rise
> and expansion of Boko Haram in Nigeria.[15]

Having laid a general basis for fighting terrorism,
especially the Boko Haram insurgency in Nigeria, we
now take a detailed look at parts of a blueprint of what
can, in effect, be an organic strategy for eliminating Boko
Haram in Nigeria.

6.1: Political and Structural Repositioning

Nigeria must build a strong and enduring foundation
for the nation to thrive and weather the violent challenge
posed by Boko Haram. There is an abiding need to build

---

15 **Nathaniel Manni**, *"Boko Haram: A Threat to Africa and Global Security"*,
Global Security Studies, Fall 2012, Volume 3, Issue 4, PP 44-54, at page 51, available at http://www.globalsecuritystudies.com/Manni%20BH%20FINAL.pdf

strong democratic institutions and to strengthen existing ones. A true nationalist spirit must be cultivated in, and imbibed by, Nigerians. The present system of ethnocentric identity based relationship must be discarded if there is to be any chance of unifying the country behind a common purpose and direction. **James Forest** offers the following thoughts on the need to move Nigeria and Nigerians in a different direction:

> Overall, the politics of ethno-centric identity undermine the strength of civil society and contribute to an unhealthy political culture, myopic mistrust across ethnic lines, corruption, and a whole host of other problems. Unless a new, more nationalist ethos is embraced throughout the country, Nigeria will not be able to meet anyone's expectations for a successful future – especially their own.[16]

He therefore identifies the United States as an example that building a melting pot of a nation is the only option available to Nigeria in order to solve its enduring ethnic and sectarian issues. He concludes that:

> Compared to the U.S., where the "melting pot" approach of cultural integration has been encouraged for centuries and has fostered a sense

---

16 James J.F. **Forest**, *Confronting the Terrorism of Boko Haram in Nigeria*, JSOU Report 12-5, Published in 2012 by the Joint Special Operations University in Florida, USA, 1-178, at page 42, available at http://www.jsou.socom.mil

of national pride in being "American" across many diverse ethnicities, the situation in Nigeria seems hopelessly counterproductive to nation-building. Addressing this system of structural ethnic cleavages should also be a priority of Nigeria's government.[17]

Chris Kwaja articulates the institutional frailties that presently beset Nigeria. He contends that:

Institutional fragility of the institutions of the state in terms of their ability and capacity to manage diversity, corruption, rising inequality between the rich and poor, gross violations of human rights, environmental degradation, contestations over land, have been some of the underlining causes of violent conflicts in Nigeria since the enthronement of democratic rule in 1999. All these are further compounded largely due to the failure of the Nigerian state to live up to its primary responsibility of providing security and welfare for its citizens. Thus, as a consequence of all these, the state is consumed by internal violence, its credibility and legitimacy are being questioned by the citizens [...] The reality of the situation is that since the citizens have lost confidence in the capacity of the state to both manage ethnic and religious diversity

---

17 Ibid at page 112

on one hand, and provide protection for them on another hand, they have resort to alternative sources of security...[18]

The Nigerian government therefore must win the hearts and minds of its citizens by showing that the government truly fulfills a function in the society, *to wit*, protecting the welfare of the citizens through the provision of security and other critical social infrastructures. The Nigerian government needs to win back the trust, respect and confidence of Nigerians before it could have any chance of effectively curtailing and eventually eliminating the scourge of terrorism. **Kwaja** does not mince words in articulating the people's loss of confidence in the Nigerian government. He points out that:

The inability of the state to effectively perform its core functions of providing or guaranteeing security for the people as well as act as regulator has led to a weakening of its bargaining strength and capacity in relation to the ethnic and religious groups in society. In this light, loyalty to ethnic or religious cleavages is being placed far and above the state, in view of the fact that people prefer to be seen and described based on the ethnic or religious groups they belong rather

---

18 **Chris M.A. Kwaja**, *Strategies for [Re]Building State Capacity to Manage Ethnic and Religious Conflict in Nigeria*, The Journal of Pan African Studies, vol.3, no.3, September 2009, at page 107, available at http://www.jpanafrican.com/docs/vol-3no3/3.3strategies.pdf

than their status as citizens of Nigeria.[19]

Without legitimacy and respect of its citizens, the Nigerian government cannot hope to win this existential fight against terrorism. If Nigerians do not feel a sense that its government cares about their welfare and is willing to live up to its social contract with its citizens, they will not have faith in its ability to win this battle and will, as a consequence, throw their support, or their sympathy, to the terrorists. **James Forest** recognizes this stark reality when he asserts that "legitimacy is central to ensuring security; if corruption is not tackled effectively, and the use of force among military and police is viewed as illegitimate by locals, the counterterrorism effort against Boko Haram will be much more difficult and much less successful than it should be."[20] **Ibrahim** and **Kazah-Toure** add that:

> The legitimacy of the state is linked to its capacity to present itself as a provider of necessary public goods and more important, a neutral arbiter that guarantees the security of all sections of society. When the state is generally perceived as serving the particularistic interests of one group, it starts losing its legitimacy, and indeed, its authority. As state capacity declines, fear of 'the other' rises and inhabitants of the state resort to other levels of solidarity such as the religious, ethnic and

---

19 **Chris M.A. Kwaja**, supra, note 18, at page 109

20 **Forest**, supra, note 16, at page 112

regional forms in search of security.[21]

Thus, the willingness and propensity of Nigerians to first identify their religious and/or ethnic affiliations ahead of their nationality is a reflection of their loss of confidence in the ability of Nigeria to fulfil its civic obligations to its citizens. Put in another way, Nigerians are wont to believe that their religion and/or ethnicity will offer them better protection and afford them a better path to support and succour. Nigerians consequently trust their religious and/or cultural groups to better protect them and better fulfil their emotional, if not material, needs. Their primary allegiance is thus to their ethnic and/or religious groups. Therefore, "it seems evident that strengthening trust and legitimacy between state and citizen should be a top priority for the Nigerian government."[22]

As a precursor to seeking a lasting solution to terrorism in Nigeria, a genuine national debate and final agreement on the basis of our federalism and the nature of the relationship between the federal government and the constituent states must be had. **Udama** hits the nail on the head with the following thoughts:

There should be a national dialogue involving all ethnic groups that will determined [sic] how

---

21 **Ibrahim, Jibrin, Kazah-Toure, Toure**, *"Ethno-religious Conflicts in Northern Nigeria*, The Nordic Africa Institute, PP 1-5, at page 2, available at http://www.nai. uu.nai.se/publications/news/archives/042ibrahimkazah/

22 **Forest**, supra, note 16

this country should be governed given its multi ethnic diversity in terms of culture, religion and traditions. It will encourage all Nigerians to re-new their commitments to brotherly love, tolerance, forbearance, moderation, goodwill and mutual understanding.[23]

Douglas et al offer their own take on the need to consult widely on the best political structure for the nation. According to them:

Focus should now be on a just and sustainable political order and ways in which this can be brought about, giving due weight to the fears, needs, and aspirations of the various social and interest groups in the country. There is growing consensus that a unitary system of government is not suited to a socially diverse country like Nigeria. A federal democracy, turning on a measured dose of fiscal autonomy for the federating units, not unlike the provisions of the country's independence constitution, is recommended. This will help diversify the revenue base of the country by enhancing domestic taxation as non-oil producing areas would be forced to find alternative ways to boost

---

23 **Udama, Rawlings Akonbede**, *Understanding Nigeria Terrorism, its Implications to National Peace, Security, Unity and Sustainable Development: A Discuss*, IOSR Journal of Humanities And Social Science (IOSR-JHSS) Volume 8, Issue 5 (Mar. – Apr. 2013), PP 100 – 115, at page 114, available at http://www.iosrjournals.org

the exchequer.[24]

Basil Ekot joins the band of advocates for a greater autonomy for the federating states. He says that "the argument proffered in Nigeria today is that at least at the state level, there should be some autonomy. Each state should be allowed to operate its own constitution so as to enable them to identify areas of interest within one Nigeria."[25] He asks and offers an answer to a pertinent existential question:

> The question for Nigeria today is what direction is to be taken regarding religious conflicts. Religious tolerance and associated conflicts could be curbed in Nigeria if true federalism is allowed to prevail. This will be a situation where the component states will enjoy some autonomy within the one federal bloc. In a democratic system especially with the federal system of government which Nigeria is trying to run, people need the allowance to express their true national consciousness.[26]

---

24 **Oronto Douglas, Ike Okonta, Dimieari Von Kemedi, Michael Watts,** *Oil And Militancy In The Niger Delta: Terrorist Threat or Another Colombia?, Working Paper No. 4, 2004, Economies of Violence Working Papers Series*, Institute of International Studies, University of California, Berkeley, USA, The United States Institute of Peace, Washington DC, USA, Our Niger Delta, Port Harcourt, Nigeria, PP 1-12, at pages 9-10, available at http://www.geography.berkeley.edu/.../NigerDelta/...

25 **Basil Ekot**, *Conflict, Religion and Ethnicity in the Post-Colonial Nigerian State*, The Australasian Review of African Studies, Volume 30 Number 2 December 2009, pp 47-67, at page 49, available at http://www.federalism-bulletin.eu/User/index.php?PAGE=Sito_it/boll...

26 Ibid

The election process in Nigeria must be revised and strengthened to ensure that it guarantees and protects the ability of Nigerians to use it as an instrument of dictating the direction of government and as a control mechanism over the political elite. It must be made a truly free and fair exercise.

In summary, the political structure of Nigeria should be tweaked so it becomes a proper representation of the hopes and aspirations of its constituent parts. If this defective structure is not addressed, then these violent episodes will continue to be an enduring part of life in Nigeria. The present attitude and dispositions of the political elite to the presidential system of governance in Nigeria needs to be addressed. The do-or-die attitude of politicians towards electioneering is destructive and threatens the very survival of the democratic system and by implication, the very survival of the nation. **Paul Francis et al** aptly identify this fault line in the following passage:

> Political authority in a culture of "winner takes all" carries with it almost unconstrained and unquestioned control by office holders over public resources, creating a personalized, unicentric field of power relations. Alliances and loyalty to those in power may be seen as the best or only way of accessing resources. With so much at stake, the incentives to manipulate elections to

gain political office are powerful [..]. While only a minority is served by such a highly unequal system of spoils, the patrimonial power of those who do benefit makes reform very difficult to achieve.[27]

Without good governance, Nigeria has no hope of putting its house in order to enable it win the existential fight against Boko Haram. And without restructuring the existing political structure, good governance is not attainable.

6.2: Strong Anti-Corruption Implementation

Fighting corruption should be at the top of any agenda for winning this battle for the hearts and minds of alienated Nigerians, particularly the vulnerable youths and the economically impoverished poor. The ruling elite will improve its chance of winning the hearts and minds of Nigerians in the north, and thus undercut the propaganda and recruitment tools of terrorist groups, by tackling corruption. According to **Francis** and **Sardessai**:

Transparency in the use of public funds is central to making all levels of government accountable to citizens. Improving transparency

---

27 **Paul Francis, Deidre Lapin, Paula Rossiasco,** *Securing Development And Peace In The Niger Delta: A Social and Conflict Analysis for Change,* Study prepared for publication by the Woodrow Wilson International Center for Scholars Africa Program and Project on Leadership and Building State Capacity, 1-160, at page 58, available at http://www.wilsoncenter.org/sites/default/files/AFR_110929_Niger%20Delta_0113.pdf

and accountability will complement the task of improving economic management, particularly at the state and local levels. State governments have enormous resources at their disposal. Mismanagement and corruption have resulted in these resources being diverted from where they are most needed. The publication of state and local budgets will enhance levels of community oversight. Furthermore, official budgetary oversight needs improvement.[28]

Bentley et al urge that beacon light be shone against government corruption. They contend that "purging the Nigerian government of corruption is possibly the most important change required for successful management."[29] They insist that:

The government needs to increase transparency, or openness, of its policies and actions to foster trust and collaboration with international organizations, corporations and local interest groups. [I]nternational institutions (especially a more active United Nations) should hold the Nigerian government accountable for its actions by monitoring the government and sanctioning abuses."[30]

---

28 **Francis, P, Sardesai, S.**, *"Republic of Nigeria: Niger Delta Social and Conflict Analysis"*, May 2008, at page 47, Document of the World Bank Sustainable Development Depart, Africa Region, available at http://www.sitesources. wprldbank.org/EXTSOCIALDEV/.../Niger_Del...

29 **Chris Bentley, Matt Hintsa, Mimi liu, Liz Moskalenko, Stacey Ng**, *The Oil Crisis in the Niger River Delta*, available at http://www.africanafrican.com/.../ Crisis_in_Niger_River_Delta(1).doc, at page 13

30 Ibid

Nathaniel Manni takes the position that:

> Should Nigeria work in conjunction with the international community to improve human rights and fight corruption within Nigeria, it is possible that those in northern Nigeria who find Boko Haram's ideology appealing – due to a sense of disenfranchisement and hopelessness among northern Muslims – will no longer tolerate/support the group's violent agenda. Once this has been accomplished it is possible that the group could be eliminated relatively easily by Nigerian security forces.[31]

Chris Newsom offers up an intriguing way of putting the feet of Nigerian government officials to the fire and thus discourage them from corrupt practices. He suggests that:

> Foreign embassies could issue travel visas for Nigerian officials only on evidence of a clean bill of conduct while in office, then maintain an open online portal where the public could post issues about official performance. Civil society could supply the portal with relevant information, both positive and negative.[32]

---

31 **Nathaniel Manni,** supra, note 15, at page 47

32 **Chris Newsom**, *"Conflict in the Niger Delta: More Than a Local Affair"*, United States Institute of Peace, Special Report 271, June 2011 PP 1-19, at page 14, available at http:www.usip.org/.../conflict_Niger_Delta.pdf...

This novel idea is quite attractive given the penchant of Nigerian officials and politicians to make frequent overseas trips, especially to launder stolen and embezzled funds or to seek medical care. This will make it harder for the corrupt predators to launder their stolen loot in foreign banks, to seek medical help, or to flee overseas to avoid criminal prosecution in Nigeria.

Another aspect that needs to be addressed is the idea of returning recovered funds to the state governments from which the corrupt official stole the money in the first place. What typically happens is that the returned funds are either promptly stolen by the incumbent, or in most cases, the funds somehow find their way back to the official(s) from whom they were recovered. This is made possible by the fact that in most cases, the convicted official was instrumental to putting the seating officials in the positions that they presently occupy. A good example is the case of the disgraced and convicted criminal who was the impeached governor of Bayelsa State. He was not only subsequently pardoned by a President [who was his deputy Governor at the time of his impeachment and subsequent conviction for corrupt practices] but it appears as if all the properties confiscated from him, as a result of his conviction and sentence, have been returned to him. A good way to get around this problem is to place all funds and properties recovered from corrupt officials into a special development fund, to be administered by a special agency. Funds recovered from officials of each state should then be used to fund projects in such state, as the case may be.

Efforts should be made to strengthen anti-corruption outfits such as the Economic and Financial Crimes Commission and Independent Corrupt Practices Commission, by granting more autonomy, fiscal independence, secure tenure for investigators and prosecutors, in order to better fight corruption and bring corrupt officials to book. Efforts should be made to tighten the loopholes in the enabling laws, as well as court procedures, that presently make it possible for corrupt officials facing prosecution to delay, frustrate, and obfuscate their trial, by filing frivolous motions, interlocutory appeals, and constant adjournments, to foster speedy trials of corrupt officials.

The Penal and anti-corruption laws should be amended to increase the penalty for corruption and to enhance seizure penalties [especially interim seizures during trial] to enable the court seize assets of corrupt officials and their cohorts, and prevent them from using stolen funds to pay for expensive defense teams to frustrate their trial.

As an added bonus, a "whistle-blower" incentive programme can be devised, whereby any person who assists the government, by reporting a corrupt official, or who assists in the detection of corruption, and/or testifies in the trial and conviction of a corrupt official, will be paid a percent [for instance, 10%] of whatever funds and or property that is recovered from the corrupt official as a result.

6.3: Legal Approach

No matter how one cuts it, terrorism is a crime that falls within the ambit of law enforcement. Terrorists are violent criminals that the law needs to punish and terrorism is a criminal activity that the law needs to discourage. After all is said and done, Nigeria should address terrorism through the legal prism. **Dos Santos** makes a case for de-escalating the violence by tuning down the government's brutal counter-terrorism activities and transforming it into a holistic law enforcement action, using mostly civilian policing rather than the military. He says that:

> From the Nigerian side, a good starting point would be the lifting of the state of emergency, the withdrawal of military forces and their replacement by police and security forces advised and trained by international actors. This would likely result in less abuse of power – thus addressing part of the popular disgruntlement towards public authorities which has been feeding violence – and, paradoxically, probably drive Boko Haram to soften its aggressive stance

in the absence of an immediate threat.[33]

The first step in fighting terrorism therefore is to pass effective legislation against terrorism, or in the case of Nigeria, revise and enhance the 2001 Act and the 2003 Amended Act to give it more teeth and narrowly tailor it to catch the most violent terrorists while choking the sponsors, facilitators, sympathizers, and enablers of terrorism. Merely copying versions of Anti-terrorism laws and provisions from other jurisdictions or regional entities, without fine-tuning them to reflect the peculiar and unique nature of Nigeria's environment, will end up exacerbating the problem rather than supply a cure.

The second step is to mount an aggressive and sustained prosecution of terrorists, their sponsors, enablers and sympathizers. It is instructive to note that till date, Nigeria has only prosecuted just a handful of suspected terrorists, even though it has been in sustained military conflict with terrorists for a dozen years and literally thousands have been scooped up by security forces in violent theatres. Like we discussed elsewhere in this book, it does appear, and anecdotal evidence suggests, that most of the people that have been rounded up have been summarily executed and some may have been detained in undisclosed locations. Or perhaps a good number of them have been let loose into the society. This

---

33 **Gustavo Placido Dos Santos**, *Boko Haram: Time for an Alternative Approach*, Portuguese Institute of International Relations and Security, IPRIS Viewpoints, April 2014, 1-3, at page 3, available at http://www.opendemocracy.net/

is problematic. Law enforcement must be transparent in its handling of suspected terrorists. Suspects must be given access to legal representation and must be tried in court or tribunal, or they must be allowed to go home. The practice of rounding people up and summarily executing them is illegal and must be stopped.

The third step is to choke terrorists' access to funds and kill off their ability to resupply and to operate, by strictly implementing the provisions of all relevant Anti-Money Laundering and Terrorism financing laws on the books. According to the **2013 FATF REPORT**:

> Terrorists and terrorist organisations depend on funds for their personal, operational, and organisational needs. Detecting and cutting off their source of funding are critical steps in denying them the ability to operate. Apprehending, investigating, and prosecuting the financiers of terrorist groups and terrorist acts will serve as a deterrent to others. The freezing, confiscation, and seizure of terrorist assets will equally have a deterring effect. More importantly, understanding and addressing the issue of terrorist financing is critical because of the destructive effects of terrorism on peace, security, and development.[34]

---

34 FATF Report, *Terrorist Financing In West Africa*, October 2013, at paragraph 1.2, available at http://www.fatf-gafi.org/.../...

Conducting a top-to-bottom review of the current
security forces strategy in the fight against terror with
a view to holding the members of the security forces,
who abuse their authority and deprive Nigerians of the
human and constitutional rights, responsible for their
actions is called for. The brutality and egregious human
rights abuses of security agencies in the north-east of
Nigeria should be investigated and dealt with, to gain
the trust of Nigerians to the government's counter-
terrorism actions. **Professor Hussein Solomon** draws a
vivid portrait of the activities of the Nigerian security
forces in the north-east in the face of the Boko Haram.
He says:

> Counterterrorism effort are also proving
> counterproductive because of the brutality
> unleashed by the security forces – in the process,
> losing hearts and minds. The Joint Military Task
> Force (JTF) in Borno State, for instance, has
> resorted to unlawful killings, dragnet arrests
> and extortion and intimidation of the hapless
> residents of Borno. Far from intelligence-
> driven operations, the JTF simply cordoned off
> areas and carried out house to house searches,
> at times shooting young men in these homes.
> Similar tactics were pursued by the JTF at
> homes searched in the Kaleri Ngomari Custain
> area in Maiduguri on 9 July of 2011. Twenty-

five people were shot dead by security services, women and children were beaten, homes were burnt and many more boys and men were reported missing. Such excesses on the part of the security services can only contribute to the further alienation of citizens from the state and its security forces – something that Abuja can ill afford. This situation is compounded by the fact that the Nigerian soldiers and police patrolling in northern states are national, not local, and therefore are unlikely to share either ethnic or cultural backgrounds with the local population who view themselves as being under siege in an occupation by 'foreign forces'.[35]

Special enquiries on use of force by security agencies in the north-east should, therefore, be constituted to address abuses of power by security agents in the region and elsewhere. An investigation of the circumstances surrounding the killing of hundreds of alleged Boko Harm members, including their leader Yusuf, while in Police custody, in July 2009, and prosecution of responsible members of the security forces who carried out the dastardly acts should be made possible by the Nigeria government. This is an important prelude to having a decent chance of engaging Boko Haram in a dialogue that may lead to the resolution of this destructive insurgency. **Anyadike** charges that the "tactics

---

35 **Professor Hussein Solomon**, *Boko Haram: What is to be Done? Research on Islam and Muslims in Africa*, January 16, 2015, 1-7, at page 3, available at http://www.muslimsinafrica.files.wordpress.com/2013/09/topbanner_isl_mus_afr6.jpg

employed by government security agencies against Boko Haram have been consistently brutal and counterproductive."[36] We agree.

Roland Marchal points out that:

To date, there has been no condemnation by the federal government of the police officers involved in the killing of Mohammed Yusuf while in police custody. Such failures to address abuses by security services continue to reinforce the feeling of neglect by the central government and the impunity of its security organs. Until the state improves its own law enforcement agencies and proves that the rule of law also applies to them, there is little hope for an accommodation between them and the general population."[37]

Udombana issues Nigerian courts a marching order. He charges them with the responsibility of holding the government in check in its anti-terrorism operations so as to safeguard and protect human rights. He counsels that:

Like the Strasbourg[38] Court, African judiciaries should work to ensure that states stay within the

---

36 **Anyadike, Nkechi O.**, *Boko Haram and National Security Challenges in Nigeria; Causes and Solutions*, Journal of Economic and Sustainable Development, ISSN 2222-1700 (Paper) ISSN 2222-2855 (Online)Vol.4, No.5, 2013, page 12, at page 22, available at www.iiste.org

37 **Roland Marchal**, *Boko Haram and the resilience of militant Islam in Northern Nigeria*, NOREF Report, June 2012, Published by Norwegian Leacebuilsing Resource Centre, available at http://www.peacebuilding.no/.../dc58a110fb362470133354efb8fee228.pdf , at page 5

38 Euphemism for the European Court of Human Rights

boundaries of constitutional and international law in their counter-terrorism campaigns. They should resist indefinite detentions and should give unambiguous signals, whenever occasions arise, that torture and other inhuman treatments are repugnant to reason, justice, and humanity and illegal at all times and in all circumstances, the war on terrorism notwithstanding. The right to be free from torture is one of the highest values protected by customary international law. Conventional international law further codifies these intransgressible principles in the Convention against Torture and other human rights instrument, universal and regional.[39]

In conclusion, terrorism is a crime that can be controlled with proper law enforcement practices and criminal justice due process. Terrorists can be rounded up, investigated and prosecuted in court. A properly administered law enforcement and criminal justice process will go a long way to putting the Boko Haram insurgency in check.

6.4: Retooling Nigeria's Policing and Security Apparatus

Care should be taken in the recruitment, training and remuneration of the police and other law enforcement agents. The quality of this nation's law enforcement

---

39 **Nsongarua J. Udombana**, *Battling Rights: International Law And Africa's War On Terrorism*, 13 Afr. Y.B. Int'l L. 67 2005, at page 127, available at http://www.ssrn.com/abstract=1806304

and security services is an embarrassment. The law enforcement and security services lack quality, professionalism and decorum. They are corrupt, inept, incompetent, and lack motivation. If truth be told, they are poorly trained and poorly remunerated. The **U.S. House of Representatives** in its **Homeland Committee Majority Report**, urges that, "the Nigerian government should be putting greater emphasis on the professionalization of its police and armed forces and prosecuting abuses carried out by its own forces."[40] Other than poor quality, lack of training and miserly pay, we also have the issue of lack of proper equipment to enable them succeed. Law enforcement in Nigeria is still in the dark ages. There is virtually no forensics, no surveillance capabilities, no electronic and other modern law enforcement training and equipment. The Nigerian security forces are merely a glorified band of bodyguards for politicians, the elite, and businessmen/women that can afford their "baby-sitting" services. **Francis, Lapin** and **Rossiasco** offer a pathway for reforming and retooling the Nigerian security forces to better equip them for the arduous task of protecting the lives, livelihoods and properties of Nigerians. They offer the following priorities:

Priorities could include stronger administration and regular payment of salaries to all security

---

40 **Boko Haram**: *Growing Threat to the U.S. Homeland*, Report prepared by the Majority Staff of the Committee on Homeland Security of the U.S. House of Representatives, September 13, 2013, at page 25, available at http://www.homeland. house.gov/sites/homeland.house.gov/files/documents/09-13-13-Boko-Haram-Report.pdf

forces; systematic penalties for unprofessional, violent, or corrupt conduct; ending the practice of privately financed police details for protecting elites and their families; training on the use of intelligence and other non-violent, unarmed methods; and guidance in building relationships with ordinary citizens and creating working partnerships with community security groups. Overall, the most effective approach for curtailing personal and economic crime would consist of joint efforts between members of security services, community leaders and civic conflict management groups.[41]

Lt. Gen. Dambazau, [rtd] offers an insightful advice on how to reinvigorate and revamp the Nigerian police. He counsels that we:

[N]eed to have a professional policing outfit that is well-trained, equipped and funded to carry out law enforcement and order maintenance critical for the security of any nation. The public has a lot of distrust of the police to the extent that people would rather not report their complaints to them; and sometimes individuals take the laws into their own hands because they simply do not trust the police. There is the urgent need to re-examine the recruitment policy that would

---

41 **Paul Francis, Deidre Lapin, Paula Rossiasco**, supra, note 27, at page 110

ensure strict vetting or background checks for potential recruits; thereafter the training of successful recruits must go beyond the initial training at the Police College. At every level of their career, training must be continuous, including such specialized training in criminal investigation and forensic science.[42]

Dambazau concludes by surmising that:

> The task before us now is to have a well-grounded professional police that could enforce law, maintain order, and properly investigate crimes by observing the rule of law. [...] This is the very first step of overcoming the security challenges in Nigeria, but this does not preclude the fact that the country requires a reform of the entire [law enforcement and security] sector.[43]

The government should do well to bring law enforcement practices in Nigeria back from the dark ages to modernity, by recruiting the right candidates, offering them 21st century training, and equipping them with the right technological tools, and holding them accountable for misconduct. Most importantly, they must be paid living wages.

---

42 **Abdulrahman Dambazau, Lt. Gen. [Rtd]**, supra, note 1, at page 8
43 Ibid at page 9

6.5: Strong Coercive Anti-terrorism Approach [The Hammer Approach]

Nigeria's counter-terrorism "strategy" in the north-east region of the country is all about extreme violence and nothing else. Rather than reduce terrorism, it drives it, forces victims to sympathize with terrorists, and in some cases turns victims to terrorism recruits and enablers. The brutality of the security forces creates more problems than it solves. It is a runaway mayhem in the name of counter-terrorism. The **United States Department of State** gives Nigeria's law enforcement agencies a fail in their counter-terrorism action and offers the reasons for their failure. In its **2013 Reports on Terrorism**, the **United States Department of State** points out that:

> Among the problems that deterred or hindered more effective law enforcement were: lack of coordination and cooperation between Nigerian security agencies; a lack of biometrics collection systems and the requisite data bases; corruption; misallocation of resources; the slow pace of the judicial system, including a lack of a timely arraignment of suspected terrorist detainees; and lack of sufficient training for prosecutors and judges to understand and carry out the Terrorism (Prevention) Act of 2011 (as amended).[44]

---

44 U.S. Department of State, Country Reports on Terrorism 2013, 1-21, available at http://www.state.gov/j/ct/rls/crt/2013/224820.htm

Professor Hussein Solomon chimes in with the following assessment:

> Counterterrorism efforts are hobbled by the incapacity of the Nigerian Police Force (NPF) to gather intelligence and undertake scientific investigations. According to Amnesty International, most police stations do not document their work. There is no databases for fingerprints, no systematic forensic investigation methodology, only two forensic laboratory facilities, few trained forensic staff and insufficient budgets for investigations. Under the circumstances police tend to rely on confessions, which form 60 per cent of all prosecutions.[45]

Modern terrorism is a largely sophisticated and often high technology driven activity. Nigeria cannot fight it with 19th century equipment and tactics. Without a well thought-out strategy and the right equipment and attitude, no amount of brute force can erase terrorism and the environment that breeds it.

This is not to say that coercion is not a crucial part of a good counter-terrorism strategy. It is crucially important, but it must be cleverly tailored and be even handed to get the job done. Most importantly, it must not be the sole content of a good counter-terrorism

---

45 **Professor Hussein Solomon**, supra, note 35, at page 2

strategy. That said, the Nigerian government should send out a strong signal that terrorism can never be accepted as an avenue for resolving disputes, or as a means of forcing policy or governmental action. Terrorism can never be tolerated no matter the motivation for it, or the philosophy that drives it. The government should consider a comprehensive military strategy by deploying the clear and hold strategy in order to win a sustainable peace against the Boko Haram insurgency. By clear and hold is meant, the forces clear a particular geographical location of terrorists and they leave some force there until proper security is in place to prevent the retaking of the area by terrorists. As a disclaimer, we must point out, at the outset, that we do not subscribe to this strategy as a stand-alone strategy. It must be implemented in conjunction with all or some of the other approaches discussed in this chapter, for it to be effective.

A few simple strategies will not only consolidate the security gains in the north-east but will erase the Boko Haram menace. First is to set up a Tactical Strike Force that will have the mobility and ordnance to respond quickly to any threats in any part of the affected areas of the north-east within 5 – 15 minutes. **Christian Akani** shares the same sentiments. He proposes that:

> [T]here should be a special anti-terrorist Squad made up of all the law enforcement agencies. This Squad should be given training, logistics and support in line with global practice and should be

specifically charged with the duty of prosecuting, intelligence gathering, and coordinating with the other agencies and foreign states on how to combat terrorism. All information about terrorism can be addressed to them for necessary action. This will circumvent overlap of responsibilities, [...] and specialization.[46]

They should be trained and equipped to bring swift and overwhelming force to bear on any terrorist threat in the area. A "Clear and Hold" strategy could be deployed in the area to retake and hold villages, hamlets and towns that are presently under the sphere of Boko Haram. This could be a strategy similar to the one the United States deployed in Fallujah in the heydays of the Sunni insurgency in Iraq.[47] The United States used this strategy to fight Suni insurgents in the City of Fallujah in Iraq and recorded success. The Infantry, in collaboration with Mobile Police Force, and backed by aerial support, should comb the villages dislodging the Boko Haram fighters and freeing these strongholds from the terrorists. The counter-terrorism force must, however,

---

46 **Christian Akani,** *2011 Terrorism Act in Nigeria: Prospects and Problems,* Online International Journal of Arts and Humanities, Volume 2, Issue 8, pp. 218-223, at page 223, October, 2013, available at http://www.onlineresearchjournals.org/ IJAH

47 After the overthrow of the Saddam regime in Iraq by the U.S. and the Allied forces, some radical members of his Sunni tribesmen who felt marginalized by the new Shia dominated leadership, alied with terrorist elements to forment an insurgency against the allied forces and the interim government. These insurgents staked out in the city of Falluja, amonst other areas. The allied forces had to device a means of recapturing Falluja by dislodging and clearing them out to enable normalcy to return to the area.

be equipped with up-to-date equipment and be properly trained in counter-terrorism. The past few years have seen Nigerian forces totally humiliated by Boko Haram fighters, who were reportedly better equipped than their Nigerian army counterparts. Lack of equipment and proper logistics leads to low morale and desertion. It is even more desperate when the forces are denied proper pay and emoluments. **Professor Hussein Solomon** makes an unflattering assessment of Nigeria's pay structure for its security forces. He says:

> While Nigeria's armed forces are allocated US$6billion of the annual budget, this hardly benefits the ordinary Nigerian soldier whose monthly pay was suddenly halved to N20,000 Nigerian naira (approximately US$130) in July 2014. Ordinary soldiers have to go into battle against Boko Haram rockets and mortar rounds, in 'soft' Hilux trucks, since the money for armoured personnel carriers inexplicably dried up. In addition, each soldier engaging in frontline duty is supposed to receive a 1,500 Nigeria naira daily allowance and food is to be provided. However, this allowance does not get to them and often, neither does the food. Under the circumstances, desertions are increasing.[48]

After dislodging Boko Haram from an area, a small interim protective force should be stationed to guarantee

---

48 **Professor Hussein Solomon**, supra, note 35, at page 3

security to the area until governmental institutions are up and running. They can then re-establish rural governments in the area and set up crucial and critical social infrastructure, such as schools, medical clinics, pipe-borne water and graded roads (using both the Youth Job Corps and the Engineering and Construction Corps of the Army) to win back the confidence and support of the people and give them a stake in keeping the area, Boko Haram free. The government should fight for the hearts and souls of the various communities in the affected areas. This war cannot be won solely on brute force. It can only be won by carrying the people along through provision of real alternatives to what Boko Haram offers. **Dambazau** agrees and submits that:

> Popular support is required by both security forces and insurgents in order to win the "Hearts and minds' of the people. While the Boko Haram insurgents use coercion, monetary inducements, brainwashing, and propaganda to acquire popular support, government should address the socio-economic problems, educate to remove ignorance, and engage the youth in vocational skills, just like it is currently happening in the Niger Delta.[49]

Intelligence must be a very critical aspect of this strategy. Sleeper agents could be recruited, trained and embedded within the rank and file of the Boko Haram organization, to act both as conduit of vital information to the

---

49 **Abdulrahman Dambazau, Lt. Gen. [Rtd]**, supra, note 1, , at page 13

security forces, as well as instruments of sabotage within the sect itself. Counter-terrorist organizations all over the world deploy this strategy. A former Nigerian Army chief, **Lt. Gen Dambazau [rtd]**, makes the same point. He argues that:

> No doubt that counter-terrorism and counter-insurgency (CTCOIN) operations require adequate information or Intelligence on the terrorists or insurgents disposition; their habits; their source of support, including weapons, funding, and mercenaries; their ideology and ultimate goals (intentions); capabilities, including their strengths and weaknesses; membership and recruitment strategy; mode of operation; leadership; motivations; affiliations; etc[50]

He rhetorically asks "How much of these do we know of Boko Haram? How coordinated is the information gathered by the various intelligence agencies? How objective is our assessment of the situation?"[51] And answers in the negative. He believes that Nigeria has been "unable to properly assess and define the actual scenario."[52] Without understanding the nature and calibre of threat Boko Haram poses, it will be impossible to defeat it by merely flying blind. Nigeria needs to fight

---

50 Ibid at page 12
51 Ibid
52 Ibid

smart and not just hard, in order to defeat the insurgency. Surveillance should be a critical component of counterterrorism operations in the north-east. Without a strong surveillance capability, the security forces will only be flying blind. An elaborate electronic monitoring and aerial drone surveillance of confirmed and suspected Boko Haram members will yield invaluable tactical information that could be used to predict future terrorist actions and identify potential terrorist targets. With the ready availability of sophisticated, but cheat drones, the counter-terrorism forces should be able to saturate the skies above suspected Boko Haram enclaves and monitor and track identified and suspected members and thereby gather crutial information. Confirmed and suspected members of Boko Haram should be put under intense surveillance to track their movements, activities and interactions. With proper judicial authorization and supervision, telephone and other digital devices of known and suspected members can be monitored to track their activities and to obtain evidence of terrorist activities. Arrested members can be electronically tagged and released, in the hope that upon return to the group, their monitored activities can lead the security forces to their den.

Efforts should be made to infiltrate the sect by injecting "sleeper agents" and former members to spy on the sect and feed critical information back to the security forces. These agents can also sabotage the sect from within. In appropriate cases, they can be authorized to "neutralize" terrorists who are about to execute a terrorist act, especially to save the lives of innocent victims. "Reformed" members of the sect can be trained as agents and encouraged to rejoin the group and act as sources of critical nformation for the security agencies.

The federal government should reconsider the necessity of continuing to maintain large military formations in several urban cities in the south, where they are virtually idling away. What is the necessity of maintaining divisions and battalions in places like the 2nd Div Ibadan, the 82nd Div Enugu, Ikeja cantonment, Bonny Camp, Artillary brigade Obinze, the Onitsha battalion Command, etc, when there are no serious security challenges in and around those locations? Would it not serve the security interest of the country better, if those military sites are closed down and the personnel relocated to flash point communities such as the north-east, southern Kaduna, Plateau State, Niger and Benue States, where there are continuing and sporadic clashes and security challenges? The Nigerian civil war ended over 50 years ago, therefore, there is no real need to continue to maintain these "occupation" forces anymore. Especially given the fact that we need all available military resources in areas where there are real security challenges.

Another questionable decision of the Nigerian government was the discontinuation of the use of "military contractors" [mercenaries, if you will] in counterterrorism operations in the north-east. The Jonathan Administration used the services of "military contractors" but the practice was halted by the Buhari Administration. In an existential battle, such as the one between Nigeria and Boko Haram, all options should be on the table. There is no negative implication, as far as I am concerned, in using the services of highly experienced and seasoned "military contractors" to supplement the efforts of the regular Nigerian troops in the war theatre. If the most powerful nation in the world, the United States of America, can use the services of "military contractors" in Iraq and Afghanistan, there is no shame in Nigeria borrowing the practice.

Hand in glove with tactical operations, must be a well-choreographed public relations and public enlightenment campaign, to reverse the misinformation propaganda that Boko Haram has fed the locals over these years. The public relations campaign will emphasize that the counter-terrorism activities to rid the area of the Boko Haram scourge is neither an anti-North nor an anti-Islam fight. Rather, it is a fight to rid the area of terrorists and reactionary elements.

One cannot over-emphasize the importance of

coordination between and collaboration among all security and other agencies involved in this war against the scourge of terrorism.

Abubakar's warning is very apt on this imperative. He says that:

> It is clear that Nigeria has put in place legal and administrative framework to combat money laundering and terrorist financing. However, combating money laundering and terrorist financing cannot succeed where law enforcement agencies operate in isolation from one another. There is need for the agencies to operate in a coordinated fashion and communicate regularly with one another.[53]

A successful implementation of this strategy will militarily defeat Boko Haram and facilitate the rebuilding of the social infrastructures of the north-east and speed up the resuscitation of the zonal economy and thus erase the environment that bred and nurtured Boko Haram in the first place.

We must caution that in pursuing a strong counter-terrorism strategy, the security forces must be circumspect and must respect the human rights of

---

53 **Ibrahim Abdu Abubakar**, *An Appraisal of Legal and Administrative framework for Combating Terrorist Financing and Money Laundering in Nigeria*, Journal of Law, Policy and Globalization, Vol.19, 2013, page 26-37, at page 35, available at www.iise.org

suspected terrorists as well as innocent victims around. **Omotola's** admonition comes in handy here. He has warned that "[a]s human rights are violated in the war against terrorism, the national security situation is further pushed to the margin. This takes the form of heightened political tensions, human rights activism and the radicalization of struggles."[54] He surmises that "[o]ne inevitable conclusion is that, while the security approach to terrorism is important and indeed indispensable, it should be handled with care to avoid escalated unintended consequences."[55] He urges that it is "better to pursue counter-terrorism measures from a human rights perspective. This approach will tackle the root causes of terrorism directly, including asymmetrical power relations, global inequality, rising poverty and so on."[56] **Professor Hussein Solomon** cautions that "the employment of force should not be at the expense of the political and developmental responses to counter-terrorism.[57] Rather the military should complement these other legs of a holistic counterterrorism strategy."[58] **Sarah Margon** of **Human Rights Watch**, offers the following beacon of light to the Nigerian government in their counter-terrorism efforts to tackle the Boko Haram

---

54 J. **Shola Omotola**, *Assessing Counter-Terrorism Measures In Africa: Implications For Human Rights And National Security, Conflict Trends*, Issue 2 (2008), African Centre for the Constructive Resolution of Disputes (ACCORD), Umhlanga Rocks, South Africa, at page 48, available at http://www.mercury.ethz.ch/serviceengine/Files/ISN/101869/.../chapter+7.pdf

55 Ibid

56 Ibid

57 **Professor Hussein Solomon**, supra, note 35,

58 Ibid

insurgency:

> In the near term, making sure old habits aren't repeated requires that Abuja[59] authorities take a serious look at what a military response to Boko Haram should look like. For starters, it needs to be part of a wider plan that includes governance, accountability and development. But within the security realm, the U.S. and other donor governments should impress upon Nigeria the need to act in accordance with its international legal obligations, including ensuring the security of the population in affected areas. By working quietly with communities to address local concerns, authorities in Abuja could help reverse the alienation of communities in the north. Nigeria's senior military leaders also need to reject outright the harassment and abuse of these communities, or the destruction of their property as a military strategy. Clear guidelines for how to protect – not prey on – vulnerable communities would be helpful.[60]

The Nigerian government should rethink the unbridled use of force as the sole means of fighting terror, because it does not work. **Agbiboa** does not believe that unbridled use of force will solve the problem of terrorism. He

---

59 Euphemism for the government of Nigeria
60 **Sarah Margon**, supra, note 2,

says that "reliance on hard power to fight religious terrorism misunderstands the nature of the violence and makes the threat considerably worse."[61] He suggests a "non-killing approach that identifies the motivations and grievances of terrorist groups and seeks to meaningfully address them."[62] In other words, he recognizes that Nigeria cannot kill her way out of terrorism. Other approaches must be deployed in conjunction with military counter-terrorism measures.[63] **The UN Security Council Resolution 1456**[64] urges in the strongest of terms the need for states to ensure compliance with international obligations such as observance of human rights, refugee and humanitarian law, in their counter-terrorism operations. **David Cortright** warns of over-reliance on coercive action. He cautions that:

> The use of military force and an over-reliance on law enforcement measures can be counterproductive and could drive third parties toward militancy. The goal instead should be to isolate hardcore elements and separate

---

61 **Daniel E. Agbiboa**, *Is Might Right?*, supra, note 9, at pages 55-56

62 Ibid at page 56

63 **Agbiboa**, ibid, argues at pages 56-57, that "A security-only military strategy typically leads to benefits for radical Islamists. They gain critical experience in tactics and create new networks of support as well as social bonds among disparate groups that enable future collaboration. This strategy also gives them opportunities to raise funds and acquire weapons and other accoutrements. Moreover, the use of military force as a counterterrorism strategy is frequently ill-advised because it is inevitably indiscriminate and often results in the alienation of precisely those individuals in a given community whom we do not want radicalized."

64 United Nations Security Council, Security Council Resolution 1456 (2003), S/RES/1456, New York, 20 January 2003, para. 6

them from their potential support base. This requires a political approach that addresses deeply felt grievances, promotes democratic governance, and supports sustainable economic development.[65]

Professor Guiora discusses the constant temptation facing law enforcement in the face of terrorism; the temptation to sacrifice civil and political rights in favour of fighting terror. He points out that:

> Terrorism, in its broadest articulation, is the constant threat faced by decision makers mandated with ensuring that national institutions are sufficiently prepared to act both proactively and reactively; preferably the former, if need, the latter. The public demands solutions and no accommodation with terrorists. However – public demands notwithstanding – operational counterterrorism cannot be justification for discarding civil and political rights. Benjamin Franklin's much cited words of wisdom 'any society that would give up a little liberty to gain a little security will deserve neither and lose both' capture the essence of this constant and unremitting tension.[66]

---

65 **David Cortright**, *A critical Evaluation of the UN Counter-Terrorism Program: Accomplishments and Challenges*, A Crime and Global Paper presented at: Global Enforcement Regimes, Transnational Organized Crime, International Terrorism and money Laundering, held at the Transnational Institute (TNI) in Amsterdam, 28-29 April 2005, available at http://www.tni.org/crime , at page 21

66 **Professor Amos N. Guiora**, *Due Process and Counterterrorism*, available at http://www.ssrn.com/abstract=1680009, at pages 1-2

Udombana points out the fact that anti-terrorism efforts and respect for human rights are not mutually exclusive.[67] They can co-habit the same space. He urges that "there can be no trade-off between effective action against terrorism and the protection of human rights."[68] In other words, "anti-terrorism measures and human rights need not be mutually exclusive, since both are concerned in the defence or procurement of an objective good."[69] **David Cortright** makes the case for the protection of human rights and strengthening democracy as an antidote for terrorism. He argues that:

> A strong case can be made that protecting human rights and strengthening democracy are essential over the long term to the fight against terrorism. Protecting human rights and guaranteeing the freedom to voice dissenting view without government interference can help to prevent the rise of political extremism. The most effective weapons in the fight against terrorism are persuasive not coercive. Guaranteeing political opportunity and democracy will do more to counter the threat from terrorism than strengthening protective and law enforcement measures.[70]

---

67 **Nsongarua J. Udombana**, *Battling Rights: International Law And Africa's War On Terrorism*, 13 Afr. Y.B. Int'l L. 67 2005, available at http://www.ssrn.com/abstract=1806304

68 Ibid at page 119

69 Ibid

70 David Cortright, supra, note 66, at page 19

Oluwafemi et al make a strong case for development of and investment in Nigeria's cyber security capability. They reviewed the nation's vulnerability both to cyber-attack and more generally to physical and infrastructural attacks by terrorists and offer a pathway to closing the barn door. They submit that, "Terrorism thrives on unrestricted accessibility to some components on the cyberspace."[71] And that "[...] the battle to confront terrorism must begin at the cyberspace."[72] Thus, "A secure cyberspace will hamper the continuous boom and smooth running of terrorist activities. In other words, a secure cyberspace is an effective anti-terrorism measure."[73] They make bold to state that:

> Cybersecurity is the offensive way (otherwise known as a preventive measure) of combating terrorism. The security of the cyberspace is as crucial more than ever to the survival of mankind as the physical space is. This simply translates to the fact that the security of the cyberspace is not only necessary for the prevention of cyber attacks, but also physical and other forms of attacks that can be organized or coordinated via the cyberspace. From a counter-terrorism point of view, cybersecurity, as a tool, is necessary for intelligence gathering.[74]

---

71 **Osho Oluwafemi, Falaye Adeyinka Adesuyi, Shafi'I M. Abdulhamid,** *Combating Terrorism with Cybersecurity: The Nigerian Perspective*, World Journal of Computer Application and Technology 1(4): 103-109, 2013, at page 106, available at http://www.hrpub.org

72 Ibid

73 Ibid

74 Ibid

Whatever approaches we deploy in this battle against terrorism, care must be taken to ensure that we do not inadvertently destroy the very basis of our existence as a nation, or undermine our hard fought democratic system of government. We must also not prosecute this war in a way to derogate from our guaranteed constitutional and human rights, otherwise, the terrorists will have won by default, if they force us to descend with them to the gutters. **David Anderson** says and we agree that:

> The distortive effects of terrorism are undeniable: but they need not disable our compasses. Special rules must be reserved for those circumstances in which they are operationally or procedurally necessary; the protections provided by our constitution and by civil society must continue to evolve; and an intangible but largely healthy culture of executive restraint must continue to be fostered. If all this can be achieved – and why should it not be – we may keep our bearings in spite of all.[75]

6.6: Economic Incentives

It is evident that the lack of economic opportunities bred frustration and hopelessness in and exposed the teeming uneducated, unemployed and neglected youth to the

---

75 **Anderson, David, Shielding the Compass;** *How to Fight Terrorism Without Defeating the Law* (June 15, 2013), at page 19, available at SSRN: http://www.ssrn. com/abstract=2292950

prey of terrorists and violent criminal gangs. **Dos Santos** suggests, "Guaranteeing basic living conditions and providing vocational and entrepreneurial skills may pre-empt large numbers of youths becoming susceptible to Boko Haram's appeal."[76] Addressing the economic plight of this vulnerable segment of the Nigerian population is needed in order to stem the tide of domestic terrorism in the north-east of Nigeria, and indeed elsewhere in the country. **Frey** and **Luechinger** posit that "an obvious possibility (in fighting terrorism) is to raise opportunity costs by increasing income in peaceable occupations."[77] Because in most cases, "the more an individual can gain from participating in an ordinary activity, the less he or she is inclined to engage in terrorism."[78]

In the medical services sector, efforts should be made to establish avenues to train and deploy primary healthcare workers and deploy them to villages, hamlets, and other interior regions of the country, particularly in the north-east. This will create training and employment opportunity for the teeming population of youths, especially young women and girls. The governments, at every level, should provide critically needed skills and career training to the teeming poor, desperate

---

76 **Gustavo Placido Dos Santos**, supra, note 33, at page 2
77 **Bruno S. Frey and Simon Luechinger**, *How to Fight Terrorism: Alternatives to Deterrence*, December 2002, working Paper No. 137, institute for Empirical Research in Economics, University of Zurich Working Paper Series, PP 1-23, at page 9, available at http://www.iew.unzh.ch/wp/
78 Ibid

unemployed youth, as a viable alternative to taking to violence. **Roland Marchal** recognizes that "farming and agribusiness investment may still be an area of productive investments that could also generate substantial employment opportunities for the local populace."[79] Part of the package that the government should consider is an economic empowerment of citizens especially the teen population in the northeast.

Ayodeji Bayo Ogunrotifa underscores the importance of addressing socio-economic imbalance in Nigeria. Economic imbalance breeds violent confrontation as both an outlet of frustration and a means of waging a class war against the dominant elite class. He is not convinced that merely resolving the Boko Haram insurgency would mean that Nigeria has weaned itself of future episodes. He cautions that:

It is likely that if Boko Haram is resolved either through military actions or dialogue, the use of individual terrorism by sectarian groups is likely to emerge in the future as long as the endemic socio-economic problems caused by global capitalism remained and unaddressed. In as much as the socio-economic crisis remain, aggrieved members of the lumpen class who

---

79 **Roland Marchal**, *Boko Haram and the Resilience of Militant Islam in Northern Nigeria*, NOREF Report, June 2012, at page 5, Published by Norwegian Leacebuilsing Resource Centre, available at http://www.peacebuilding.no/.../dc58a110fb362470133354efb8fee228.pdf

could no longer tolerate the series of frustration they suffer will find solution in joining or forming sectarian groups and resort to the use of individual terrorism as a response to the state of affairs.[80]

David Cortright advocates economic empowerment as an antidote to terrorism. He believes that:

Closely related to the challenge of enhancing political participation is the need to expand economic and social opportunity. Because political extremism and violence grow out of joblessness and lack of opportunity, a process of sustained, equitable economic development is essential to reducing the breeding grounds for terrorism [. . .] Democracy, human rights, and economic opportunity are the antidotes to terrorism, and they should be promoted actively as core strategies for preventing the rise of political extremism.[81]

Ajayi takes the view that a critical step towards solving this scourge is to tackle the underlying economic situation that fuels it. He believes that "government must address the problems of mass unemployment, poverty and illiteracy concretely in order to deplete the ranks of malcontents who constitute a ready pool of foot

---

80 **Ayodeji Bayo Ogunrotifa,** supra, note 8, at page 55
81 **David Cortright,** supra, note 66, at page 22

soldiers for criminal activities."[82] **Nwankpa** suggests the use of "socio-economic intervention (through development of infrastructure, job creation and poverty alleviation) by the government, as well as improved governance and genuine fight against corruption, [as] very useful in addressing the Boko Haram crisis, particularly toward creating a disincentive for the largely impoverished youth to be recruited into the sect."[83] **Francis, Lapin** and **Rossiasco** offer, "skills training, internships, or apprenticeship, jobs, self-employment, and business credit according to personal interests and abilities"[84] as the way to go, in searching for solutions to the grave unemployment problem in these areas where terrorists thrive.

The Nigerian government will do well to use the excess funds from crude oil sales, during the fat years, and parlay it to the diversification of the economy in order to better serve the overall interests of the Nigerian people, especially during the lean years. **Francis** and **Sardessai** make this point when they observe that, "Non-renewable resources by their definition are not infinite and it is

---

82 **A.I. Ajayi**, *'Boko Haram' and terrorism in Nigeria: Exploratory and Explanatory notes*, Global Advanced Research Journal of History, Political Science and International Relations Vol. 1(5) pp. 103 – 107, at page 107, July, 2012, available online http://garj.org/garjhpsir/index.htm

83 Nwankpa, Michael, *The Politics Of Amnesty In Nigeria: A Comparative Analysis Of The Boko Haram And Niger Delta Insurgencies*, Journal of Terrorism Reasearch, Volume 5, Issue 1, 1-6, at page 4, available at http://www.ojs.st-andrews.ac.uk/index.php/jtr/rt/printerFriendly/830/709

84 **Paul Francis, Deidre Lapin, Paula Rossiasco**, supra, note 27, at page 116

important that the government takes advantage of this current increase in revenue flows. The challenge is to take the opportunity of high commodity prices and use the resources wisely and efficiently for the benefit of all citizens."[85]

To confront the economic problems the youth of Nigeria are facing, especially to address unemployment and lack of social mobility, these specific steps are germane and we recommend them:

6.6.A: Creation of National Youth Job Corps

The government should consider setting up a National Youth Job Corps, especially in the north-east (where youth unemployment and their susceptibility to recruitment into terrorist groups are highest), to employ the bourgeoning population of unemployed youths and young adults and give them opportunity to earn stipends. They can be used in rebuilding and reconstructing damaged and destroyed public buildings, facilities, and infrastructure such as schools, medical centre, churches, mosques, police stations and barracks, army barracks, government buildings, roads and bridges. The corps can employ most of the youths, including secondary and post-secondary school graduates. Such a scheme will automatically create employment for between 2 and 5 million young men and women and give them

---

85 **Francis, P, Sardesai, S.**, supra, note 28, at page 47

opportunity to earn a small stipend and thus divert them away from violent crimes and terrorism. While they participate in the job corps, they will receive careers and skills training that will allow them acquire marketable skills and gain other real world job experiences.

6.6.B: Career Training, Apprenticeships, and Internships

Education of and skills training for the youth of Nigeria is the key to draining the pool of available candidates for terrorists. **Diala's** advice is that:

[T]he government both at States and Federal level should start doing something about the poor educational system in the country. Less privileged citizens should be able to have access to financial support and scholarship from the government so that they can acquire formal education that would help them chart a cause for their future. The government should concentrate more on the Northern region of Nigeria where the condition of education has reached a state of moribund. Where people are illuminated through education they will not see terrorism as a good venture. They will have regard for their own lives and that of other around them.[86]

---

86 **Diala Barnabas Chinaedu**, *New Trend In Terrorism In Nigeria: 'Boko Haram Sect'* – *The Villain Of The Piece*, pp 1-19, available at http://www.ssrn.com/abstract=1932061

Ekanem and **Ekefre** identify ignorance as the driving force behind the large pool of youth membership of Islamic terrorist groups. They contend that:

> Lack of proper education is the major reason for religious conflicts and violence in Nigeria. This is because proper education will equip religious adherents with better understanding of the dynamics of religion. Education helps to liberate the minds of religious adherents of all dogmas that tend to generate and create intolerance, fundamentalism and extremism. It places the adherents in a position to question certain religious views and dogmas that will be against the views of others.[87]

As a long term strategy to confront unemployment, especially among the youth and young adult population of Nigeria in general, and the north-east region in particular, the various governments should have a hard look at Nigeria's educational system, which places undue emphasis on tertiary education, even when most of what is taught in those institutions does not train the students for the jobs of today. The governments should consider building new, or converting some of the existing tertiary institutions, to institutions that train students for careers,

---

87 **Ekanem, Samuel Asuquo, Ekefre, Ekong Nyong,** *Education and Religious Intolerance in Nigeria: The Need for Essencism as a Philosophy,* Journal of Educational and Social Research, Vol. 3 (2) May 2013, PP 303-310, at page 305

such as in building construction; arts and crafts; electrical technology; environmental control technology; welding and metal works; machinists; construction management; carpentry and woodworking; hospitality and tourism; massage therapy; nursing and ancillary medical services; chef; photography and cinematography; computer programming, computer assembly and repairs; heating, ventilation, and cooling [HVAC]; fashion design; hair and beautification; agriculture and animal husbandry.

These are careers that can lead to real jobs, and failing that, can put the graduates in a position to self-employ themselves by accessing micro-finance facilities. In addition to training the youths and young adults in these careers, a national apprenticeship programme can be designed, in collaboration with medium to large scale private businesses all around the nation, to inspire and mentor these youths and expose them to real world job experiences. NGOs, civil society organizations, faith and religious organizations, and multinational corporations, can also play a large part in the apprenticeship and mentorship program. This sort of apprenticeship program is very prominent in Germany and accounts for the dominance of Germans in technical and mechanical knowhow.

As an intermediate step, the government can solve the problem of youth unemployment by diversifying the economy, especially through investment in farming, horticulture, fisheries and animal husbandry. Nigeria, especially in the troubled north-east, is blessed with abundance of fertile arable land and grass fields. The government can invest heavily in agro-business and grow the sector, not only to feed the nation and reduce the dependence on imported food, but to produce enough for export abroad. This sector potentially can provide employment for a large segment of the Nigerian youth, especially those in rural areas. A large scale national scheme can encourage farmers and fishermen and women, with micro-loans, supply of mechanized farming and fishing equipment, as well as technical education, on the best techniques and approaches to engender better yields and increased returns on investment.

Trans-National corporations can be offered tax and other incentives to come and invest in the agro-business in Nigeria. Crash trainings can be made available to youths and young adults in this sector and thus provide another outlet to employ the teeming population of unemployed youth. Those that show real aptitude can be encouraged with micro-loans and other support services to go into agriculture. Older and more experienced farmers can mentor the younger ones. Beneficiaries of the micro-loan programmes can be made, as a condition of obtaining the micro-finance, to employ one or more of the youth in their farms or fish farm businesses. This agriculture scheme potentially can provide employment and livelihood for hundreds of thousands of young Nigerians who are presently unemployed. **Omoluwa Olusegun** suggests that, "agriculture and cooperative societies should be empowered to provide funds and imputes to rural farmers. This will reduce the level of poverty in the affected societies, and also enable parents to be economically viable to take care of their children."[88]

6.7: Social Services and Infrastructural Incentives

Winning the hearts and minds of the citizens through the provision of critical social infrastructure, such as roads, portable water, electricity, medical services, schools, and security, are a *sine qua non* to defeating terrorism and eliminating the environment that makes it possible for it to thrive. **Professor Guiora** advocates the use of "soft" measures as a veritable tool for fighting terrorism. He urges that:

> Counterterrorism should be simultaneously viewed from two distinct perspectives. One branch of counterterrorism is operational measures ranging from detention to imposition of administrative sanctions to killing suspected terrorists. The other branch is comprised of 'soft' measures ranging from building schools

---

[88] **Omoluwa Olusegun**, *Functional Education: A Tool For Combating Terrorism In Nigeria*, International Journal of arts & Humanity Science (IJAHS), Volume 1 Special Issue 1, (Nov-Dec 2014), PP. 35-39, at page 39, available at http://www.ijahs.com

and hospitals to economic investment and infrastructure development. The latter's target audience are those who can be dissuaded. These are individuals who understand terrorism does not benefit their families or communities but are dependent on concrete measures demonstrating that the benefits of progress and modernity outweigh the harm terrorism inflicts.[89]

The government needs to invest heavily in infrastructural development. The nation needs work on its road network, the rail development, water, electricity, medical services, and schools. Excess funds from crude oil revenues in times of improved oil prices should be taken and invested in infrastructural development rather than distributed to states and local governments where the funds are promptly stolen and/or mismanaged.

Investment in infrastructure not only addresses the sources of grievances against the state, but it actually improves the business environment for small, medium and large business, and will ultimately result in the creation of much needed jobs to employ the teeming mass of unemployed youths while also improving the quality of lives for Nigerians. So, it is all a win-win situation for the nation.

---

89 **Professor Amos N. Guiora,** *Due Process and Counterterrorism,* available at http://www.ssrn.com/abstract=1680009, at pages 2-3

6.8: Dialogue and Other Non-Violent Avenues for Conflict Resolution

Terrorism and violent opposition to the Nigerian state can also be addressed by the creation of peaceful channels for addressing legitimate aspirations of aggrieved ethnic or religious groups. **Udama's** view is that:

> Violence is a reaction to individual or groups acts of despair and of a people that sees no future because it is vastly ignored or frustrated by government unfair practices. There is the urgent need to identified [sic] and justly resolve the political, economic and social grievances nursed by the aggrieved. Most of these deeply felt grievances are legitimate which resulted from manipulations of rules and processes to favour certain persons [. ..] These varieties of factors have alienated a veritable numbers of persons or groups and have made the resort to violence inevitable.[90]

Dialogue with a view to a political solution is the way to go. **Alao et al** offer peaceful dialogue as an antidote to terrorism. Their suggestion is that "Government approach to handling political or other related crises as peace approach is more successful than security approach."[91] **Nwanegbo** and **Odigbo** add that:

---

90 **Udama,** *Rawlings Akonbede*, supra, note 23, at page 114

91 **Alao, David Oladimeji, Atere, Clement Olusegun, Alao, Oluwafisayo,** *Boko Haram Insurgency In Nigeria: The Challenges and Lessons*, Singaporean Journal of Business Economics and Management Studies, Vol.1, No.4, 2012, 1-15, at page 11,

There is need for government and stakeholders to explore alternative avenues (basically dialogue) rather than force to find lasting solution to the security lapse and the menace of Boko Haram if actually Nigeria wants to develop. This is because use of force approach appears to have been inflaming the crisis and diverting attention from the fundamental issues that nurtures and propels the insurgence.[92]

David Cortright offers his own insightful approach to tackling terrorism. He takes the position that:

Because terrorism is primarily a political phenomenon, the strategies for preventing it must focus on political issues as well. Isolating hardcore militants and reducing the legitimacy of terrorist methods requires a strategy of conflict transformation: recognizing the injustices that terrorist groups exploit and engaging with affected parties to resolve grievances through political rather than military means. Demonstrating that political means are available to meet a community's deeply felt needs can convince those

---

available at http://www.singaporeanjbem.com/pdfs/SG_VOL_1_(4)/1.pdf

92 **Nwanegbo, C. Jaja, Odigbo, Jude,** *Security and National Development in Nigeria: The Threat of Boko Haram,* International Journal of Humanities and Social Science Vol. 3 No. 4 [Special Issue – February 2013] 385-291, at page 290, available at http://www.ijhssnet.com/journals/Vol_3_N0_4_Special_Issue.../29. pdf

who support militancy to resolve their grievances through political bargaining rather than armed violence. Where contending groups are involved in dialogue and political engagement, they are less likely to resort to violence.[93]

Oronto Douglas et al take the view that:

In order for Nigeria's federal democracy to be meaningful to ordinary people and their social and economic needs, a new compact between state and society, in which the civic, political and social rights of the people are not only clearly spelled out but are made justiceable, will have to be worked out. A socially and economically-empowered body politic will encourage active citizens, eager to participate in public affairs. And broad and active participation in public affairs by an enlightened citizenry is the secret of good policy.[94]

In conclusion, **David Cortright** offers a blueprint for building an environment that displaces terrorism as a means of pushing a point of view or fighting against perceived injustice or denial of entitlement. He argues that, "Citizens who have opportunities to dissent and

---

93 David Cortright, supra, note 66, at page 21

94 **Oronto Douglas, Ike Okonta, Dimieari Von Kemedi, Michael Watts**, supra, note 24, at page 10

petition for redress are less likely to resort to violence to make themselves heard."[95] **Ibrahim Sada Ladan-Baki** believes that "the state is secure only when the aggregate of people organized under it has a consciousness of belonging to a common sovereign political community; enjoy equal political freedom, human rights, economic opportunities, and when the state itself is able to ensure independence in its development and foreign policy."[96]

6.9: Cultural and Religious Groundwork

The government, community and religious leaders, together with civil society, should collaborate and cooperate to present a common front in this existential fight against terrorism.[97] **Robert Dowd** makes a case for collaborative efforts between the state and civil society in turning Nigeria into a proper melting pot. His position is that:

> While religious diversity and integration cannot be manufactured, there are important roles for state and civil society actors to play in carefully fostering diversity and promoting religiously integrated societies. For example, state actors

---

95 **David Cortright**, supra, note 66, at page 22

96 **Ibrahim Sada Ladan-Baki,** *Corruption And Security Challenges In Developing Countries*, International journal of Politics and Good Governance Volume 5, No. 5.2 Quarter II 2014, 1-19, at page 6, available at http://www.onlineresearchjpournals.com/ijopagg/art/149.pdf

97 **James J.F. Forest**, *Confronting the Terrorism of Boko Haram in Nigeria*, Joint Special Operations University Press, 2012, 1-178, available at http://www.jsou.socom.mil

can pass and enforce laws that open the way for geographic territories to become more religiously diverse by ensuring public schools and other institutions, such as the military, are religiously integrated. If there are interreligious tensions within a state, policymakers may develop political institutions that incentivize moderation and accommodation between religious groups. Besides the state, civil society also has a crucially important role to play in promoting religiously integrated communities. Interreligious voluntary associations tend to promote mutual understanding and tolerance, increasing the likelihood that geographic areas become religiously diverse and integrated. Such associations deserve greater attention and support than they typically receive.[98]

Religious tolerance should be part of the centrepiece of any effort to curb radical Islamic terrorism, such as the Boko Haram insurgency. Imams and other influential religious leaders and teachers must recognize that they have a crucial role to play in dousing tensions, stimulating tolerance and in giving proper direction for the youths seeking guidance. **Robert Dowd** suggests that "the preferred course of action for religious leaders in highly diverse settings is to promote religious tolerance and state neutrality in religious affairs. To

---

98 **Robert Dowd**, *Religious diversity and Violent Conflict: Lessons from Nigeria*, The Fletcher Forum Of World Affairs, Vol.38.1 Winter 2014, pp 153-168, at pages 165-166, available at http://www.fletcherforum.org/.../38-1.D...

do otherwise would be to open the way for mutually assured destruction."[99] **Udama** recognizes that "religious beliefs plays significant role in Nigeria social unrest" and therefore recommends "a well orchestrated against hate and violence campaign ... be carried out in order to change the mindset of various groups of terrorists."[100] He suggests that "it is vital that the clerics of the various religions should teach and continue to preach the right doctrines and good morals to their adherents."[101] **Basil Ekot's** "bottom line is how to manage a state that ensures religious freedom."[102] He submits that "it is not enough to have a constitution that declares Nigeria a secular state when it is clear that this declaration is not acceptable to a large section of the state's population."[103] He urges that Nigerians need to "transcend this religious divide"[104] and see their country as the main focus rather than differences in religious beliefs. **James Forest** has no doubt that "the major contributors to the demise of Boko Haram will be Muslim community leaders and nongovernmental leaders with local legitimacy, more so than the heavy-handed tactics of the police and military."[105] He believes that religious and community leaders' contributions are needed by

---

99 Ibid at page 158

100 **Udama, Rawlings Akonbede**, supra, note 23, at page 113

101 Ibid

102 Basil Ekot, supra, note 25, at page 64

103 Ibid

104 Ibid at page 65

105 **James J.F. Forest,** supra, note 16, at page 120

Nigerian government to de-legitimize Boko Haram and thus diminish the pool of potential recruits and sympathizers to their cause. He points out that "efforts like the Interfaith Mediation Council are crucial for ensuring that Boko Haram's attempts to provoke sectarian violence do not succeed."[106] And that "credible religious leaders can pose a threat to the abilities of Boko Haram to spread its ideology, and as such are an asset in any counterterrorism effort."[107]

Religious and Civic education, and sensitization of the rural population, are tools that will help cultivate a better society.[108] **Ekanem** and **Ekefre** argue that "dogmatism as a product of indoctrination can be cured through education that seeks to liberate the minds and remove all forms of mental cobwebs gathered through cultural and religious activities and beliefs. Through education the perception of religious adherents could be altered positively."[109] **A.I. Ajayi**[110] offers a blueprint for sensitizing the citizenry on the truth about religion and its lack of endorsement of terrorism. He suggests that "one way of divesting terrorism of religious coloration is through well packaged information and mass education

---

106 Ibid at page 102

107 Ibid

108 Ibid at page 95

109 **Ekanem, Samuel Asuquo, Ekefre, Ekong Nyong**, supra, note 88, at page 306

110 **A.I. Ajayi**, *'Boko Haram' and terrorism in Nigeria: Exploratory and explanatory notes*, Global Advanced Research Journal of History, Political Science and International Relations Vol. 1(5) pp. 103 – 107, July, 2012, available online http://garj.org/garjhpsir/index.htm

about the subject with particular attention being focused on the fact that no known religion endorses terrorism overtly or tacitly."[111] He however cautions that "as long as acts of terrorism are glorified by indiscreet mass media coverage it will be difficult to curtail."[112] He believes that the mass media "have a responsibility not to sensationalize acts of terrorism but to condemn them in unmistakable terms."[113] **Popoola** makes the case for the media as a strategic partner in the fight to checkmate violence and terrorism in Nigeria. He argues that "as the fourth estate of the realm and trustees of the public, the media are strategically placed as the main institution that could help in educating and enlightening the citizenry about the danger of indiscriminate violence."[114]

Working with community leaders and religious leaders to foster good neighbourliness, respect for each other and tolerance, is a key step for the Nigerian government. There is need to hold those who fan the embers of conflict to account. Often, politicians and community leaders, in their search for relevance and access to power, resort to instigating conflict and violence. **Kwaja** believes that "ethnic and religious identities in themselves do not create conflicts"[115] but that "it is the politicization of

---

111 Ibid at page 106
112 Ibid
113 Ibid at page 107
114 **I.S. Popoola**, *Press and Terrorism in Nigeria: A Discourse on Boko Haram,* Global Media Journal, African Edition 2012 Vol 6 (1) PP 43-66, at page 61, available at http://www.globalmedia.journals.ac.za

115 **Chris M.A. Kwaja**, *Strategies for [Re]Building State Capacity to Manage Ethnic and Religious Conflict in Nigeria,* The Journal of Pan African Studies, vol.3, no.3, September 2009, at page 112, available at http://www.jpanafrican.com/docs/vol3no3/3.3strategies.pdf

these identities"[116] that is the problem. He charges that:

> Such identities become problematic when access to opportunities in the political system in terms of power and resources are dependent on membership of a particular ethnic or religious group, as well as when the state is relatively weak in terms of its capacity to protect its citizens and provide for their basic needs. The Nigerian experience as it relates to ethnic and religious conflicts has become a major phenomenon as politics is defined along ethnic and religious fault-lines.[117]

Civil society and non-governmental groups and institutions have crucial roles to play in addressing some of the forces that drive terrorism in northeast Nigeria. **James Forest** makes a case for civil society to fill some of the developmental and conflict resolution voids left in the society by the absence of good governance. He says:

> While government is surely expected by its citizens to lead the fight against terrorism, there are many kinds of nongovernmental entities that can also help address the kinds of conditions that give legitimacy to the grievances articulated in a terrorist group's ideology. Further, in several cases, nongovernmental actors may be perceived

116 Ibid
117 Ibid

on a local community level as having more legitimacy than the government, and as such they are in a unique position to have influence in those communities. In the struggle against Boko Haram, these entities play an important role in providing services and development assistance to compensate for the deficiencies of the state.[118]

In other words, civil society, non-governmental groups and institutions, can help pick up the slacks left by government and fill the void created by bad governance.

6.10: Truth and Reconciliation Approach

Another approach to erasing the environment that breeds terrorism and terrorists in Nigeria, is to make a genuine effort to heal the wounds caused by the ruthless counter-insurgency and counter-terrorism activities of law enforcement agencies and the military, in the north-east of Nigeria. Ethnic, sectarian and religious conflicts and animosities that have festered for generations need to be put on the table, discussed and hopefully resolved. The time has come to constitute a "Truth and Reconciliation Committee" that will help air and put to rest, these past and current ugly events. This will go a long way to helping heal wounds, reconcile the nation and open a lasting dialogue on how to live in harmony in a heterogeneous ethnic and religious nation. The South

---

118 **James J.F. Forest**, supra, note 16, at page 96

African experience proves that honestly talking about past and current violent events and an honest showing of remorse heals wounds and helps both the victims and their victimizers turn the corner on ugly experiences and avoid a repeat episode.

Even the more recent so-called "Oputa Truth and Reconciliation Panel" recorded some modest achievements. At least it shone some light on some of the misdeeds of the past military administrations.[119] Truth and reconciliation will engender an honest debate and possible resolution of the enduring ethnic and religious tensions and other outstanding societal conflicts in Nigeria. It will help highlight and, hopefully, eliminate simmering suspicion, jealousy and unhealthy rivalries between and amongst the various ethnic and religious groups in the country and convince all sections that they need to cohabit in peace and harmony with each other because they share one nation and one destiny. It will facilitate making Nigeria a true melting pot of religions, ethnicities and languages.

6.11: Amnesty

The Nigerian government should intensify efforts to fashion out and implement an amnesty programme for

---

119 See "Truth Commission: Nigeria" available at http://www.usip.org/publications/truth-commission-nigeria; Justice In Perspective, "Nigeria: Human Rights Violations Investigation Commission (Oputa Panel), available at http://www.justiceinpesrpective.org.za/africa/nigeria/human-rights-violations-investigation-commission-oputa-panel.html

the Boko Haram insurgents in the north-east, to see if it can pacify the sect and thus end the carnage in the region. The drastic decline in the Niger delta militancy is a clear indication of the positive attributes of amnesty as a tool of conflict resolution. The amnesty programme for the Niger delta offered militants, career and job training with monthly stipends, in return for giving up arms and abandoning militancy. Many of their leaders secured lucrative security contracts from the government and the oil industry. That apparently was sufficient incentive to persuade them to abandon militancy. Amnesty has been deployed as a useful tool in several hotspots around the world to resolve violent conflicts including terrorism. It has been used in Afghanistan, Pakistan, Saudi Arabia, Columbia, Iraq, Northern Ireland and Sri Lanka, to name but a few. The time has come to deploy amnesty as a tool for potentially resolving the Boko Haram question in the north-east of Nigeria.

We believe that amnesty as a resolution scheme is one of the several tools in the resolution basket that must be explored in all and every attempt to find resolution to a conflict. It may well be that after efforts are made, that particular situation is found not appropriate for amnesty or the party to whom it is extended rejects it. One can never close the door on amnesty as a tool for resolving conflict. Dealing with terrorism requires a multi-dimensional approach and that must necessarily include amnesty.

It appears that amnesty for Boko Haram has not gained traction, due partly to the intransigence of the sect leadership, but also because of the apparent double standards of some entrenched sections of the Nigerian leadership. These people, some from the Niger delta region, are convinced that somehow the Niger delta militancy is justified and therefore entitled to amnesty, whereas the Boko Haram insurgency is not. Without going into the justification or lack thereof, of these two groups of violent events, the fact still remains that terrorism can never be justified as a legitimate course of seeking remedy to an action or inaction of government. Second, we cannot discount any approach that has a potential for resolving an intractable violent confrontation. On that score alone, all options must be on the table, as far as the Boko Haram is concerned. The alternative is much too grim to contemplate. **Muhammed Kabir Isa** rightly indicts the discriminatory approaches of the Nigerian government towards armed groups in the country. He says that:

> The state seems to lack a common approach of dealing with armed non-state groups. Although the state responded with massive and unprecedented force to the Boko Haram uprising and the Niger Delta insurgence, it has so far extended amnesty only to the Niger Delta militants. It is obvious that the presence of

natural resources such as oil has influenced the different approaches taken by the government to address militant uprisings in different regions of the country.[120]

Frey and **Luechinger** suggest that bargaining with terrorists in a bid to increase their opportunity costs for remaining terrorist will incentivize them to abandon terrorism and rejoin the society. They cite the examples of the Red Brigade in Italy and the Red Army Faction in Germany, to substantiate their point that "persons engaged in terrorist movements can be offered incentives such as money, reduced punishment and secure future life if they are prepared to leave the organization they are involved with and are prepared to talk about it and its project."[121] If it worked for these other nations, and it has been shown to work, to a large extent, in the Niger delta, then it must be genuinely explored in the north-east of Nigeria.

---

120 **Muhammed Kabir Isa,** *Chapter 11: Militant Islamist Groups in Northern Nigeria,* available at http://www.mercury.ethz.ch/.../MilitiasRebelsIslamistMilitants_Chapter+11.pdf , at page 334; According to UN Office for the Coordination of Humanitarian Affairs, Analysis; Carrot or Stick? – Nigerians divided over Boko Haram, available at http://www.irinnews.org/printreport.aspx?reportid=95874 [last visited on 12/7/2014], "To underline Abuja's alleged lack of sincerity, the major effort by the federal government to solve the Niger Delta crisis – where amnesty and rehabilitation packages were offered to the militants that took on the oil companies, and development funding was thrown at the region – is contrasted with its approach to the north. The sole initiative so far has been a promised US$26 million to build 400 schools for Almajiris – children sent to Islamic madrasas by their families, but who must beg on the streets for their upkeep."

121 **Bruno S. Frey and Simon Luechinger,** *How to Fight Terrorism: Alternatives to Deterrence,* December 2002, working Paper No. 137, institute for Empirical Research in Economics, University of Zurich Working Paper Series, PP 1-23, at page 12, available at http://www.iew.unzh.ch/wp/

Although **Nwankpa** agrees that "conciliation and negotiation are very powerful tools for mitigating terrorism,"[122] he takes the position that the Boko Haram sect is unsuitable for an amnesty programme much like the one extended by the Nigerian government to the Niger delta militants. He argues that whilst the Niger delta militants somehow deserve such a programme, Boko Haram, in his own analysis, are underserving. We disagree. Amnesty is not about who deserves what, in our opinion, but is about seeking solutions to a complex problem. Amnesty, as we have said earlier, is only but a tool in the box set of possible prescriptions for conflict resolution. You do not dismiss a therapy outright solely on the basis of your subjective assessment of who deserves what. Terrorism is a very destructive ailment and every available therapy ought to be tried on it to see if that would supply a cure. To do otherwise is plain foolery.

6.12: Victims Compensation

The Nigerian government should try to devise a mechanism for compensating the families of the victims of Boko Haram, as well as the families of the alleged Boko Haram members who were extra-judicially executed by the security forces. The compensation scheme should include paying damages for those that lost their lives,

---

122 **Nwankpa, Michael**, *The Politics Of Amnesty In Nigeria: A Comparative Analysis Of The Boko Haram And Niger Delta Insurgencies*, Journal of Terrorism Reasearch, Volume 5, Issue 1, 1-6, at page 4, available at http://www.ojs.st-andrews.ac.uk/index.php/jtr/rt/printerFriendly/830/709

including members of the security forces; medical and other support care for the wounded; and financial compensation for those who lost real estate, businesses, jobs, personal properties and those who were displaced from the violent theatres in north-east Nigeria. The untold human suffering by people in north-east Nigeria cannot go unaddressed. Their suffering needs to be ameliorated. **Ayodeji Bayo Ogunrotifa**, quoting **Aliyu Tilde**,[123] makes a convincing case for the thesis that, the runaway violence that presently characterizes the Boko Haram insurgency in the north-east of Nigeria could have been avoided had the government taken early steps to address the question of victims of the extra-judicial killing of members and families of the sect in July of 2009. According to him:

> In the analysis of the origin of Boko Haram insurgency, Aliyu Tilde [...] observed that 'sect leader (Muhammed Yusuf) wrote series of letter to the Borno state government and the Borno commissioner of police. He called for the compensation of the family of those who were killed by the police during the funeral procession. He followed his letter with practical visits to the police but all appeal fell on deaf ears. He then called severally to the IG of police and the Yar'adua administration to intervene but to

---

123 **Aliyu Tilde** (2012) *"The new challenges of Boko Haram in Nigeria."* Available at http://www.nigeriavillagesquare.com/aliyu-u-tilde/the-new-challenges-of-boko-haram.html

date; nothing was done to the culprits. He began to send threat to the government and the police. He castigated the Yar'adua government and called Yar'adua an oppressor and declared the government as unjust. For those Muslim leaders and scholars who opposed his threat against government, he declared them as hypocrite and even declared some as unbelievers. He and his member [sic] began to arm themselves while receiving support from many who sympathized with them and had grievance against the jungle justice of the Nigerian police.[124]

One can see the progression from civil appeals, neglect to act, and ultimately threats, and then inception of violence.

Agbiboa offers a first step in preparing the ground for a constructive engagement of Boko Haram in a dialogue that may conduce to a lasting resolution of the insurgency. According to him, Boko Haram were disposed to engaging the government in an amicable resolution of their grievances after the events of July 2009 and that "among the proximate demands of Boko Haram are the release of all its prisoners and the prosecution of those responsible for the killing of their founder."[125] These

124 Ayodeji Bayo Ogunrotifa, supra, note 8, at page 49

125 **Agbiboa, Daniel E,** *Peace at Daggers Drawn? Boko Haram and the State of Emergency in Nigeria*, Studies in Conflict & Terrorism, 37:41-67, 2014, at page 56, available at http://www.researchgate.net/...Peace_at_Daggers_Drawn_Boko_Haram_and_t...

are not outrageous demands but a decent starting point in engagement which the Nigerian government failed to take advantage of. Substantially, the same demands were restated by the group two years later when they met with former President Olusegun Obasanjo on 16 September 2011, to wit, release of their members in prison; stop indiscriminate arrest of their members; pay compensation to the families of their members killed by security forces and; the prosecution of members of the police that executed their former leader Muhammad Yusuf.[126]

The Nigerian government should tackle head-on, the humanitarian crisis that has been brought on by Boko Haram. Refugees and internally displaced peoples should be given assistance in the short term, but in the mid to long-term, efforts should be intensified to stabilize their home bases and make efforts to return them to a safe and viable environment for them to pick up their shattered lives. So far, the government is not even addressing the refugees and internally displaced persons. The **U.S. Department of Justice** points that out in their report. According to them, "the Convention [referring to the African Union Convention for Protection and Assistance of Internally Displaced Persons in Africa (Kampala Convention) of October 2009] requires state parties to find permanent solutions to displacement 'by promoting and creating satisfactory

---

126 Ibid at page 59

conditions for voluntary return, local integration or relocation on a sustainable basis and in circumstance of safety and dignity." So far, however, it seems that Nigeria has done little to assist the IDPs."[127] The fact that effort was made to enable the displaced persons in the north-east to vote in some of the most recent national elections is an indication that it is logistically possible to address the resettling and rehabilitation of the large pool of displaced Nigerians in the north-east. What seems to be missing is the political will to bring that about.

6.13: Effective Border Controls and Better Handle on Arms Smuggling

We pointed out in Chapter 3, that Nigeria's porous borders and the ability of arms smugglers and terrorists to move freely to and from bases in the neighboring nations of Niger, Chad and Cameroon, has been a great enabler for Boko Haram in the north-east. Control of the national borders, especially against inflow of arms and rogues from neighbouring nations, is therefore a critical piece of any strategy to successfully stem terrorism in northern Nigeria. **Dambazau** articulates the challenges posed by smuggling through our porous borders. He asserts that:

---

127 **Hanibal Goitom,** *Nigeria: Boko Haram, Report for the U.S. Department of Justice,* July 2014, The Library of Congress, 1-11, at page 11, available at http://www.justice.gov/.../nigeria/2014-010...; African Union Convention for the Protection and Assistance of Internally Displaced Persons in Africa (Kampala Convention) art. 5, Oct. 22, 2009, 49 I.L.M. 86, available on the United National High Commissioner for Refugees (UNHCR) portal, REFWORLD, at http://www.unhcr.org/4ae9bede9.html

The challenge we have relates to the strategy to be adopted for not only to clean the mess created by the presence of drugs and arms, but also to prevent them from further infiltration through our borders. Like the problem we have with weak police institution, we also have similar problems with the Immigration and Customs, the two main institutions policing our borders.[128]

The link has been made between terrorism, smuggling and organized crimes. Terrorism cannot be effectively controlled and/or eliminated without controlling smuggling and organized crime syndicates that dominate that scene. **Udombana** makes the case that "there are parallels between terrorism and organized crimes, including the illicit traffic of arms, drugs and money laundering; and like these other crimes, terrorism threatens the stability of societies and security of individuals."[129] **Dr. Adigbuo** posits that "the sub-region's [ECOWAS] ill-governed spaces have expectedly attracted terrorist groups by providing access to transport systems, safe havens and venues for transnational funding."[130] **Rose C. Uzoma** advises that "it is vital that security agencies monitor the activities of visitors and immigrants in Nigeria while at the same

---

128 **Abdulrahman Dambazau, Lt. Gen. [Rtd]**, *Overcoming Nigeria's Security Challenges*, supra, note 1, at page 10

129 **Nsongarua J. Udombana**, supra, note 39, at page 74

130 **Dr. Ebere Richard Adigbuo**, *The New ECOWAS Counter Terrorism Strategy and Arms Trade Treaty, Journal of International Affairs and Global Strategy Vol.25*, 2014, 46-54, at page 53, available at http://www.iiste.org

time protecting national security and ensuring the right of entry to foreigners."[131]

For the Nigerian security forces to have any chance of crushing Boko Haram, the nation's borders should be effectively controlled and secured, by restricting the smuggling of funds, supplies, arms, and fighters. Efforts should be made to collaborate with the governments of the neighbouring nations to ensure proper control of shared borders.

6.14: Regional & Transnational Collaboration

The cross-border menace of Boko Haram in Northern Cameroon, Chad and Niger show clearly that the Boko Haram insurgency has become a transnational problem. The solution to it therefore requires transnational collaboration and cooperation. It has been suggested that "because of the cross-border nature of international terrorism, national counter-terrorism efforts [should] rely heavily on international cooperation – the exchange of information; the sharing of intelligence and cooperation between intelligence agencies; and on mutual assistance in investigation, prevention, and prosecution of terrorists."[132] Because of the cross-border operations

---

131 **Rose C. Uzoma**, *Religious Pluralism, Cultural Differences, and Social Stability in Nigeria*, Brigham Young University Law Review [Summer 2004] 651-664, at page 664, available at http://www.digitalcommons.law.byu/cgi/viewcontent.cgi?article=2179...

132 United Nations Office of the Special Adviser on Africa , "Africa and International Counterterrorism Imperatives," Expert paper prepared by the Office of the Special Adviser on Africa, at page 10, available at http://www.un.org/africa/.../OSAA-TerrorismPaper-12Nov2010...

of Boko Haram it is no longer a national problem. It has gone regional. Scores of people have been killed in northern Cameroon. People have also been kidnapped in Cameroon by the group, including the wife of the Deputy Prime Minister[133] In addition to their cross-border operation, is their ability to move back and forth across the Nigerian borders with Niger, Chad and the Cameroon and to move arms and fighters between these neighbouring nations. Given the transnational nature and capabilities of Boko Haram, a transnational approach to curtailing their operations and reach, is called for. **Professor Hussein Solomon** offers a pathway. He says that:

> [T]here is a discernible Boko Haram presence in Chad, Cameroon, Mali, and Niger. Currently each of these countries is trying to unilaterally take on Boko Haram. Whilst some successes have been achieved ... it is clear that neighbouring states need to think along the lines of joint military operations, sharing intelligence, coordinating border crossings, as well as starving Boko Haram of its financial resources emanating locally and abroad to conducts [sic] its terror campaign.[134]

Babjee Pothuraju has reasons to fear that "due to its rapidly expanding attack capability, Boko Haram is on

---

133 **Charlotte Alter,** *"Third attack Since 22 Militants were Sentenced to Prison in Cameroon Friday"*, TIME, July 28, 2014, available at http://www.time.com/3045718/boko-haram-cameroon-nigeria/

134 **Professor Hussein Solomon**, supra, note 35, at pages 1-2

a trajectory to become the next international jihadist franchise group in the region."[135] Thus it "has transformed Boko Haram into a regional problem, one that requires a response not only from the Nigerian government, but also from the country's neighbours."[136] It therefore follows that:

> International counter-terrorism efforts are likely to succeed only with significant improvement in cross-border cooperation and collaboration, exchange of information, and intelligence sharing. In essence, States must be able to protect their borders and must have the capacity to provide mutual assistance to each other in the investigation, apprehension and prosecution of terrorists, thereby denying safe haven to them and their supporters."[137]

Coordination with regional and trans-national organizations such as the UN, the AU and ECOWAS, in the fight against terrorism is called for. The expertise and funding capacities of these organizations will go a long way to helping Nigeria stem the Boko Haram insurgency. **Udombana** highlights the fact that "the OAU Terrorism Convention is significant in its focus on

---

135 **Babjee Pothuraju**, supra, note 4, at page 8

136 Ibid

137 United Nations Office of the Special Adviser on Africa , *"Africa and International Counterterrorism Imperatives,"* Expert paper prepared by the Office of the Special Adviser on Africa, at page 10, available at http://www.un.org/africa/.../ OSAA-TerrorismPaper-12Nov2010...

international mutual cooperation, including the sharing of information and mutual legal assistance."[138] Nigeria should take advantage of the technical and logistical assistance available to it from the AU and ECOWAS in its efforts to fight terrorism. Nigeria should press for the implementation of the ECOWAS Arrest Warrant regime to enable her reach fugitives in Chad, Niger and other West African nations. **Dr. Adigbuo** believes that, "if implemented, the ECOWAS Arrest Warrant ... will strengthen cross-border cooperation among law enforcement agencies and eliminate safe havens for terrorists and other criminals. In particular, it will enable ECOWAS states [such as Nigeria] to pursue terrorists across borders."[139]

Nigeria should also take advantage of the opportunities offered by the Trans-Sahara Counterterrorism Partnership [TSCTP].[140] Nigeria should consider leveraging its membership of the partnership to obtain assistance in the areas of counter-terrorism capacity building, investigation, intelligence gathering and sharing, monitoring and countering terrorism financing, and the interdiction of cross-border smugglers and terrorists.

---

138 **Nsongarua J. Udombana**, supra, note 39, at page 110

139 **Dr. Ebere Richard Adigbuo**, supra, note 130, at page 52

140 TSCTP was established in 2005 and designed, with the US funding, to build capacity and cooperation of military, law enforcement, and civilian actors across North and West Africa to counter terrorism. Membership of the partnership include Algeria, Burkina Faso, Cameroon, Chad, Mali, Mauritania, Morocco, Niger, Nigeria, Senegal, and Tunisia: U.S. Department of State, Bureau of Counterterrorism, Country Reports on Terrorism 2013, 1-21, available at http://www.state.gov/j/ct/rls/crt/2013/224820.htm

The Nigerian government should put in motion, efforts at collaboration with neighbouring nations, such as Niger, Chad and Cameroon, in tracking arms and terrorists and in exchange of information and strategic training. This is echoed by the UN Special Representative for West Africa, **Mohamed Ibn Chambas**, after the sacking of Baga by Boko Haram. He was quoted as saying that the four African nations most threatened by Boko Haram must set aside their distrust of each other and work on a command structure and a strategy to defeat Boko Haram. He stressed that "the countries should not be left to tackle it individually. That has been the approach so far and it is not winning the fight."[141]   Currently, it appears as if some level of collaboration between the Nigerian, Cameroonian, Chadian and Nigerien forces are pushing back the Boko Haram gains. The neighbouring nations must build on these recent successes and forge a real sustained alliance.

As an interim measure, the Niger Republic, Chad, Cameroon, and Nigeria, should form a strategic Interim Anti-Terrorism Joint Security Task Force to checkmate the advance of Boko Haram and give Nigeria an opportunity to encircle and round up the sect. The Task Force should collate and share intelligence, maintain data, do joint training and exercises. In the long run, ECOWAS should consider forming an ECOWAS

---

141 UN: African states must unite against Boko Haram, REUTERS, 2015-01-15, at page 1, available at http://www.news24.com/Africa/News/African-states-must-unite-against-Boko-Haram-201...

Counter Terrorism Force [ECO-FORCE] to counter terrorism throughout the sub-region. The force could be drawn from armed forces of member states based on size of countries and their level of development. The force will be funded by ECOWAS and funds and expertise can be solicited from the UN, EU, USA, Russia, China, Japan, AU and other developed nations, and from multinational organizations around the world. ECO-FORCE could have two bases, one each in a Francophone and an Anglophone country. The force will train and supply logistics and expertise to anti-terrorism squads of member nations. The force will be mobilized to assist member nations facing terrorism attacks. The force can also be used for the protection of peace-keeping staff in ECOWAS peace-keeping activities in the region.

In light of the foregoing discussion, we make the following recommendation:

•   That the government convene a real and broadly representative Constitutional Assembly, to design a new Republic, which will address the relationship between the central government and the federating states;

•   The Nigerian government should make anti-corruption efforts a priority;

•   The government should make a concerted effort to improve governance, and thus reinstate the citizens' trust in their government;

•   Alternative legal avenues should be created and

made available for Nigerians to voice their discontent with or dissent from their government, as well as an avenue to resolve inter and intra sectarian conflicts. This should include ensuring access to courts, and the maintenance of the independence of the judiciary;

• The excesses of the security forces in the north-east regions of the country, should be thoroughly investigated and any officer(s) found culpable should be prosecuted, and if found guilty, jailed and dismissed from service. In other words, the government should sanitize the law enforcement and security agencies;

• The security forces and the police force should be retrained in modern security and law enforcement operations. They should be provided with the right up-to-date tools and expertise with which to work. The government should also ensure that these men and women are paid adequate living wages;

• The problem of unemployment, lack of access to social mobility by the youths of Nigeria must be addressed by instituting youth job corps and setting up of skills training institutions, apprenticeship programmes and mentorship;

• Diversification of the Nigerian economy to grow the economy and create jobs must be a priority of government;

• Religious, tribal, and community leaders should be alert to their responsibilities not to preach hate and divisiveness, rather they should encourage their followers and adherents to be good and responsible citizens of a truly united nation, Nigeria;

•   The Nigerian government needs to create a fund from which to address the issue of compensation for victims of terrorism. At the same time, the humanitarian catastrophe that has enveloped the north-east region of the country should be addressed through a collaborative effort of the government, civil society, regional, and international organizations, and donor nations;

•   Nigeria should make haste to secure her borders from smugglers, violent criminals, and terrorists;

•   Nigeria should forge alliances, collaborate with, and seek assistance of her neighbours, regional, and multinational organizations, in her existential fight against terrorism;

•   To top it off, the Nigerian security forces should bring the fight to Boko Haram by intensifying its effort to retake, clear and hold, the territories currently under the sway of these terrorists in the north-east, and thus give the government the opportunity to bring normalcy to these troubled parts.

Chapter 7
Summary

Terrorism has become the latest fad. This in no way diminishes its danger and potency. Although terrorism is practically as old as humanity itself, it has taken a pre-eminent place in world affairs, on the heels of the terrorist attacks on the World Trade Center, the Pentagon, and the fields of Pennsylvania in the continental United States, on that fateful morning on September 11, 2001. Following that harrowing experience, the world woke up to a new paradigm. The era of the "War against Terrorism." Leading **Andrew C. Orr** to argue that:

Ten years after September 11th, it seems almost absurd to argue that terrorism is a law enforcement matter. The scale, sophistication, and complexity of the al Qaeda threat has long-since evolved into something more substantial. Perhaps the first step is recognizing that groups like al Qaeda are really game changers in the world of international law, much like the internet was a game changer in the world of information and communication.[1]

The horrors of 9/11, and the feeling of empathy towards the victims, spurred a global outrage that conduced to a flurry of political, legal, and legislative action to de-legitimize terror as a tool of agitation, political or otherwise. It also led to heightened and concerted legislative and military action to confront terror, and to punish those who perpetrate or sponsor it. With the active and pushy influence of the United States, Great Britain, and even Russia, and buoyed apparently by the guilt of seeing all those horrific images coming out of the World Trade Center in New York, the United Nations led the march in the world-wide effort to confront terrorism head-on. With the passage of **Resolution 1373 of 2001,** the UN galvanized and mandated the entire international community to change its outlook on terrorism, and to move terrorism from the realms of "law enforcement" to the rarified heights of "war." The resolution mandated nations to pass appropriate legislation to punish terrorism and its perpetrators; to block funding for terrorists by legislation; and to cooperate and coordinate efforts on sub-regional, regional and multilateral bases to effectively police and eliminate terrorism. **Sudha Setty** says that "Resolution 1373, in an arguably unprecedented step for the Security Council, mandates that member states

---

1 **Orr, Andrew C.,** *"Unmanned, Unprecedented, and Unresolved: The Status of American Drone Strikes in Pakistan Under International Law,"* 44 Cornell Int'l L.J. (2011) PP 730-752, at page 752

combat terrorism in numerous ways, work cooperatively with other member states to share information related to security issues, and report to the Counter-Terrorism Committee – established for the purpose of overseeing progress in fulfilling the mandate of Resolution 1373."[2]

While there is unanimity in the condemnation, and belief in the infamy, of terrorism, as well as the need to eliminate it, the problem is that there does not seem to be a corresponding unanimity on what terrorism really is. Governments and those in power are wont to define terrorism broadly, for the most part, as a leeway to punish and eliminate dissent and opposition. Peoples, groups, and communities, that are pursuing legitimate aspirations for nationhood, are leery of an expansive definition of terrorism. Countries in the middle-east who are sympathetic to the cause of the Palestinian people are, quite understandably, weary of an expansive definition of terrorism that might "criminalize" the aspirations of the Palestinian people to control their own land and to be an independent nation.

Further complicating the controversy around a universal definition of terrorism is the fact that even nations themselves cannot agree on one definition, and do in fact end up having multiple definitions of terrorism by different units of the same government. A typical example is the United States. Although the US is a

---

2 **Sudha Setty,** *What's In A Name? How Nations Define Terrorism Ten Years After 9/11,* **U. Pa. J. Int'l L,** Vol. 33:1 [2011], at page 12, available at http://www.ssrn.com/abstract=1858327

leading light and an arrowhead of the push for forceful response to "terrorism," it does not have a uniform and single definition of terrorism. Several agencies of the US government have defined terrorism in different formats and to varying degrees. The United Nations itself has not helped matters. It mandates nations to legislate against terrorism without defining terrorism to aid clarity, thus leaving nations to their own devices.

The question of where to draw a line between fighting for freedom and acts of terrorism, is throwing wrinkles into attempts to forge a common articulation of what terrorism is. One school of thought argues that oppressed peoples have a right to fight for their freedom, using whatever tools they can find, including violence. Whilst another school of thought insists that all use of violence to shock, intimidate and coerce a government to act or forgo action, is terrorism. Add to that, the controversy around whether or not a government can commit, enable or sponsor terrorism. Quite predictably, most governments, particularly dictatorships, create the appearance that all governmental actions ought to be classified as legitimate, no matter how violent. The tendency, therefore, is that because legislative functions belong to the government, most terrorism legislation denounce actions of others outside of government [non-state actors], particularly dissenters and opposition elements, whilst ignoring those of the government and their supporters.

What we therefore end up with, is a situation where terrorism is defined to reflect the biases and predilections of those responsible for drafting the law. One is then left, in an attempt to study terrorism, with the only option of looking at how others have defined terrorism, including international, regional, and sub-regional organizations, to make a sense of the boundaries of the term "terrorism." It does then appear, from a reading of the various definitions, that the hallmark of terrorism is that it aims to shock, intimidate, or awe the victims and/or other target audience, and is intended to force action or inaction. It is often classified either by the act itself, or by the intent of the perpetrator(s). The final element is, that the violence or threat thereof, must be for the purpose of advancing a point of view, to push an ideal, or to advance a political, religious, social, or cultural point of view. Gratuitous violence alone will not suffice.

Nigeria is a nation laden with ethnic, cultural, religious, and linguistic fault lines, and is therefore susceptible to terrorism. Because of the nature of its founding by colonial Great Britain, Nigeria is a hastily thrown together contraption of different peoples, ethnicities, languages, and religions. Because there was no negotiated union, and no terms of association, these different interests have had to battle for ascendancy. This tussle has got more vicious with the exit of Britain, the only glue that held the nation together in colonial times. These latent and subterranean tremors are now seeking to erupt into a full-blown sectarian conflict, and possibly a civil war, due in part to the activities of Boko Haram in the north-east region of Nigeria.

The Boko Haram insurgency in the north-east region of Nigeria, is the latest and most potent of a trend of religious radicalism that flares up periodically in the north. It is a throwback to the Maitasine insurrections of the 1980s in Kano and several other cities in northern Nigeria. Although it is not quite clear when and who founded the Boko Haram religious sect, the climate of opinion seems to suggest that the sect was founded in 2002 by one Muhammed Yusuf. The sect is essentially a culmination of the growing radical Salafism movement that drew its inspiration from the Iranian revolution of 1979. **Osaghae & Suberu** draw a link between the surge of radical and fundamentalist activities of the post Iranian revolution and the emergence of radical Islamic movements in northern Nigeria that gave rise to Boko Haram. According to them:

> Following the Iranian Islamic revolution of the 1970s, there was a surge of radical and fundamentalist activities especially among Muslim youths. This was the context within which some fundamentalist Muslim sects, notably the Maitatsine, Izala movement, the Muslim Brothers

or Shiites, and most recently the Talibans emerged to demand, amongst others: purist Islam based on Sharia law; the eradication of heretical innovations; and the establishment of an Islamic state or theocracy. The activities of these sects were a major precipitant of the religious conflicts that proliferated the Northern political landscape in the 1980s and 1990s.[3]

Recounting the history of Boko Haram, **Don North** writes:

Its genesis began with a handful of Muslim clerics who followed the extremist Islam of the Saudi Arabian Wahhabis and Salafists. Boko Haram morphed slowly into its form today feeding on the poverty and illiteracy of northern Nigeria to form its ideology of fundamentalism and hatred. Poverty-stricken and disillusioned youth believing they had nothing to lose began to huddle under the black jihadi flag.[4]

The sect was originally a non-violent movement that railed against modern institutions and the decadence and failure of the established Muslim orders in the north. The sect advocates the establishment of an islamic state based

---

3 **Osaghae, Eghosa E., Suberu, Rotimi T.**, *A History of Identities, Violence, and Stability in Nigeria*, Queen Elizabeth House, University of Oxford, Crise Working Paper No. 6, January 2005, 1-27, at page 11

4 **Don North**, *Behind the War with Boko Haram*, Consortiumnews.com, November 16, 2014, 1-27, at page 10, available at http://www.consortiumnews.com/2014/11/16/behind-the-war-with-boko-haram/

on the tenets and dictates of the Quran. Although there were periodic minor violent skirmishes between the sect and authorities in several cities in the north, things came to a head in July 2009. A violent confrontation between the sect and security forces over a minor traffic infraction led to loss of lives on both sides of the conflict. Following the altercation, and apparently irked by their losses, the security forces went on a rampage, rounding up suspected members of the sect, including Yusuf and some members of his family, and extra-judicially executing hundreds of sect members in front of the police station, often in full public view. This singular act turned the movement from a largely peaceful organization to a full-blown violent insurgency.

The sect initially called for the arrest and prosecution of the killers of their leaders and members; compensation to the families of the victims; and the release of members still detained. Although these were fairly reasonable demands, they were ignored in the belief that the sect could be easily eliminated with brute force. **A.F. Ahokegh** says:

> Yet the situation would not have been what it is today if not for the extra-judicial killings carried out by government. Whilst Boko Haram started as a non-violent breakaway group, persecution and aggressive crack-downs from the security services brought about their violent response.

Boko Haram was at first a small and controllable problem, but the issue escalated in 2009 after heavy crackdowns were ordered by President Yar'Adua. The crackdown was brutal and disproportionate; around 700 innocent people were killed, some of them publicly executed on suspicions that they were members of Boko Haram [...] The killing of their leader, Mohammed Yusuf actually made the group increases [sic] its rate of violent activities [...] Following the killing of their leader the movement went underground but emerged a year later with renewed attacks. Even at this point the situation was controllable, yet the government response was heavy-handed.[5]

A dozen years later the sect is alive and growing, and at a stage, reportedly in control of a swathe of territory the size of Belgium. The sect, now proscribed as a terrorist organization, uses suicide bombing, assassinations, kidnapping, beheading, arson, rape, and bank robbery, as their mode of operation. Over 35,000 lives have been lost so far and the killing continues unabated on a daily basis. Hundreds of thousands of victims have been injured in the insurgency. Millions have been displaced and tens of thousands are refugees in neighbouring nations, as a result of the insurgency. Property loss and damage, infrastructural and business losses, social and economic

---

5 **A. F. Ahokegh**, *Boko Haram: A 21st Century Challenge In Nigeria*, European Scientific Journal, September edition vol.8. No.21, 46-55, at page 52, available at http://www.eujournal.org>Home>Vol8,No21(2012)>Ahokegh

dislocations, are all estimated in billions of dollars. The activities of the sect have become a potent existential threat to the Nigerian nation. Speaking to the issue of Boko Haram insurgency, the **U.S. House of Representatives** says:

> While Boko Haram began as, and maintains elements of, a basic Islamic movement, it has evolved into a hardened and sophisticated terror network. The challenge for Nigeria and its partners is to arrest and incarcerate or eliminate Boko Haram operatives, while at the same time shrinking their broad public sympathy among northern Nigerian Muslims. This is a complex obstacle, and requires multiple simultaneous efforts to enhance the capacity of Nigeria's police and military, restore the trust in Nigeria's government among large segments of its population, and provide viable solutions to the long-term problems faced by many Nigerians in the north.[6]

Bad governance, institutionalized corruption, massive unemployment, poverty and the feeling of increased marginalization and isolation, have allied with radical Islam in the north-east, to create a perfect storm in the

---

6 *Boko Haram: Growing Threat to the U.S. Homeland*, **Report prepared by the** Majority Staff of the Committee on Homeland Security of the U.S. House of Representatives, September 13, 2013, at page 39, available at http://www.homeland. house.gov/sites/homeland.house.gov/files/documents/09-13-13-Boko-Haram-Report.pdf

name of Boko Haram. According to the U.S. **House of Representatives**:

> A number of factors have been attributed to the fueling of Boko Haram's violence and fanaticism, including a feeling of alienation from the more-developed, predominantly Christian, southern region of Nigeria; pervasive poverty; rampant government corruption; incompetent and brutal security services; and the belief that relations with the West are a corrupting influence. These grievances have led to sympathy for Boko Haram among the local Muslim population despite the group's violent tactics.[7]

The environment that breeds terrorism, and factors that drive it, are important to understand in order to fashion an effective counter-terrorism strategy. Several factors have been identified as creating the environment that drives Nigerians to terrorism, and also helps swell the pool of potential recruits. According to **Abimbola, J.O.,** and **Adesote, S.A.,**

> The activities of the Islamic group especially since 2009 in the area have not only constituted a major security threat to the nation, but has also make [sic] the area the most dangerous place to live in the country. The activities of this sect are

---

7 Ibid at page 8

capable of disintegrating the country. Thus, the need to find lasting solution to the grievance of this Islamic group is paramount.[8]

Some of these factors include structural-political, economic, religious, corruption, legal. **Nathaniel Manni** reaches the heart of the matter in his search for the drivers of terrorism in Nigeria. He finds that:

> Systemic corruption within the Nigerian government, government instability, widespread poverty, and continuous sectarian strife within the state, have created the perfect storm for the spread of terrorism within Nigeria; a situation that Boko Haram has continued to use to its advantage. With many Nigerians living in poverty, while government officials enjoy the lion's share of oil revenue within the country, Boko Haram has enjoyed widespread support in the Muslim north, due to the fact that many in the region believe Boko Haram's objective – the establishment of an Islamic state in Nigeria – is the only possible remedy for the nation's woes.[9]

---

8 **Abimbola, J.O., and Adesote, S.A.**, *Domestic Terrorism And Boko Haram Insurgency In Nigeria, Issues And Trends: A Historical Discourse,* Journal of Arts and Contemporary Society, Volume 4, September 2012, 11-29, at page 16, available at http://www.cenresinpub.org,

9 **Nathaniel Manni**, *"Boko Haram: A Threat to Africa and Global Security"*, Global Security Studies, Fall 2012, Volume 3, Issue 4, PP 44-54, at page 45, available at http://www.globalsecuritystudies.com/Manni%20BH%20FINAL.pdf

The most basic driving force behind terrorism in Nigeria is the defective foundational structural underpinning of the nation. The founding of Nigeria was such that a foundation was laid for endemic and sustained internal competition and conflict. Nigeria is essentially several ethnic, cultural, religious, and linguistic entities, thrown together without any negotiated and/or agreed basis for the union. The forced union was held together by the force and cunning of colonial Britain. Once independence was achieved, the cracks began to show, and simmering animosity and suspicion began to bubble up in episodes of violence and conflict. Matters were and are not being helped by the fact that the political elite have mired the nation in extreme bad governance, where corruption and nepotism hold sway.

The second factor that drives terrorism is the endemic and systemic corruption that has put the nation under a stranglehold. It is no exaggeration to state that corruption is amock in Nigeria. It has become a cancer that has spread throughout all aspects of life, and throughout all segments of the Nigerian society. Corruption is no longer an exception to the rule, it has become the exception that drives the rule. The tendency of the political elite to manage the nation's enormous wealth as if it is their personal largesse is really tugging at the hearts of many Nigerians. The unwillingness and/or inability of the government to confront this run-away corruption is a source of extreme frustration for the teeming population of youths and young adults who are suffering most for the politicians' profligacy. This frustration is manifested through terrorism and violent crimes, such as kidnapping for ransom.

Religion is another driver of terrorism in Nigeria. The radical salafi movement that has its origin in the middle-east and gained prominence with the success of the Iranian revolution of 1979, spread southwards into North Africa and across the Sahel region into northern Nigeria. The frustrated unemployed youth in northern Nigeria are being driven into radicalized interpretation of the Quran by these charismatic Salafists. This movement inspired the Maitasine insurrection of the 1980s, and is the philosophical and doctrinal basis for the Boko Haram insurgency in the north-east of Nigeria.

Another key driver of terrorism in Nigeria is extreme poverty, unemployment, and lack of social mobility, particularly in the north-east region of the country. The enormous revenues that Nigeria derives from oil activities, have not translated to any improvement in the standard of living or quality of life of the people of Nigeria. **Diala** blames the lack of education and consequent lack of opportunity for social mobility for the allure of terrorism to the Nigerian youth. He suggests that:

> Most of the people who join terrorist groups such
> as Boko Haram are largely illiterates who do not

have formal education. They become cheaply coerced into terrorism because they do not realize anything wrong in destroying the lives of other people. Assuming they had basic education, they would not be easily brainwashed.[10]

Hopelessness, frustration, and desperation, have driven the teeming population of youths and young adults in the northeast, into the Boko Haram insurgency. **A.F. Ahokegh** says:

> In Nigeria, it is ironical that democracy, which should be the channel for reducing the problem of competition for resources, through the provision of basic facilities, has instead created a situation of poverty. Out of hopelessness, the Nigerian masses have resorted to threatening the nation's security by killing innocent citizens.[11]

The dearth of critical infrastructural and social amenities, are added grievances that terrorists offer as their reasons for taking up arms against the nation. Electricity, portable water, paved roads, medical clinics and services, and good schools, are in critical short supply and therefore greatly diminish the standard and quality of lives of Nigerians, particularly the youth.

---

10 **Diala, Barnabas Chinaedu**, New Trend In Terrorism In Nigeria: 'Boko Haram Sect' – The Villain Of The Piece, [2011] 1-19, at page 13, vailable at http://www.ssrn.com/abstract=1932061

11 **Akoghe** supra, note 5, at page 47

The government's brutal counter-terrorism strategy, rather than control the violent situation has exacerbated it. The "coercion only" strategy, which merely aims at brutally quelling the insurgency, has so far fallen short. It has rather driven the terrorists to more aggressive and more devastating levels of violence and brutality, including suicide bombings. Rather than garner cooperation for the government and separation from the terrorists, the brutal tactics of the security forces have driven away the sympathy of the victims, and has swelled the ranks of the terrorists.

The absence of legal avenues and channels to address legitimate grievances, has elevated terrorism to a viable option to settle scores, and as an outlet for dissent. Brutal put-downs of peaceful demonstrations and non-violent expressions of dissent, have forced peaceful and non-violent movements to transition to militancy and violent insurgency.

Matters are not being helped by the porous Nigerian borders, particular in the borders with Cameroon, Niger, and Chad, where smuggling of arms, fighters, and funds, enable the Boko Haram insurgency, and sustain their longevity. Nigeria cannot protect her interior from terrorists if it cannot protect her borders and frontiers.

Domestic terrorism has had a very serious negative impact

in Nigeria and on Nigerians. Without a doubt, terrorism poses an existential threat to the nation, given the fact that it threatens to create a breakaway nation(s) out of Nigeria, and that it is also creating the sort of instability that is likely to conduce to a sectarian civil war in the country. The Boko Haram sect had at a point declared a swathe of territory under its control, a sovereign Islamic Caliphate. Even if the sect is unsuccessful in its lofty aspirations, its activities are potentially likely to elicit reprisals from victims, survivors, and their ethnic and/or religious groups, against Muslims in the north and elsewhere, thus leading to a sectarian conflict and civil war. In either scenario, their activities are an existential threat to the Nigerian nation. Even the nation's national elections had been impacted by the activities of terrorists in the northeast, leading to the postponement of scheduled presidential elections in February 2015.

Nigerians have paid dearly in terms of lives lost and injuries sustained due to terrorism. To-date, by all estimates, over 35,000 lives have been lost and hundreds of thousands of people have been injured. It is estimated that between 3 and 5 million Nigerians have been internally displaced and over 150,000 Nigerians are seeking refuge in neighbouring countries of Niger, Chad and Cameroon. The social and psychological impact of the massive loss of lives, injuries and dislocations to Nigerians are incalculable. It will take generations to resolve the huge social problems terrorism has thrown up in Nigeria. Speaking of the impact of domestic terrorism in Nigeria, the **U.S. Department of Justice** says that "reports indicate that Boko Haram violence has affected over fifteen million people, caused the displacement of about six hundred fifty thousand, and claimed over five thousand lives in northeast Nigeria."[12]

In terms of the economy, the activities of the Boko Haram insurgents have led to the loss of infrastructure, business dislocations, and personal property damages and losses, estimated to be in the billions of dollars. Additionally, the nation has tripled its defence and security budgets, at the expense of other sectors, in a bid to confront the scourge of terrorism. Several key sectors of the Nigerian economy are under great stress, including agriculture, tourism and hospitality, education, and telecommunication.

Infrastructures in the north have borne the brunt of the Boko Haram mayhem. Schools have been destroyed, and facilities looted and burnt. Government offices and buildings have been damaged, or destroyed. Military barracks and hardware have been sacked and looted. Churches and mosques have been damaged, destroyed, or burnt. Cell towers have been destroyed. Newspaper offices were bombed. Medical clinics are targeted and critical medical services forced to shut down. In other words, infrastructures that are in short supply are further diminished by the activities of these terrorists. Moderate gains that had been recorded in the area of education in the

---

12 **Hanibal Goitom**, *Nigeria: Boko Haram*, Report for the U.S. Department of Justice, July 2014, The Library of Congress, 1-11, at page 6, available at http://www.justice.gov/.../nigeria/2014-010...

north-east region have been set back decades, because of the activities of Boko Haram. The continuing destruction of desperately needed infrastructures is further lowering the quality of lives of the people in northern Nigeria.

As a direct consequence of terrorism, Nigerians have suffered human rights abuses and curtailment of their constitutional rights in the hands of the Nigerian security agencies. Innocent and hapless victims of terrorism have often borne the brunt of reprisal actions from law enforcement and security agents. Innocent Nigerians have often been caught between the proverbial "rock and a hard place" in the nation's counter-terrorism efforts.

On the international front, terrorism has become a terrible blight on Nigeria's international image. The activities of the Boko Haram sect have actually put Nigeria on the terrorism map of the world. Nigeria is fast becoming synonymous with terrorism on the world stage and is actually being lumped in the same category of terrorism infested nations that include Afghanistan, Yemen, Syria, Iraq, and Somalia, to name a few.

Terrorism has, and continues to, deal debilitating body blows to Nigeria and Nigerians. In the north-east region where the Boko Haram sect holds sway, terrorism is continuing to stall Nigeria's effort to develop and improve the standard and quality of lives of Nigerians. Economic activities continue to be interrupted, lives continue to be lost, dislocations of people and businesses continue unabated, and palpable fear envelopes the nation. The **U.S. House of Representatives Committee on Homeland Security** calculates the enduring impact of the Boko Haram insurgency in the following passage:

> [A[ccording to former U.S. Assistant Secretary of State for African Affairs Johnnie Carson, 'Boko Haram has created widespread insecurity across northern Nigeria, increased tensions between various ethnic communities, interrupted development activities, frightened off investors, and generated concerns among Nigeria's northern neighbors.' Through these activities, it is the goal of Boko Haram 'to humiliate and undermine the government and to exploit religious differences in order to create chaos and to make Nigeria ungovernable.' This continual degradation of the quality of life in northern Nigeria – already quite low – weakens the state's legitimacy in the eyes of its citizens. But it is not merely poverty and corruption that play a role. Nigeria's law enforcement and military forces attempting to eradicate Boko Haram have very likely engaged in atrocious human rights abuses, even as they fight the ruthless and bloody Boko Haram.[13]

---

13 **U.S. House of Representatives Committee on Homeland Security** supra, note 6, at page 24

What might then be done to tackle and, hopefully, eliminate Boko Haram? In exploring this task, it is important to bear in mind that terrorism is an organic problem. It is not enough to kill off the hardened terrorists or even several terrorist groups. It is critical to exorcize the factors that fertilize, breed, and nurture terrorism, in order to completely eliminate the scourge. Anything less will be only a temporary setback for terrorism and will allow terrorism to recur ad infinitum. It has been suggested that given the organic nature of terrorism that what is needed is a holistic approach. We therefore agree with **Udombana** that "terrorism will remain a delicate, sophisticated, and complicated problem, demanding concerted efforts and holistic strategies to confront it."[14] **Dambazau** echoes the case for a multi-dimensional approach to dealing with modern terrorism in Nigeria. He asserts that:

> Nigeria's security challenges are multi-dimensional, therefore overcoming them requires a multi-dimensional strategy. There is no doubt however that whatever strategy is adopted would depend on good governance, because the majority of these challenges are the consequences of lack of transparency and accountability in governance; poorly observed rule of law; violations of fundamental human rights; high incidence of corruption; and general indiscipline.

---

14 **Nsongarua J. Udombana**, *Battling Rights: International Law And Africa's War On Terrorism*, 13 Afr. Y.B. Int'l L. 67 2005, at pages 129-130, available at http://www.ssrn.com/abstract=1806304

In addition our political and criminal justice institutions have become weak, while our values have been degraded.[15]

Continuing, he posits that "security and development are like Siamese twins, sharing the same internal organs, therefore neither can exist without the other."[16] What is needed, therefore, is the right mix of approaches to countering terrorism. An approach that combines an attempt to address the factors we reviewed in chapter three, mixed with strong coercive anti-terrorism operation. As we suggested elsewhere in this book, Nigeria cannot kill her way out of terrorism. **James J.F. Forest** offers up a compact menu that we believe will assuage the hunger to take to terrorism. He says that:

In addition to putting an end to corruption, the government must also address the many grievances mention earlier by becoming more transparent, efficient, and effective with regard to delivery of services, rule of law, accountability, and justice for all. It must foster nationwide respect toward all religious faiths, equitable distribution of resources, improvements in education and economic opportunity, and much more.[17]

---

15 **Abdulrahman Dambazau, Lt. Gen. [Rtd]**, *Overcoming Nigeria's Security Challenges*, available at http://www.iuokada.edu.ng/.../Overcoming%20Nigerias%20 Security%20Chall..., at pages 13-14

16 Ibid

17 J**ames J.F. Forest**, *Confronting the Terrorism of Boko Haram in Nigeria*, Joint Special Operations University Press, 2012, 1-178, at pages 93-94, available at http://www.jsou.socom.mil

In simple terms, **James Forest** is saying that if the Nigerian government lives up to its responsibility and does what government is set up to do, it will go a long way to addressing the grievances in society that find expression in terrorism. **Manni** adds that:

> Nigerian government must be encouraged to make much needed political measures such as fighting corruption, reducing poverty and improving human rights. Should these steps be taken, the main factors which have been attributed to Boko Haram's survival will be eliminated; seriously curbing the group's ambitions in the region, and improving African and global security.[18]

The first thing that needs to be addressed is Nigeria's political structure. A real constitutional convention/conference is needed to give Nigerians, of all stripes, the opportunity to discuss and come up with the right kind of federalism that hopefully protects the interests of minorities, while allowing each region or geopolitical bloc enough independence to grow at its own pace, using a substantial percentage of its own resources for the benefit of its own peoples. Aside from political restructuring, is the need to build a good governance structure that recognizes that the government is there to take care of the governed, and not those who are fortunate to govern. That, indeed, is the bane of Nigeria.

---

18 **Nathaniel Manni** supra, note 9, at page 46

Corruption is the third wheel of governance in Nigeria. Institutionalized corruption is driving the wheels of state off the developmental rail. No real progress can ever be recorded in any bid to address the underlying drivers of terrorism, without an effective handle on Nigeria's runaway corrupt establishment. Politicians, the military establishment, and the business elite, are collaboratively stripping flesh off Nigeria's corpus. The vultures must be tamed in order to right the ship of governance. The anti-corruption institutions should be strengthened, and allowed to operate independently of the executive and legislative branches of government.

The government should establish and enhance avenues and outlets for Nigerians to voice dissent, and to challenge bad governance. In this vein, the Judiciary should be made truly independent, to convince Nigerians that they have a real forum where they could vent whatever grievance they have against their government, or fellow citizens, and thus obviate the need to resort to terrorism and violence.

With regard to fighting terrorism, the government must recognize that, by and large, terrorism is a law enforcement issue and that terrorists are criminals that must be dealt with under the law. To this end, the government should strengthen and faithfully implement the provisions of the anti-terrorism and anti-laundering laws, in order to fight terrorism, its sponsors. and enablers. In so doing, the government should recognize and respect the human and constitutional rights of its citizens, including suspected terrorists. Blanket deprivation and denial of peoples' human and constitutional rights in the name of counter-terrorism, rather than result in success, often leads to escalation and swelling of the ranks of the terrorist groups. In this vein, all the members of the security forces that took part in extra-judicial executions of suspected terrorists and/or other victims, as well as those who burnt and looted people's properties should be investigated and tried in court for their crimes.

Nigeria's security apparatus needs to be retrained, retooled, and re-energized, to bring it from the dark ages, where it presently is, to modernity. Nigeria's security forces are poorly trained, ill-equipped, and miserably remunerated, to do the arduous task of safeguarding and protecting the nation and its citizens. Effort should be made to recruit suitable candidates, and to train them in modern law enforcement and counter-terrorism methods. The government should also provide them with the right mix of equipment and technological know-how, to enable them operate in the digital age. Care should also be taken to pay them well, at the very least a living wage, to prevent corruption and graft.

A critical part of any counter-terrorism strategy must be a strong coercive operation. Unrepentant terrorists and violent criminals should be taken down, if they cannot be safely apprehended and tried. The security forces should target areas under the sway of terrorists with surgical operations, to dislodge the terrorists, clear and hold all territories recovered from terrorists, and earnestly begin the arduous task of re-instituting governance and infrastructures in the affected areas. Care should be taken to avoid or minimize civilian casualties, and innocent victims must never be re-victimized by the security forces, in reprisal attacks on suspicion of sympathizing with the terrorists. We agree with **Babjee Pothuraju**, that "there is no purely military solution to the problem of Boko Haram."[19] What, however, "is essential to incapacitate the group is not Nigerian military prowess but a long-term response to address the issue in all its complexity, including the root causes of radicalization." [20]He takes the view that the solution to the Boko Haram issue lies in a "mix of security and development."[21] **Agbiboa** surmises that:

An effective counterterrorism policy in Nigeria must go beyond a security-only killing strategy to embed counterterrorism in an overarching national security strategy that appreciates the broader context in which Islamist radicalization

---

19 **Babjee Pothuraju**, *Boko Haram's Persistent Threat in Nigeria*, Backgrounder, March 19, 2012, at page 9, Institute For Defense Studies & Analyses, New Delhi, India, available at http://www.idsa.in/.../ThreatinNigeri...

20 Ibid

21 Ibid

occurs and seeks to meaningfully and non-violently alter it. In other words, Nigeria must shift away from a security policy that makes counterterrorism the prism through which everything is evaluated and decided.[22]

The primary aim of the military action against the terrorists in the north-east should be to retake, clear and hold territories under the sway of Boko Haram. To arrest and prosecute any indicted terrorist and enabler. And to reintroduce governmental institutions and social infrastructures in any such cleared area.

Religious, tribal, and community leaders, should work cooperatively and collaboratively to build trust, unity, and good neighbourliness, among all sections in the Nigerian society. They should educate their followers on the need to respect their neighbours and fellow citizens. Nigerians must be made to understand that everybody has a stake in building a strong, virile, cohesive, and progressive nation. Rancour, distrust, animosity, and envy, only stall the ability of the nation to advance, and to better cater for all its citizens. The governments, at all levels, should invest in education, skills and careers training, for the ever expanding population of children and young adults in Nigeria, to help them acquire the necessary

---

22 **Daniel E. Agbiboa,** *Is Might Right? Boko Haram, the Joint military Task Force, and the Global Jihad,* Journal of Military and Strategic Affairs, Volume 5, No. 3, December 2013, PP 53-72, at page 68, available at http://www.mercury.ethz.ch/serviceengine/Files/.../Ch+3+Might+Right.pdf

attitudes and skills to live in and interact with people from backgrounds different from theirs. Education helps eliminate prejudice, broadens horizons, and eliminates apathy. Education can free these impressionable youth from the clutches of mischief makers and radical groups.

In the area of the economy, the nation should diversify its economy from its present mono-reliance on crude oil exploitation. Other sectors should be given heightened attention, in order to grow the economy and improve the citizens' quality of life. Sectors such as agriculture and solid minerals, should be invested in massively, at least to generate the much needed employment for Nigeria's teeming army of unemployed youths and young adults. And speaking of unemployment, the frightening unemployment level among this susceptible group should be addressed with a youth job corps programme, together with the provision of skills and careers training opportunities.

Nigeria's infrastructure is very poor. Nigeria needs to invest massively in infrastructural development, particularly in the areas of power generation, road and rail networks, schools for skills and careers training, medical clinics and hospitals. The right mix of investment in these critical sub-sectors, will not only grow the economy, but will also help create jobs while also improving the quality of life for Nigerians.

The kind of amnesty program created for the Niger delta militants should also be extended to the insurgents in the north-east. Amnesty is a tool in every counter-terrorism chess box that must be explored, at the very least, to dislodge members of terrorist groups that are not yet hardened, and those who are still seating on the fence.

A fund should be created to pay victims of the insurgency in northern Nigeria. All displaced Nigerians should be returned home, given assistance to resume their shattered lives, or relocated to safe locations, if their homes are no longer safe or habitable. Those taking refuge in neighbouring countries should be assisted to return to their homes, if possible, or relocated to other safe areas within Nigeria's borders.

Nigeria must secure her borders to prevent smuggling and cross-border criminality. Nigeria would do well to cooperate with her neighbours, in a bid to build stronger regional and transnational collaboration, and to garner assistance in fighting this scourge. Nigeria must not feel shy to ask for help, be it logistical, technical, financial, and material, from international organizations and donor countries. Terrorism is, for the most part, a transnational problem, requiring transnational cooperative and collaborative solution.

In conclusion, solving the problem of terrorism in Nigeria requires the right mix of approaches, in a holistic bid to find an anti-dote. The strategy must balance the use of coercive force with programs to address the underlying political, social, and economic factors, that drive terrorism. **David Cortright** agrees that "the larger struggle to tame terrorism, however, will require a more comprehensive and holistic strategy that combines preventive and protective measures that devotes as much attention to dissuasion as to denial."[23]

Post-Script

To demonstrate the enduring nature of the existential threat that Boko haram poses to the Nigerian nation, as late as 26 April 2021, the Executive Governor of the Niger State, a state that borders the Federal Capital Territory of Nigeria, raised the alarm that Boko Haram had taken over the Kaure area of Shirr local government in his state and had hoisted their flag and forced the surrounding communities into membership of the sect. Kaure is less than two hours' drive to Abuja, Nigeria's capital city.[24]

---

23 **David Cortright**, *A Critical Evaluation of the UN Counter-Terrorism Program: Accomplishments and Challenges*, A Crime and Global Paper presented at: Global Enforcement Regimes, Transnational Organized Crime, International Terrorism and money Laundering, held at the Transnational Institute (TNI) in Amsterdam, 28-29 April 2005, available at http://www.tni.org/crime , at page 22

24 **Annie Nwosu**, *Boko Haram Elements Have Taken Niger State – Governor Bello cries out*, Daily Post, Published on April 26, 2021, available at http://dailypost.ng/2021/04/26/boko-haram-elements-have-taken-over-niger-state-gov-bello-cries-out/

Bibliography

Journal Scholarly Articles

Ahokegh, **A. F.** *Boko Haram: A 21st Century Challenge In Nigeria*, European Scientific Journal, September edition vol.8. No.21, 46-55, available at http://www.eujournal. org>Home>Vol8,No21(2012)>Ahokegh

Ajayi, **A.I.** *'Boko Haram' and terrorism in Nigeria: Exploratory and explanatory notes*, Global Advanced Research Journal of History, Political Science and International Relations Vol. 1(5) pp. 103 – 107, July, 2012, Available online http://garj.org/garjhpsir/index.htm

Abdulrahman Dambazau, Lt. Gen. [Rtd], *Overcoming Nigeria's Security Challenges*, available at http://www.iuokada. edu.ng/.../overcoming%20Nigeria%20Security%20Chall...

Abdulaziz, Ibrahim and **Harun a Umar**, *Amnesty: Nigeria massacre deadliest in history of Boko Haram*, AP January 9, 2015, available at http://www.news.yahoo.

com/7-kids-reunite-parents-lost-nigeria-islamic-upris-
ing-094251667.html?soc_src=mediacontentsharebut-
tons&soc_trk=ma

Abimbola, J.O., and Adesote, S.A., *Domestic Terrorism
And Boko Haram Insurgency In Nigeria, Issues And Trends:
A Historical Discourse*, Journal of Arts and Contemporary
Society, Volume 4, September 2012, 11-29, at 13, available at
http://www.cenresinpub.org

Abubakar, Abdu Ibrahim, *An Appraisal of Legal and
Administrative framework for Combating Terrorist Financing
and Money Laundering in Nigeria*, Journal of Law, Policy and
Globalization, Vol.19, 2013, page 26-37, available at www.
iise.org

Adebayo, Anthony Abayomi, *Implications of 'Boko Haram'
Terrorism on National Development in Nigeria: A Critical
Review*, Mediterranean Journal of Social Sciences, Vol 5 No.
16, July 2014, PP 480-489, available at http://www.mcser.org/
journal/index.php/mjss/article/download/3330/3284

Adekunbi Olukemi Johnson Odusanya, *The Challenge Of
Democratic Governance In The African Region: The Nigerian
Experience,* OIDA international Journal of Sustainable
Development 06:06 (2013), 11-22; Available
at http://www.ssrn.com/link/OIDA-Intl-Journal-
Sustainable-dev.html

Adeyinka Peters Ajayi, *The Economic Impact Of Crisis And
Militancy On Tourism Destination Development In Niger-*

Delta, Asian Journal of Management sciences and education Vol. 1. No. 1, page 127 at page 129, April 2012, sourced from www.leena-luna.co.jp

Adigbuo, **Richard Ebere, PHD,** *The New ECOWAS Counter Terrorism Strategy and Arms Trade Treaty,* Journal of International Affairs and Global Strategy Vol.25, 2014, 46-54, available at http://www.iiste.org

Afeno, Odomovo S. *The Boko Haram Uprising And Insecurity In Nigeria; Intelligence Failure Or Bad Governance?*, Conflict trends 35, available at http://www.academia.edu/.../The_Boko-Haram_Uprising_and_I...

African Union Counter Terrorism Frame work, available at http://www.peaceau.org/en/page/64-counter-terrorism-ct

Agbiboa, Daniel E, *Peace at Daggers Drawn? Boko Haram and the State of Emergency in Nigeria, Studies in Conflict & Terrorism*, 37:41-67, 2014, available at http://www.researchgate.net/...Peace_at_Daggers_Drawn_Boko_Haram_and_t...

Agbiboa, Daniel Egiegba, *The Ongoing Campaign of Terror in Nigeria: Boko Haram versus the State, Stability*: International Journal of Security and Development, [S.I.], v. 2, n. 3, p. Art. 52, Oct. 2013. ISSN 2165-2627. Available at: http://www.stabilityjournal.org/article/view/sta.ci/145

Agbiboa, Daniel E. *Is Might Right? Boko Haram, the Joint Military Task Force, and the Global Jihad*, Journal of Military and Strategic Affairs, Volume 5, No. 3, December 2013, 53-

71, available at http://www.mercury.ethz.ch/serviceengine/ Files/.../CH+3Might+Right.pdf also available at http://www. inss.org.il/index.aspx?id=4538&articleid=6649

Akani , Christian, *2011 Terrorism Act in Nigeria: Prospects and Problems,* Online International Journal of Arts and Humanities, Volume 2, Issue 8, pp. 218-223, October, 2013, available at http://www.onlineresearchjournals.org/IJAH

Akpan, Patrick L. Onwuka, Ebele Mary, Onyeizugbe, Chinedu, *Terrorist Activities And Economic Development In Nigeria: An Early Warning Signal,* OIDA International Journal of Sustainable Development 05: 04 (2012), 69-78 , available at http://www.papers.ssrn.com/.../SSRN_ID2173041_co...

Alao, David Oladimeji, *Boko-Haram Insurgency In Nigeria: The Challenges And Lessons,* Singaporean Journal of Business Economics and Management Studies Vol.1, No.4, 2012, available at http://www.singaporeanjbem.com/pdfs/SG_VOL_1_(4)/1.pdf Anderson, David, Shielding the Compass; How to Fight Terrorism Without Defeating the law, 1-19, (June 15, 2013) , Available at SSRN: http://www.ssrn.com/abstract=2292950

Anyadike, Nkechi O., *Boko Haram and National Security Challenges in Nigeria; Causes and Solutions,* Journal of Economic and Sustainable Development, ISSN 2222-1700 (Paper) ISSN 2222-2855 (Online)Vol.4, No.5, 2013, page 12, available at www.iiste.org Atta Barkindo, "Join the Caravan": The Ideology of Political Authority in Islam from

Ibn Taymiyya to Boko Haram in North-Eastern Nigeria, Perspectives On Terror, Vol 7, No 3 (2013), PP 1-10, accessed from http://www.terrorismanalysts.com/pt/index.php/pot/article/view/266/html

Bender, Jeremy and **Armin Rosen**, *Boko Haram Just Pulled Off One Of The Deadliest Terrorist Attacks In History*, Business Insider, January 9, 2015, available at http://www.businessinsider.com/boko-harams-deadliest-terrorist-attack-2015-1

Bentley, Chris. Matt Hintsa, Mimi liu, Liz Moskalenko, Stacey Ng, *The Oil Crisis in the Niger River Delta,* available at http://www.africanafrican.com/.../oil_Crisis_in_Niger_River_Delta(1).doc

Blakesley, Christopher l. *Ruminations on Terrorism: Expiation and Exposition,* 10 New criminal law review 554 (2007) published by William S. Boyd school of Law, University of Nevada Las Vegas, accessed from http://ssrn.com/abstract=1151019 *Constitutive Act of the African Union*, available at http://www.au2002.gov.za/docs/key_oau/au_act.htmDaniel Agbiboa, The Ongoing Campaign of Terror in Nigeria: Boko Haram versus the State, Stability: International Journal of Security and Development, Vol 2, No 3 (2013) sourced from http://www.stabilityjournal.org/rt/printerFriendly/st.cl/145

Chase, Eric, *Defining Terrorism: A Strategic Imperative, Small Wars Journal*, Jan 24 2013 accessed from http://

smallwarsjournal.com/print/13722 Eugenia Dumitriu, The E.U.'s Definition of Terrorism: The Council Frame-work Decision on Combating Terrorism, German Law Journal, Vol. 05 no. 05 page 585, available at http://www.germanlawjournal. com/index.php?pageID=11&artID=435 Gustavo Placido Dos Santos, Boko Haram: Time for an Alternative Approach, Portuguese Institute of International Relations and Security, IPRIS Viewpoints, April 2014, 1-3, available at http://www. opendemocracy.net/

Cortright, David, *A critical Evaluation of the UN Counter-Terrorism Program: Accomplishments and Challenges*, A Crime and Global Paper presented at: Global Enforcement Regimes, Transnational Organized Crime, International Terrorism and money Laundering, held at the Transnational Institute (TNI) in Amsterdam, 28-29 April 2005, available at http://www.tni.org/crime
Defining Terrorism, WP 3, Deliverable 4, October 1, 2008, COT Institute for Safety, Security and Crisis Management, at page 1,available at www.transnationalterrorism.eu

Diala, Barnabas Chinaedu, *New Trends In Terrorism In Nigeria: 'Boko Haram Sect' – The Villain Of The Piece*,[2011], available at http://ssrn.com/abstract=1932061

Ebienfa, Imomotimi Kimiebi, (2011): *Militancy in the Niger Delta and the Emergent categories*, Review of African Political economy, 38:130, 637-643, available at http://www. kimiebi.blogspot.com/2012/.../militancy-in-niger-delta-and-emergent.htmlLevitt, Mathew, and Jacobson, Michael

(2008), The Money Trail: Finding, Following, and Freezing Terrorist Finances, Washington Institute for Near East Policy, Washington DC, United States, available at http://www. washingtoninstitute.org/...

Ekanem, Samuel Asuquo, Ekefre, Ekong Nyong, *Education and Religious Intolerance in Nigeria: The Need for Essencism as a Philosophy*, Journal of Educational and Social Research, Vol. 3 (2) May 2013, PP 303-310, available at http:// www.mcser-org.ervinhatibi.com/journal/index.php/jesr/ article/.../168/159

Ekanem, Samuel Asuquo, Jacob Abiodun Dada, Bassey James Ejue, *Boko Haram And Amnesty: A Philo-Legal Appraisal*, International Journal of Humanities and Social Science

Eke, Chijioke Chinwokwu, *Terrorism and the Dilemmas of Combating the Menace in Nigeria*, International Journal of Humanities and Social Science, Vol. 3 No. 4 [Special Issue – February 2013] 265-272

Ekot, Basil, *Conflict, Religion and Ethnicity in the Post-Colonial Nigerian State*, The Australasian Review of African Studies, Volume 30 Number 2 December 2009, pp 47-67, available at http://www.federalism-bulletin.eu/User/index. php?PAGE=Sito_it/boll...

Ewi, Martin and **Kwesi Aning**, *Assessing the Role of the African Union in Preventing and Combating Terrorism in Africa*, African Security Review 15.3, Institute of Security studies, www.issafrica.org/.../01-oct-2006-assessing-the-role-of-the-africa-unio...

Frey, S. Bruno and **Luechinger, Simon,** *How to Fight Terrorism: Alternatives to Deterrence,* December 2002, working Paper No. 137, institute for Empirical Research in Economics, University of Zurich Working Paper Series, PP 1-23, available at http://www.iew.unzh.ch/wp/

Goitom, Hanibal, *Nigeria: Boko Haram,* Report for the U.S. Department of Justice, July 2014, The Library of Congress, 1-11, available at http://www.justice.gov/.../nigeria/2014-010...

Guiora, Amos N., *Due Process and Counterterrorism,* available at http://www.ssrn.com/abstract=1680009

Hardy, Keiran and Williams, George, *What is Terrorism? Assessing Domestic Legal Definitions (February 7, 2013)* UNSW Law Research Paper No. 2013-16; UCLA Journal of International Law and Foreign Affairs, Vol.16, 2011; UNSW Law Research Paper No. 2013-16. Available at SSRN: http://ssrn.com/abstract+2213332

Ibrahim, Jibrin, Kazah-Toure, Toure, *"Ethno-religious conflicts in Northern Nigeria,* The Nordic Africa Institute, PP 1-5, available at http://www.nai.uu.nai.se/publications/news/archives/042ibrahimkazah/

Isa, Kabir Muhammed, Chapter 11: *Militant Islamist Groups in Northern Nigeria,* available at http://www.mercury.ethz.ch/.../MilitiasRebelsIslamistMilitants_Chapter+11.pdf

Nathaniel Manni, "Boko Haram: A Threat to Africa and Global Security", Global Security Studies, Fall 2012, Volume 3, Issue 4, PP 44-54, available at http://www.globalsecuritystudies.com/Manni%20BH%20FINAL.pdf also at http://www.start.umd.edu/pubs/STARTBackgroundReport_BokoHaramRecentAttacks_May2014_O.pdf

ISS Seminar Report, Pretoria: *The Threat of Boko Haram and the Challenges to Peace, Security and Unity in Nigeria,* Held 2 February 2012 in Pretoria, South Africa; Sourced from http://www.issafrica.org/events/iss-seminar-report-pretoria-the-threat-of-boko-haram-and-the

Karolyi, George Andrew, *The Consequences of Terrorism for Financial Markets: What Do We Know?* (May 7, 2006. Available at SSRN: http;//ssrn.com/abstract=904398 or http://dx.doi.org/10.2139/ssrn.904398

Kwaja, Chris M.A. *Strategies for [Re]Building State Capacity to Manage Ethnic and Religious Conflict in Nigeria,* The Journal of Pan African Studies, vol.3, no.3, September 2009, available at http://www.jpanafrican.com/docs/vol3no3/3.3strategies.pdf

Ladan-Baki, Ibrahim Sada, *Corruption And Security Challenges In Developing Countries,* International journal of Politics and Good Governance Volume 5, No. 5.2 Quarter II 2014, 1-19

Loimeier, Roman (2012), *Boko Haram: The Development of a Militant Religious Movement in Nigeria, in: Africa Spectrum,*

47, 2-3, 137-155 at pages 140 et seq, available at http://www. africa-spectrum.org

Marchal, **Roland,** *Boko Haram and the resilience of militant Islam in Northern Nigeria,* NOREF Report, June 2012, Published By Norwegian Leacebuilsing Resource Centre, available at http://www.peacebuilding.no/.../ dc58a110fb362470133354efb8fee228.pdf

National Consortium for the Study of Terrorism and Responses to Terrorism, *Boko Haram Recent Attacks,* Background Report, May 2014, 1-8, available at http:// www.start.umd.edu/pubs/STARTBackgroundReport_ BokoHaramRecentAttacks_May2014_O.pdf

Nmah, **Patrick,** *Religious Fanaticism, a Threat to National Security: The Case of Boko Haram Sect,* p106, available at http://dx.doi.org/10.4314/uja.v13i1.7

Norman, **Paul, PHD.,***The United Nations and Counter-terrorism After September 11: Towards an Assessment of the Impact and Prospects of Counter-terror 'Spill-Over' into International Criminal Justice Cooperation,* Paper to British Society of Criminology Conference 6-9th July 2004, University of Portsmouth, available at http://www.britsoccrim.org/new/ volume7/004.pdf

Northern Nigeria: Background To Conflict, Africa Report No. 168 – 20 December 2010, International Crisis Group, available at http://www.academia.edu/.../NORTHERN_ NIGERIA_BACKGR...

Nwanegbo, C. Jaja, Odigbo, Jude, *Security and National Development in Nigeria: The Threat of Boko Haram*, International Journal of Humanities and Social Science Vol. 3 No. 4 [Special Issue – February 2013] 385-291, available at http://www.ijhssnet.com/journals/Vol_3_N0_4_Special_Issue.../29.pdf

Nwankpa, Michael, *The Politics Of Amnesty In Nigeria: A Comparative Analysis Of The Boko Haram And Niger Delta Insurgencies*, Journal of Terrorism Reasearch, Volume 5, Issue 1, 1-6, available at http://www.ojs.st-andrews.ac.uk/index.php/jtr/rt/printerFriendly/830/709

Odoemelam, Chinedu Christian, Kidafa Ibrahim, Onyebuchi Alexandra Chima and Agu Oluchi Sussan, *Influence Of The Boko Haram Security Threat In Nigeria*, On The Level Of Interest In Mainstream Media News Among Postgraduate Students At The University Of Nigeria, Nsukka, Global Journal of Interdisciplinary Social Science at page 2, available at http://www.gifre.org

Ogbonnaya, Ufiem Maurice, Ehiagiamusoe, Uyi Kizito, *Niger Delta Militancy and Boko Haram Insurgency*: National Security in Nigeria, Global Security Studies, Summer 2013, Volume 4, Issue 3, available at http://www.academia.edu/.../Niger_Delta_Militancy_Boko_Hara...

Ogege, Sam Omadjohwoefe, *Insecurity and Sustainable Development: The Boko Haram Debacle in Nigeria*, American International Journal of Social Science, Vol.

2 No.7; October 2013, 82-88, available at http://www. aijssnet.com/journals/Vol_2_No_7_October_2013/10.pdf

Oladimeji, Moruff Sanjo, Oresanwo, Adeniyi Marcus, *"Effects of Terrorism on the International Business in Nigeria"* *International Journal of Humanities and Social Science*, Vol. 4, No. 7(1); May 2014, 247-255, available at http://www.ijhssnet. com/journals/Vol_4_No_7_1_May_2014/30.pdf

Oladunjoye, Patrick, Omemu, Felix, *Effect Of Boko Haram On School Attendance In Northern Nigeria*, British journal of Education Vol.1, No.2 pp 1-9, December 2013, Published by European Centre for Research Training and Development UK (available at www.ea-journals.org)

Ogunrotifa, Ayodeji Bayo, *Class Theory of Terrorism: A Study of Boko Haram Insurgency In Nigeria*, Research on Humanities and Social Sciences, Vol.3, No.1, 2013, 27-60, available at http://www.iiste.org

Olusegun, Omoluwa, *Functional Education: A Tool For Combating Terrorism In Nigeria*, International Journal of arts & Humanity Science (IJAHS), Volume 1 Special Issue 1, (Nov-Dec 2014), PP. 35-39, available at http://www.ijahs.com

Omotola, Shola, J., *Assessing Counter-Terrorism Measures In Africa: Implications For Human Rights And National Security*, Conflict Trends, Issue 2 (2008), African Centre for the Constructive Resolution of Disputes (ACCORD), Umhlanga Rocks, South Africa page 41, available at http://www.accord. org.za/publications/conflict-trends-20082Javier   Ruperez,

The United Nations In The Fight Against Terrorism, sourced from www.un.org/en/sc/ctc/.../2006-01_26_cted-lecture.pdf

Douglas, Oronto. Ike Okonta, Dimieari Von Kemedi, Michael Watts, *Oil And Militancy In The Niger Delta: Terrorist Threat or Another Colombia?*, Working Paper No. 4, 2004, Economies of Violence Working Papers Series, Institute of International Studies, University of California, Berkeley, USA, The United States Institute of Peace, Washington DC, USA, Our Niger Delta, Port Harcourt, Nigeria, PP 1-12, available at http://www.geography.berkeley.edu/.../NigerDelta/...

Orr, Andrew C., "*Unmanned, Unprecedented, and Unresolved: The Status of American Drone Strikes in Pakistan Under International Law*", 44 Cornell Int'l L.J. (2011) PP 730-752

Osaghae, Eghosa E., Suberu, Rotimi T., *A History of Identities, Violence, and Stability in Nigeria*, Queen Elizabeth House, University of Oxford, Crise Working Paper No. 6, January 2005, 1-27

Osho, Oluwafemi, Falaye Adeyinka Adesuyi, Shafi'I M. Abdulhamid, *Combating Terrorism with Cybersecurity: The Nigerian Perspective*, World Journal of Computer Application and Technology 1(4): 103-109, 2013, available at http://www.hrpub.org

Popoola, I.S., *Press and Terrorism in Nigeria: A Discourse on Boko Haram*, 43-66 at page 58, Global Media Journal African Edition 2012 Vol 6(1), available at http://www.globalmedia.journals.ac.za

Pothuraju, **Babjee**, *Boko Haram's Persistent threat in Nigeria*, Backgrounder, March 19, 2012, Institute For Defense Studies & Analyses, New Delhi, India, available at http://www.idsa. in/.../ThreatinNigeri...

Revealed: List of attacks blamed on Boko Haram in 2014, available at http://www.nigeriaeye.com/2014/06/revealed-list-of-attacks-blame... Robert Dowd, Religious diversity and Violent Conflict: Lessons from Nigeria, The Fletcher Forum Of World Affairs, Vol.38.1 Winter 2014, pp 153-168, available at http://www.fletcherforum.org/.../38-1.D...

Sal, **Ben,** *Definition of "terrorism" in the UN Security Council: 1985 – 2004,* Chinese Journal of International Law (2005), Vol. 4, No. 1, 141 – 166 doi:10.1093/chinesejil/jmi005 downloaded from http://chinesejil.oxfordjournals.org/ on 10/9/2014

Salawu, B., *Ethno-Religious Conflicts in Nigeria: Casual Analysis and Proposals for New Management Strategies,* European Journal of social Sciences – Volume 13, Number 3 (2010), available at http://www.eisf.eu/.../0071-Salawu-2010-Nigeria-ethno-religious-confli...

Solomon, Hussein, *Boko Haram: What is to be Done? Research on Islam and Muslims in Africa*, January 16, 2015, 1-7, available at http://www.muslimsinafrica.files.wordpress. com/2013/09/topbanner_isl_mus_afr6.jpg   Rawlings Akonbede UDAMA, Understanding Nigeria Terrorism, its Implications to National Peace, Security, Unity and Sustainable

Development: A Discuss, IOSR Journal Of Humanities And Social Science (IOSR-JHSS), Volume 8, Issue 5 (Mar. – Apr. 2013), PP 100-115, available at www.Iosrjournals.Org

Sturman, **Kathryn,** *The Au Plan On Terrorism Joining the global war or leading an African battle?*, African Security Review 11(4) 2002, page 103, available at http://www. issafrica.org/pubs/ASR/11No4/Sturman.pdf

Udombana, **Nsongarua J.,** *Battling Rights: International Law And Africa's War On Terrorism*, 13 Afr. Y.B. Int'l L. 67 2005, available at http://www.ssrn.com/abstract=1806304

Utomi, Pat, *The Niger Delta Crisis: Beyond the Price of Crude Oil*, Published by the Center for Strategic and International studies, available at http://csis.org/print/
13910, http://csis.org/story/niger-delta-crisis-beyond-price-crude-oil

Uzoma, **Rose C.,** *Religious Pluralism, Cultural Differences, and Social Stability in Nigeria*, Brigham Young University Law Review [Summer 2004] 651-664, available at http://
www.digitalcommons.law.byu.edu/cg, /viewcontent.
cgi?article=2197…

Walter, **Christian,** *Defining Terrorism in National and International Law*, accessed from http://edoc.mpil.de/
conference-on-terrorism/index.cfm

Newspapers & Magazines

Abubakar, Aminu and Ola Awoniyi, *NE Nigeria hit by Wave of Suicide Bombings as Violence Spikes*, AFP, January 11, 2015, available at http://www.news.yahoo.com/twin-blasts-market-pitiskum-ne-nigeria-residents-172536455?soc_src=mediacontentstory&soc_trk=ma

Bender, Jeremy and **Armin Rosen**, *REVEALED: List of attacks blamed on Boko Haram*, Boko Haram Just Pulled Off One Of The Deadliest Terrorist Attacks In History, Business Insider, January 9, 2015, available at http://www.businessinsider.com/boko-harams-deadliest-terrorist-attack-2015-1

Business and Financial News, Thursday March 19, 2015, available at http://www.reuters.com/print?aid=1UZ20150319

Indiatoday, In New Delhi *Boko Haram: 5 deadliest attacks by the Islamist group in* 2015, March 21, 2015, available at http://indiatoday.intoday.in/education/story/boko-haram-5-deadliest-attacks-by-the-islamist-group-in-2015/1/425031.html

Nwosu, Annie, *Boko Haram Elements Have Taken Niger State – Governor Bello Cries Out*, Daily Post, Published on April 26, 2021, available at http://dailypost.ng/2021/04/26/boko-haram-elements-have-taken-over-niger-state-gov-bello-cries-out/

Reuters, *Cameroon appeals for international military aid to fight Boko Haram*, Friday January 9, 2015, available at http://w-ww.reuters.com/assets/print?aid=USKBNOKI18920150109

The Guardian, *Boko Haram attacks – timeline*, available at http://www.theguradian.com/world/2012/sep/25/boko-haram-timlin...

The Nation Newspaper, 25th April, 2011, at pages 14-16

The Nation Newspaper, February 2, 2010, at page 8

The Nation Newspaper, January 29, 2011, at page 12

The Nation Newspaper, July 31, 2009, at page 6 The Sun Newspaper, available at http://odili.net/news/source/2015/mar/24/506.html

The Sun Newspaper, June 28, 2011, at page 4

The Sun Newspaper, September 8, 2010, at page 12; The Guardian, available at http://www.theguradian.com/world/2012/sep/25/boko-haram-timlin...

The US Department of State, Nigeria Travel Warning, August 8, 2014, available at http://www.travel.state.gov/content/passports/english/alertswarnings/nigeria...

Thenationonlineng.net/new/timeline-of-boko-haram-attacks/

National, International & Regional Legislations

Article 3, *OAU Convention On The Prevention And Combating Of Terrorism*, 1999

Boko Haram: Growing Threat to the U.S. Homeland, Report prepared by the Majority Staff of the Committee on Homeland Security of the U.S. House of Representatives, September 13, 2013, at page 25, available at http://www.homeland.house.gov/sites/homeland.house.gov/files/documents/09-13-13-Boko-Haram-Report.pdf

Council Framework on Combating Terrorism, Council of the European Union, Brussels, 18 April 2002, Art. 1

Economic and Financial Crimes (Establishment) Act, 2004

ECOWAS Counter-Terrorism Strategy And Implementation Plan, available at www.issafrica.org

EU Press Release of June 2, 2014 titled "The EU lists Boko Haram as a terrorist organization", available at

http://www.eeas.europa.eu/legal-content/EN/TXT/
PDF/?uri=0J:L:2014:160:FULL&from=EN

FATF *Report, Terrorist Financing In West Africa*, October
2013, available at http://www.fatf-gafi.org/.../...

NATO Glossary of Terms and Definitions, AAP-06 Edition
2012 Version 2.

*OAU Convention on the Prevention and Combating of
Terrorism*, 1999, available at http://www.refworld.org/
docid/3f4b14.html

*Protocol to the OAU Convention On the Prevention And
Combating of Terrorism*, Adopted by the Third ordinary
Session of the Assembly of the African Union, Addis Ababa,
8 July 2004, available at http://www.au.int/.../protocol-oau-
convention-prevention-and-c...

*Supplentary Act A/SA.3/02/113 Adopting the ECOWAS
Strategy for Combating Terrorism, and its Implementation
Plan*; See government of Ghana Official portal, accessed
from http://ghana.gov.gh/index.php/2012-02-08-08-32-47/
general-news/974-ecowas-adopts-anti...

Terrorism (Prevention) (Amendment) *Act*, 2013

Terrorism (Prevention)Act, 2011

The Money Laundering (Prohibition) Act, 2011

*U.S. Department of State, Bureau of Counterterrorism,
Country Reports on Terrorism* 2013, 1-21, at page 3, available
at http://www.state.gov/j/ct/rls/crt/2013/224820.htm

*U.S. House of Representatives Committee on Homeland Security,
Boko Haram: Growing Threat to the U.S.* Homeland, Published
by the Majority Staff of the Committee on September 13,
2013, at page 3, available at http://www.homeland.house.gov/
sites/homeland.house.gov/files/documents/09-13-Boko-
Haram-Report.pdf

UN Office for the Coordination of Humanitarian Affairs, Analysis; Carrot or Stick? – Nigerians divided over Boko Haram, available at http://www.irinnews.org/printreport.aspx?reportid=95874

United Nations Security Council, Security Council Resolution 1373 (2001), S/RES/1373, New York, 28 September 2001

UNSCR 1566 of October 2004

Books

Drukkers, Ipskamp, 2014, available at http://www.infra-nigeria.org/IMG/pdf/boko-haram-islamism-politics-security-nigeria.pdf

Forest, James J.F., *Confronting the Terrorism of Boko Haram in Nigeria*, Joint Special Operations University Press, 2012, 1-178, available at http://www.jsou.socom.mil

Mohammed, Kyari, *The message and methods of Boko Haram*, In Boko Haram: Islamism, Politics, Security and the State in Nigeria, edited by Perouse de Montclos, Marc-Antoine, 9-32 at page 13. Eschede, Netherlands: Institut Francais de Recherche en Africaque (IFRA), 2014, available at http://www.infra-nigeria.org/IMG/pdf/boko-haram-islamism-politics-security-nigeria.pdf

Reinert, Manuel and Lou Garcon, *"Boko Haram Crisis: A Chronology."* In Boko Haram: Islamism, Politics, Security and the State in Nigeria, edited by Perouse de Montclos, Marc-Antoine, 237-245 at pages 239 et seq. Enschede, Netherlands:

Cases

Cordano, Diego, The Evolution of Boko Haram: a growing threat?, Consultancy African Intelligence, Friday June 2014, PP 1-5, available at http://www.consultancyafrica.com/index.

php?option=com_content&view=article&id=1695:...

Jacobellis v. Ohio, 378 U.S. 184 (1964)
Internet Sources

North, Don, *Behind the War with Boko Haram,* Consortium news.com, November 16, 2014, 1-27, available at http://www.consortiumnews.com/2014/11/16/behind-the-war-with-boko-haram/

Human Rights Watch, *Nigeria: Boko Haram Attacks Cause Humanitarian Crisi*s [1], March 14, 2014, 1-4, available at http://www.hrw.org/print/news/2014/03/14/nigeria-boko-haram-attacks-cause-humanitarian-crisis

The united Nations, *Multilateral Responses to terrorism;* posted October 2004 by the Anti-Defamation league in its terrorism update, accessed on 10/9/2014 from http://archive.adl.org/terror/tu/tu_38_04-09.html

Sergie. Mohammed Aly and Toni Johnson, *Boko Haram, Council on Foreign Relations,* October 7, 2014, available at http://www.cfr.org/global/global.../p32137#!/?...; also available at http://www.cfr.org>Nigeria

Margon, Sarah, *How Do You Beat Boko Haram with an Army that's Almost as Evil?,* May 14, 2014, Human Rights Watch, available at http://www.hrw.org/print/news/2014/05/14/how-do-you-beat-boko-haram-army-thats-almo...

www.ingramcontent.com/pod-product-compliance
Lightning Source LLC
Chambersburg PA
CBHW060310030426
42336CB00011B/987